CLAREMONT READING
CONFERENCE

Sponsored by Claremont Graduate School

FORTY-SEVENTH YEARBOOK

Edited By
MALCOLM P. DOUGLASS

Special 1983 Conference theme:
READING READING:
50th ANNIVERSARY PERSPECTIVES

Continuing Conference theme:
READING, THE PROCESS OF CREATING
MEANING FOR SENSED STIMULI

Price $12.00

Back issues of the Claremont Reading Conference are available from two sources. Volumes still in print may be ordered from the following address: Claremont Reading Conference Yearbook, Harper 200, Claremont Graduate School, Claremont, California 91711. Write for information concerning books in print and special price list. All past Yearbooks are available through University Microfilms, 300 Zeeb Road, Ann Arbor, Michigan 48103.

ISBN #0-941742-01-6

Published by The Claremont Reading Conference
Center for Developmental Studies
Claremont Graduate School, Claremont, California 91711

Table of Contents

Introduction to the Yearbook

With this volume we bring to our readers the proceedings of the 50th annual Claremont Reading Conference, which was once again held on the campuses of the Claremont Colleges during the midwinter period (January 14th and 15th, 1983). To mark this particular milestone, two things seemed particularly appropriate to the occasion. One was to invite participants who had contributed to the programs of previous conferences, to make this event something of a reunion as well as an anniversary, and so almost all of those making presentations and contributing to this Yearbook are in fact alumni of previous Claremont Reading Conferences. A second was to ask that, where appropriate to their particular topic, some reflection on the past and the future, a retrospective and a prospective emphasis, be included if possible. After all, a Golden Anniversary ought not pass without some stock-taking. As the oldest conference devoted to the subject of reading, we perhaps may be allowed some special dispensation in this regard before getting on with the problem of reading, which unhappily, despite great strides in our advancement of knowledge *about* reading during these past five decades, and particularly within the last two of them, remains stubbornly before us.

A special feature of this Yearbook is the inclusion of an Index covering the period during which the Yearbook itself has been published. Although the Conference series itself began in the summer of 1932 (it was subsequently moved to the winter period, and thus we account for what would at first appear to be an error in arithmetic), publication of the proceedings was not commenced until 1935. However, none of the original contributions was lost, having been included in that first Yearbook. We are now able to present in this volume a comprehensive index of all of the articles included since, i.e., from 1935 to 1982. Additional separate bound copies of the Index are available for a small charge from the Claremont Reading Conference, Harper Hall 200, Claremont, California 91711.

Anyone who has been responsible for "putting on" a conference of any sort knows that it involves a great deal of preparation and many helping hands during the event itself. It is *not* a one-person affair. For the Claremont Conference, which is gauged to about 1,000 attendees and somewhere around 60 "participants" or "presenters," it is obvious that not everyone who contributed to the success of the 50th Conference could be listed here. However, I do wish especially to acknowledge the continuing support and steady help and cooperation of my academic colleagues, not just within the Faculty in Education, important as that has been, but across numerous disciplines both at Claremont Graduate School and in the five undergraduate colleges which together comprise what is known as the Claremont Colleges. Thanks are due to the many graduate students who volunteer their efforts, as they are also due the numerous active professionals in the Claremont area who give their time and energies to the Conference. Particularly important is the help they provide in arranging the only book exhibit at the Conference, a display of notable books for children and young adults (this is perhaps the only conference on Reading which does not include commercial exhibits). Saying that, there are three persons who deserve recognition either for their role in planning our anniversary conference or for past contributions, or both: Julie Robinson, Director of the George G. Stone Center for Children's Books (who directs a concurrent Young People's Reading Conference), Ethel Parker, Secretary to the Faculty in Education, and Dennis Tierney, Executive Secretary to the Faculty. Finally, one would be remiss at best if mention of the sponsor of the Claremont Reading Conference series were omitted. For fifty years Claremont Graduate School following in its tradition of supporting faculty in efforts which they deem worthy of pursuit, has sponsored this conference series. Sponsorship includes many aspects, for each of which both I, and I am sure my predecessor, Peter L. Spencer, the founder of the series and its director from 1932 to 1948, are most grateful.

Malcolm P. Douglass, *Director*
Claremont Reading Conference

Reading Reading: 50th Anniversary Perspectives

Malcolm P. Douglass

My task is to help place the Claremont Reading Conference in some kind of professional and historical perspective, at least as I see it, and in that way provide a context for the discussions which will occupy us during the 1983 meetings. A 50th Anniversary is generally thought to be an appropriate time for such reflection, and I hope that what I have to say will be informative and useful to you.

First, you may be interested to know that, beyond being simply 50 years of age, this conference series is also the oldest continuing series of meetings devoted to the subject of reading. We are, in fact, not just the oldest conference of its kind in the United States, but evidently the oldest anywhere else in the world. That this should happen here should not be so surprising if you realize that no other country has had such a long love affair, although it has often been a painful one, with the goal of universal literacy. No other country has placed such faith in the fruits of a truly literate society, none has cared more, nor done more to gain that goal, though it is yet to be reached, so a Reading Conference is really as American as apple pie.

This Conference has another distinguishing, even unique, characteristic in relation to other meetings devoted to the problem of literacy. It has been distinguished by the fact it has presented a singular and consistent message, or point of view, about the nature of the reading process since its inception in 1932. This has not been a conference series based on the principle of eclecticism; i.e., it has not been designed as a forum in which widely divergent views have been presented more or less willy nilly, as is the case with most other reading conferences. Divergent views have and will continue to find a forum here. But the end purpose remains, which is to illustrate and expand upon a broad, naturalistic, and holistic conception of the reading process.

Although this conference series commenced in 1932, it owes

its origins to a fundamental reconceptualization of the nature of reading behavior which began to take place something over 100 years ago, and which continues to this day. I am not speaking here of the old, and tired, phonics/whole-word controversy, which took shape in the 1840s after Horace Mann and several others brought back the idea from Germany that it was more meaningful to start formal instruction in reading with words themselves rather than their apparent parts. (There was also a sentence method, but its popularity in this country did not last long.) Although it is popular to think that the differences between a phonics method and a whole-word method are true differences, as well as terribly important ones — witness the editorial page of a recent *Los Angeles Times* for yet another example — it is very much the kettle calling the skillet black. (1) This is because both rely on developing the same basic process, of developing associations between sound and symbol, out of which activity meaning is supposed to be derived. In both, reading can be likened to hearing familiar sounds go off in one's head. In both, there is a subject matter to be learned as a precondition to the achievement of meaning. The learning tasks, while they may deal with a somewhat different subject matter, especially in the initial stages of instruction, are based on the same principles. And in fact they are so closely related, neither a phonics method nor a whole-word method ignores the other, except perhaps at the outset of instruction, with the importance of phonics falling quickly away even then. For my authority on that I shall turn to Jeanne Chall, who has written extensively in favor of returning to what she euphemistically calls a "code-emphasis," and in the process has brought phonics methods back some of their lost respectability. Even Chall suggests that "once a pupil has learned to recognize in print the words he knows . . . , any additional work on decoding is a sheer waste of time." (2)

To put it in a nutshell, the differences we commonly attribute to phonics and whole-word methods of teaching are minor compared to their similarities when it comes down to the kind of learning we expect will occur, and what we think is necessary to have reading occur. While the subject matter may differ a bit, at least at the beginning, both treat reading behavior as something that must, of necessity, be *invoked.*

The reconceptualization which began a century ago takes a position almost diametrically opposite. This is the view that reading is only incidentally learned in formal environments. While there will necessarily be assistance, for the most part one learns to read through practice. Where traditional methods (i.e., phonics or whole-word) perceive skills as precursors to the achievement of meaning, this view — we can call it an experiential or naturalistic one — places *meaning* at the center of the activity we call reading. Skill grows as a consequence of practice, which in turn occurs because the reader is always, first, attempting to create meanings for the things he seeks to read. With regard for the problem of assuring the presence of abilities which make initial and subsequent reading possible, the assumption here is that the environment, given that it is sufficiently rich, will allow for their natural development, and it is therefore necessary in only a few cases that it be provided. Reading is perceived not as behavior which can be obtained only by *in*voking it; rather it is a natural form of behavior which only needs to be *e*voked. In other words, it becomes present in some sufficient form quite naturally and only needs to be encouraged into a fuller being.

The view that reading is a product of normal development and that it is driven by a naturally occurring search to make meanings on the part of the reader was first articulated at length by Edmund Burke Huey in 1908. (3) In his book, *The Psychology and Pedagogy of Reading*, Huey describes what he calls a naturalistic method of teaching reading. He believed that the child would pick up reading "as naturally as the sun shines," if parents could arrange a relatively simple scenario, what we might call a "curriculum of the mother's knee." All that was needed was a caring parent, a book (with good illustrations), and a knee to sit upon while the child was being read to and encouraged to think about the ideas presented.

Huey recognized there would be some children who would not be fortunate enough to have such an opportunity. He proposed for such youngsters a school environment which reflected the home atmosphere and opportunities he thought most likely to bring about reading. If the child still didn't learn in this environment, he would provide formal instruction beginning around the age of 9 or 10. Huey's counterpart today in this regard is Hans Furth, who puts it more bluntly when he says that children before that age should in any case be learning how to *think* rather than how to *read*. (4) They will have ample time to learn to read, he has said, and will gain the skill quickly, if they are a little older. Meanwhile, they have the time to develop their intellect rather than spending it on what are nothing more than low-level mental exercises.

Following the publication of Huey's book there appeared numerous others, along with journal articles, elaborating on

Huey's naturalistic methodology. Those of us in teaching are inclined to think that it really is possible to run across something new in the educational scene, until another example such as this comes to our attention. Any brief visit to a university library will reveal that such things as the "Language-Experience Approach" to reading, although not going under that flag, will be found described in great detail in many publications during the 20s and 30s.

It was out of this milieu that Peter Spencer called the first of what has turned out to be such a long-running series of meetings, that summer in 1932. It is perhaps difficult for us today to appreciate the fact that there have been other times when new educational ideas were welcomed, perhaps not wildly so, but welcomed and encouraged. In a time when such tight restrictions are placed on individual teacher behavior, it does not seem possible that there have been periods in which it might be suggested that the school become more open to ideas. All we see today are criticisms of our efforts and suggestions that we return to another time when things were presumably more structured and under control. But that was not the climate of the early 30s or even in later periods, for that matter.

In order to understand Spencer's major contribution to the field of reading, it is necessary to appreciate the fact that we have been ignorant about the nature of reading behavior until very recently. That ignorance has not abated entirely, by any manner of means. We still know very little, virtually nothing, about *how* children actually learn to read or write, or speak or listen for that matter. But we have a mass of recent data, although still largely inferential, and it is helping dispel that ignorance. It either takes a great deal of gall, or another kind of ignorance, for someone to tell you that they know exactly how children should be *taught* to read, because by doing so they imply they know exactly *how* children learn to read. We teach, and we hope children learn. But it is still not possible for us to know whether what we did actually produced the results we see. So, we are inclined to think that if we get what we wanted (in the way of behavior), then our teaching is responsible for what may only be a serendipitous effect. On the other side of it, if the results are unsatisfactory, we place the blame elsewhere than on the teaching.

The situation is somewhat analogous to our experiences in mental testing. In the early stages of our efforts in this regard, little more than 100 years ago, doctors believed that the size of the cranial cavity was an appropriate measure of intelligence. (5)

This obviously had to be an after-the-fact measurement and could not include any actual measure of performance. Nonetheless, they went ahead, filling various cavities of skulls gathered from around the world with buckshot, refining their methodology as they went along (mainly by standardizing the size of the shot itself). Not surprisingly, the good doctors found that men were generally more intelligent than women; and some races, more intelligent than others, among other scientific "facts" which eventually took some time to dispel as we went on to measure lumps on the head instead of pouring inert material into the remains of what was once a human being. The idea that physiology was destiny in mental measurement dies hard, and is, in fact, not dead yet by any means.

The point is that, if your initial concepts are off base, so will be everything else. Now back to Spencer. He believed initial concepts which guided traditional methods of teaching reading to be invalid. I will name only three of the ideas that he disagreed with here:

1. That the achievement of meaning is dependent upon the prior development of specific skills.

2. That words themselves possess meanings which reside outside of the direct, personal experience of the learner.

3. That reading itself is an unnatural form of behavior dependent for its existence upon formal instruction.

Instead, he argued that reading itself is a generic form of behavior driven by the need to create meanings for those things in the environment for which the reader is able to develop some kind of awareness. Skill at interpreting or building meanings for such stimuli then depends upon the quality of the experiences the learners have with them. Spencer considered "reading" to be descriptive of behavior associated with any and every form of stimulation. One reads music, either its notation or its actual performance, faces, social situations, numbers, chemical formulas, and, of course, words when they are presented in their printed, as well as their aural, form. Spencer divided reading in this broad sense into two major types: primary reading, or the reading of things, and secondary reading, the reading of symbols of things. This is in some ways, as you can see, nothing more than the application of the term "reading" as we use it in everyday life. If it fits there, why does it not fit in school?

This broad conception of reading behavior is not easy to assimilate, especially if the conventional wisdom has a good hold on one's thinking. I cannot convince you of its validity; you must weigh the evidence yourself — no one else can conclude anything for you on this subject. The point I would make is that Spencer wrested the notion of reading away from its usual narrow association with literacy as skill in writing and reading, at the same time denying it a *special* role as a unique, and often contrary form of human behavior. There is not time to elaborate on this very different view — I want to concentrate here on the gist of the message — and so I would refer those of you who are intrigued by it, and what it might mean for teaching, to his book, *Reading Reading*, and of course to prior Claremont Reading Conference Yearbooks. (6) Knowing just this, however, I think it can be appreciated why the first meeting of this conference series was called "The Claremont Reading and Curriculum Implementation Conference." Reading in its broad sense expresses a legitimate concern for the total curriculum and places reading narrowly construed in every part of it. Indeed, William S. Gray, "Mr. Reading" for over half a century, in an *Elementary School Journal* article on the conference in 1945, wrote that "Spencer and the contributors to the Yearbook present a point of view that merits large emphasis in any valid conception of the total function to be rendered by schools and good teaching." (7)

One other comment seems appropriate about Spencer's work. As he developed his ideas, he evolved a model of reading behavior which I believe to be the first of its kind. We have several people appearing on our program who have participated rather extensively in model building in their particular fields of interest. Spencer, a man always ahead of his time, was, I'm afraid, ahead here too!

Spencer directed this conference series, following a star put up for him by Albert Einstein, who, when asked how he accounted for his contribution to science was reputed to have said, "I challenged an axiom." Spencer had indeed challenged an axiom. But like another person living in a somewhat earlier period, Edmund Huey, he found fewer listening than he should have. Huey's 1908 book actually languished on the shelves for 60 years, unnoticed and unread, if the still original bindings I have seen are any indication. It only really gained notice when it was republished by the MIT Press in 1968. Spencer's own ideas became widely known but were so contrary to the conventional wisdom few, including Dr. Gray, I fear, could sense how to turn them into practice. Nor did many challenge Spencer's ideas outright; they seemed implicitly logical and sensible. It was when it came to classroom practice that conventional wisdom overwhelmed us. And of course, our ignorance of language processing continued. We still believed that verbal language learning occurred in fairly discrete units and that it involved large doses of imitation and relatively low-level forms of associationism. The Pavlovian model was the accepted model. Learning was viewed as an essentially passive activity with the learner largely at the mercy of the manipulations of others.

Several developments began to take place at about the time of Spencer's retirement in 1958 which are now putting an entirely new face on matters, and they are, in my judgment, largely confirmatory of his original conceptualization of reading behavior. For me, two events are key to what is turning out to be a major knowledge explosion which is now requiring us to totally reassess what we have been doing. One was the American publication of Jean Piaget's work. Piaget had been widely known elsewhere, his books had been available in England for years, and the influence of his contribution to the understandings of thought processes is widely acknowledged there. We were not privy to his thinking, at least on any kind of wide basis, for some 25 years or more later than that. The reasons for that unconscionable delay make another story, but they lie in the refusal of American scholars to accept the validity of his research methods, a matter which has now been overcome to a considerable degree.

The second development has been the invention of the portable high fidelity tape recorder. When the capabilities of this instrument to stop language in mid-flight, so to speak, making it available for analysis, were combined with the research skills of the linguists and other scholars interested in language and cognitive development, we came into possession of an extremely valuable tool. Now, 20 or so years later, we are in possession of information almost totally unavailable to us previously regarding how children learn to speak and to write. Listening research remains moribund, however, primarily because we have yet to discover what, if any, residue there may be to this activity. With an exception or perhaps two — I think first of the miscue research — the same circumstance seems to afflict print reading. Reading leaves little or no residue detectable other than by inference, and if our newer findings, following on Spencer's theorizing, are any indication, what we have assumed is residue is at best only remotely so. Despite the many tests which we are told measure reading competence, the chances are that our ability to make such measurements is therefore probably equally suspect.

These new data point out several things of importance. One is that the verbal language functions are complexly interrelated. Development in one affects development in the others. A second is that the learner is an active participant in his own development. He is in many ways teaching himself to speak, to write, and to read. He is in a very real sense constructing his own curriculum, laying out his own learning agenda, and one would hope with a minimum of interference. Third, the search for meaning takes precedence over the development of skill in revealing meaning. Learning that is not meaningful is indeed meaningless. It possesses an extraordinarily short half-life.

The last several years of the conference series have emphasized these aspects of the knowledge explosion in cognition and language development. During that period there has been widening recognition that the problem of literacy, even narrowly conceived, requires the attention of persons from a wide variety of interests, from medicine, psychiatry, sociology, history, government, English, the arts, and other fields as well as education and psychology. I am very optimistic about our coming to understand reading better in the future.

I am less optimistic about our ability to turn theory into practice. That involves political issues of considerable magnitude. Earlier, I mentioned the presence of periods in recent American educational history when there was a reasonable, if not a considerable, acceptance of difference both in opinion as to the nature of the problems we face and with regard for how teaching should be carried out. The most recent example includes the period following the Korean War, and extending well into the late 60s. During this time, for example, considerable attention was paid to the work of Willard Olson, a distinguished educationist and developmental psychologist at the University of Michigan. (8) Olson inferred from his own research in physiological development, and that of others, that children who were placed in a relatively free but carefully arranged environment for reading instruction would engage in reading activities which would produce growth in achievement commensurate with or better than conventional instructional situations. He believed children would engage constructively in what he termed *seeking, self-selection, and pacing* activities where books were concerned and that the resulting practice would result in improved reading. Which it did.

So-called *Self-Selection Reading Programs* were very popular for a number of years, as were *individualized* and

personalized reading programs, let alone the Language-
Experience Approach to Reading with which R. Van Allen is so
closely identified. These have almost entirely disappeared from
the scene. They are not dead, but their health is in question. In
its place we find highly structured programs, little teacher
initiative in choosing what methods to use in teaching, and often
the mandating of method and materials by persons far removed
from the classroom and even the school itself. The demise of
statewide subject matter requirements, almost 15 years ago now
here in California, has led to the institution of state-wide testing
and its gradual increase, now to intolerable levels, at least for
elementary school teachers. A "silicon revolution" has led to the
development of an almost infinite array of new modes for
presenting lessons, particularly in reading print. Unfortunately,
virtually all of them are, so far, simply recapitulations of the kind
of lessons so familiar in the conventional reading textbook series.

So the current situation is mixed indeed. On the one hand we
live in exciting times. We know more about aspects of human
development related to reading than ever before. This new
knowledge augurs well where expanding our understanding of the
nature of the problem of reading is concerned. But the politics of
reading threatens to make that information unuseable in the
school. For those of us who fly the colors of the rationalist in the
hope that reason can indeed be applied to the solution of
educational problems, all I can say is that there is a great deal
more work to do in the vineyard.

REFERENCES

1 Patrick Groff, "Pho-nics: It's Not Too Late to Sound Out a Bad Error," *Los Angeles Times*, January 19, 1983 (II).
2 Jeanne Chall, *Learning to Read: The Great Debate*. McGraw-Hill, 1967, p. 307.
3 Edmund Burke Huey, *The Psychology and Pedagogy of Reading*. Macmillan, 1908 (reprinted by the MIT Press, 1968).
4 Hans Furth, *Piaget for Teachers*. Prentice-Hall, 1970.
5 Stephen Jay Gould, *The Mismeasure of Man*. Norton, 1981. See especially: Chapter 2.
6 Peter Lincoln Spencer, *Reading Reading*. College Press, Claremont, California, 1971. See also: *Claremont Reading Conference Yearbook*, Center for Developmental Studies, Claremont Graduate School, Claremont, California 91711. (Also available through University Microfilms, Ann Arbor, Michigan 48103.)
7 William S. Gray, "The Claremont Colleges Reading Conference," *Elementary School Journal*, 45:488-489, May, 1945.
8 Willard C. Olson, *Child Development* (2nd ed.). D.C. Heath, 1959.

Language, Cognitive Development, and Reading Behavior

Yetta Goodman

It is exciting to be a part of this 50th anniversary of the Claremont Reading Conference. Everytime I come back to California, it helps me remember that my views about schooling and reading started here. I did my teacher training in Southern California in the early fifties and then taught here for ten years. When I talk to my undergraduate students, they are astonished by the wondrous "new methods" I present. I always admit that the methods were the ones I learned and put into practice thirty years ago. They grew out of the progressive education movement, and there is little new about the methodology. The one major new aspect is that we have more research than ever before to support the humanistic, holistic methods of teaching the language arts, including reading and writing.

There is ample evidence that shows children learn to read and write prior to formal schooling. That is, they may not yet be reading and writing in a conventional sense, but they certainly have built all kinds of conceptualizations about the written language system before schooling takes place. It is important that curriculum development be based on this knowledge.

When educators don't take into consideration what children know when they come to school, it is possible to interfere with their language development. I believe much of the trouble children have with reading and writing in school starts when the child's own cognitive knowledge about the written language system is rejected or ignored. The children then begin to believe the fragmented notions that some teachers present about language, and they try to accommodate a system that doesn't make sense to them — to their cognitive development.

There is enough evidence at this point to know children are indeed inventing written language even earlier than the age of two. There are some people looking at children's response to written language starting at six or seven months. We need additional studies for this age group similar to the longitudinal

10

study done by Glenda Bissex on her son, Paul, age 5-11,
(Bissex, 1980) or similar to Halliday's oral language work on
Nigel (Halliday, 1982). We need longitudinal studies by parents
on their own children, or by people who can go into homes for a
long period of time and watch children's developing inter-actions
with written language.

When my granddaughter was five months old, I was holding
her in my arms as I was reading an airline schedule. As I was
flipping through the pages, she was looking at the pamphlet with
incredible intensity. If we believe as Piaget says that children act
on objects in their environment — and begin to build hypotheses
about those objects — then my granddaughter at five months was
responding in just that way, building hypotheses about written
language events.

There are seven different areas of investigation in the field of
literacy before schooling. There are ethnographic investigations.
Educational sociologists and people interested in anthropology
and education are looking at the impact of literacy on very young
children. They are studying home environments, watching parents
interacting with homework, watching what two-year-olds do when
fathers are filling out unemployment and medical forms (Leichter,
1983). Others are looking at how children respond to story telling
at home (Doake, 1981). All this ethnographic research will shed
light on the impact of literacy events on children in home
situations. Shirley Brice-Heath has spent eight years looking at
literacy development in working class communities in the South
(Brice-Heath, 1983). Her book presents the literacy development
of two southern working class communities, showing their
interaction with literacy events.

Second, there is a group of studies looking at how children
respond to print awareness in their environment: to signs, names,
and symbols of all kinds (Harste, Burke, Woodward, 1982;
Goodman and Altwerger, 1981). Also, these investigations focus
on how children respond to the handling of books (Clay, 1979).

Story research is examining how children respond to
narratives. The work of Arthur Applebee and Howard Gardner is
significant in this third area (Applebee, 1978; and Gardner,
1982).

A great deal of work is being done on children's writing
production, especially in the development of spelling. Charles
Read's work, for example, among others, is significant (Read,
1971). Others are looking at children's stories and how children
develop written narratives (Graves, 1983).

Dolores Durkin's retrospective studies focus on what happened to children who learned to read before they came to school (Durkin, 1966). Similar work has been done in England (Clark, 1978).

The sixth area has to do with the child's metalinguistic awareness. Work has been done providing insight into what knowledge about written language children have (Downing, 1981).

Finally, recent studies from Piagetian psychologists utilizing innovative Piagetian literacy tasks are showing how children respond to written language as an object (Ferreiro and Teberosky, 1979). I will discuss one such study in detail later.

I have summarized the seven areas of research into pre-school literacy. One intriguing note: I have examples of children's scribbling from many countries. In the same way the very young babble in a representation of adult oral language, when children start scribbling, their scribbling represents the orthographic structures of the written language into which they are being acculturated. This is tangible evidence of the early awareness of their written language system.

Research in literacy before schooling has been conducted in many languages, with many different alphabetic systems, in many different countries. We may disagree on some specifics, such as stage development and the kinds of specifics that children know, but generally we have all concluded that children do know about written language before they come to school. Whether they are reading and writing depends on a definition of reading and writing. From my point of view, I believe they are actually reading and writing before they come to school.

The work of Emilia Ferreiro and Ana Teberosky, Piagetian psychologists, provides specific insights that are worth a detailed discussion (1982). This work should have a tremendous impact on our understanding of what children know about written language. It is the first Piagetian look at literacy tasks by adapting the Piagetian clinical approach to the objects of literacy itself.

By the time children are three or four, the following seems to be happening: first, children know written language is not just marks on paper; rather, written language represents something external to the graphic system. They know written language says something. When a three-year-old comes up and asks, "What does this say?", that is a bit of data demonstrating this awareness. Second, to these young children both pictures and print represent ideas, but pictures and print are different kinds of representations. Children initially believe that print represents ideas, not alphabetic writing. Although they haven't yet moved into an awareness of the alphabetic writing system, they do know that written language says something.

For example, if you show a child his own name in print, "Johnny," and ask him what that says, he might well respond orally, "John Jones Jr." The child knows "Johnny" represents him whether it is called John, John Jones Jr., Johnny or even, as some children respond, "That's me." This is an example of the growing evidence that for the young child, written language is some iconic form different from a picture.

Ferreiro and Teberosky have found some interesting results among Argentinian children that we are finding with English speaking children. For instance, in order for something to be readable it must have a minimum of three letters. Less than three letters and children will say, "not readable." Most words in English are three letters or more, except for function words. Maybe function words should never have been separated from content words, but that is a linguistic argument beyond this discussion. Not only does the written word have to have three letters for the child but they have to be three different letters; "ccc" cannot be read, but "cae" is readable. There is no difference between socioeconomic classes on these two principles.

After the earlier iconic view of written language, children begin to treat written language as if it were syllabic. That is, they begin to match written language units to what they perceive are equivalent oral language units. Later on they begin to be aware of the alphabetic principles of language. They don't know syllables in the traditional grammatical sense. Children just know there is some relationship between oral and written language.

Those who teach beginning reading should remember that children are trying to match an oral equivalent with a printed word, but sometimes what they see doesn't match their scheme. For example, when Suzanne saw "The boy saw something," she read, "The boy saw some," believing that SOMETHING is SOME since it is one unit. She was looking for where "thing" was, because to her it had to be a separate unit. Teachers have noticed this characteristic for a long time, but now we have research and a theory to help us understand why such things happen. We know children are using intellectual functioning when they get into these problems; they are not simply reading deficits. Children are developing linguistic as well as functional hypotheses about written language. They come to school with a large sense about what written language is and what it can do.

Those of us who have been working with these young children agree learning to read and write is first of all building awareness of what print is and what it can do. Second, it is learning how print makes sense, especially as children begin to focus on the forms that written language takes. Almost simultaneously, children begin to make sense out of print.

I can offer two examples of making sense through and out of print. A four-year-old girl was seated next to me on a plane with her little brother, about two, seated next to her. He had his thumb in his mouth. The plane engines started to rev up and the lighted message began to flash, "Fasten Your Seat Belts/No Smoking." The little girl gave her brother a big shove and said, "Look, Bobby, get your finger out of your mouth. Don't you see what it says up there; "No bad habits!" Some people talk about kids owning their own language. That little girl owned language to the point that she could use it to control other people.

The marvelous language stories about children which occur continuously in our presence helps us understand that children are coming to school with lots of ideas about written language.

What does this mean in terms of schooling? (Goodman and Goodman, 1981). First of all, we know from the other presentations at this conference what happens in homes rich with literacy experiences for children. That is what our schools must do — provide a rich literate environment for children as early as possible.

Three-year-olds are writing. They are writing with magic markers, they are writing with pens, they are writing with crayons. Yet some schools still are mandating that children must use those great big horse-leg pencils and paper with lines six feet apart with pieces of wood still floating in it in order to write. It takes a long time to make an "A" if the child has to go from the top to the bottom with lines that far apart. Children have too many rich experiences at home to have their behavior controlled by graded pencils and paper and outmoded ideas about carefully controlled writing instruction.

I want to encourage story reading and story writing, but I also think in addition to children's literature we need to legitimize the wide range of practical literacy functions (Goodman and Goodman, 1983). Many of our working class children have many experiences with the pragmatic aspects of reading and writing. There is one working family class where the mother has a whole category system for food coupons. Her three- and five-year-olds help her file the coupons according to the aisles in the supermarket.

We should not overemphasize the simplistic filling out of forms in the name of pragmatism. Functional reading and writing are very frequent and various in our society. Things we do every day such as making lists, keeping diaries, reading and writing letters should be emphasized at school. In kindergarten or first grade, teachers should place pencils and papers in the housecorner and the wheel toy areas. Children can make shopping lists and keep track of gas usage. There are so many kinds of reading and writing to add to play. Pragmatic literacy experiences need to be a part of the curriculum for young children embedded in their other learning experiences.

Reading and writing development has nothing to do with readiness, especially as it has developed into practice in our schools. You don't get ready to read and write; you do reading and writing. The group we are hurting the most with the notion of readiness are bilingual children or children who are diagnosed in some way as using oral language in a limited fashion. We keep waiting for them to demonstrate fluent oral English. You can learn to read and write without fluent oral anything. We have to seriously consider this issue, because we hold groups of children back from reading and writing waiting for them "to be ready." Traditional readiness notions get in the way of providing rich literacy experiences for children.

We have got to learn to trust learners to learn. The work of Piaget, of Vygotsky, the research I've just summarized about literacy development show that kids are indeed actively involved in learning reading and writing before they come to school. We have to trust that learning. Our lack of trust in the process of learning to read and write makes us turn language into very artificial and very abstract bits and pieces. We can instead set up language learning environments where children are comfortable, where they are familiar with written language, where they are interacting with each other, where they have personal and social reasons to communicate through reading and writing.

REFERENCES

Anderson, Alonzo. AWAKENING TO LITERACY (Eds.) H. Goelman, A. Oberg and F. Smith. Heinemann. Due November, 1983.

Applebee, Arthur. THE CHILD'S CONCEPT OF STORY. The University of Chicago Press. Chicago and London, 1978.

Beers, James and Edmund Henderson. "A Study of Developing Orthographic Concepts Among First Graders." RESEARCH IN TEACHING OF ENGLISH. 1978, pp. 133-148.

Bissex, Glenda. GYNS AT WORK. Harvard University Press. Cambridge, Massachusetts, 1980.

Clark, Margaret. YOUNG FLUENT READERS: WHAT CAN THEY TELL US? Exeter, New Hampshire. Heinemann Educational Books, 1978.

Clay, Marie. THE EARLY DETECTION OF READING DIFFICULTIES. Heinemann Educational Books. 2nd Edition, 1979.

Doake, David B. "Book Experience and Emergent Reading Behavior in Preschool Children." Doctoral Thesis. University of Alberta, Edmonton, Alberta, Canada, 1981.

Downing, John. "What Do Children Need to Know About Language to Profit From Reading Instruction?" Paper presented at the annual convention of the International Reading Association, New Orleans, Louisiana, 1981.

Durkin, Dolores. CHILDREN WHO READ EARLY. New York: Teachers College Press, 1966.

Ferreiro, Emilia and Anna Teberosky. LITERACY BEFORE SCHOOLING, Exeter, New Hampshire. Heinemann Educational Books, 1979.

Gardner, Howard. "The Making Of A Story Teller." PSYCHOLOGY TODAY, March 1982.

Goodman, Kenneth and Yetta Goodman. "A Whole Language Comprehension Centered Reading Program." Occasional Paper No. 1. Program in Language and Literacy, University of Arizina, 1981.

  "Reading and Writing Relationships: Pragmatic Functions." LANGUAGE ARTS. Volume 60, Number 5, May 1983.

Goodman, Yetta and Bess Altwerger. "A Study of Literacy in Preschool Children." Occasional Paper No. 4. Program in Language and Literacy, University of Arizona, 1981.

Graves, Donald. WRITING: TEACHERS AND CHILDREN AT WORK. Heinemann Educational Books. Exeter, New Hampshire and London, 1983.

Halliday, M.A.K. "How Children Learn Language." *English in the 80's*, R.D. Eagleson, Ed. Papers presented at the Third International Conference for the Teaching of English, Adelaide, New South Wales, 1982.

Heath, Shirley Brice. WAYS WITH WORDS. (In press.)

Harste, Jerome, Carolyn Burke, and Virginia Woodward. "The Young Child as Writer-Reader and Informant." Indiana University. NIE Final Report, 1983.

Leichter, Hope. "Families as Environments for Literacy." AWAKENING TO LITERACY. (Eds.) H. Goelman, A. Oberg and F. Smith. Heinemann Educational Books. Due November, 1983.

Read, Charles. "Pre-school Children's Knowledge of English Phonology," HARVARD EDUCATIONAL REVIEW. February, 1971, pp. 1-34.

Why Read?

Herbert Kohl

My oldest daughter, Tonia, is an omnivorous reader. She has read the *Dune Trilogy* 15 times, and she has read all of Ann McCaffery's books. She even delved into Hemingway when she had nothing else to read, because Hemingway was in the house. Once, in despair, she was wandering around the house looking for a book. (She put on "The Clash" as loud as possible to get into a comfortable mode of reading. Now, you're thinking "You cannot listen to 'The Clash' and read at the same time." Right? Of course you can! Especially if you listen to "The Clash" 400 times and it eliminates random noise.) To keep her busy, I gave her *War and Peace*. She grabbed ahold of it and read it avidly, and fortunately it did keep her busy for about a week. After finishing it, she said, "That's one of the most wonderful science fiction novels I have ever read!" When I inquired as to what she meant by science fiction novel, she replied, "It has all these people with these strange names, living on this weird planet, trying to make love in the middle of war while they cross the Tundra. That's science fiction!" Of course she is right. Not only is she right, but it is a whole new "take" for me on *War and Peace*. It is really quite wonderful.

The point is that kids will come to classics when they are not told that they are classics. *War and Peace* is extraordinary because Tolstoy can write about people in a way that very few authors have ever written about people. But children can't appreciate that quality of work, because they are always required to list reasons why a classical work is a classic and because they do not have adequate opportunity to approach it and to feel it.

The reason Shakespeare is good is because Shakespeare is good, because he has something to say, not because the teacher says Shakespeare is good. That's the basis for my summer drama class for children from 7 to 14 years of age. Over the last four summers, we have done "Midsummer Night's Dream," "Antigone," and "Macbeth." I chose their dramas carefully for the content and then rewrote them for the kids. I chose "Midsummer Night's Dream," for instance, because it is really about adolescent love. The theme "I love her but she loves him but he loves me and then we turn into donkeys at the light of the moon and astrology determines that we fall in love with the next thing we see and then suddenly everything works out well in the end" is teenage love! So, I approached "Midsummer Night's Dream" in that way. The only problem was that we had eight kids who wanted to be Puck, so I created eight Pucks. It was very easy. I had each child memorize three lines of Shakespeare and understand what they were saying. Of course what happened was that the whole play was transformed. Puck was up in the trees; Puck was under the stage; Puck was in the audience. And, as a result, everybody was a part of "Midsummer Night's Dream."

I chose "Antigone" because it was a play about female defiance of male authority. Many of the kids that I work with can really relate to that issue, and this includes many of the males who also hate male authority. Again, the kids transformed the play: in our version, a whole group of males joined Antigone and Ismene at the end of the play and together they overthrew Creon, the King. After the performance, a couple of "type 3" teachers came up to me and said, "You can't rewrite a play." I said, "We have already done it, so I know I can." They missed the point. If you know anything about the history of literature, you know that playwrights and authors are always rewriting — there are seven versions of "Antigone," for instance. The fact is that literature is alive, and themes exist to be changed. You do not do one "take" on something, because that is an impoverishment of experience.

I picked "Tartuffe" because it is about Christian hypocrisy, and that is an issue in our society. I left the Christian movement out of it, so as not to offend some people. We just centered on hypocrisy. We set it in the court. I took "Tartuffe" and threw in some ideas from Scapin (from Moliere's "Les Fourbrieres de Scapin"), because they were very funny, and kids appreciate humor! We set the whole thing in the court of Louis XIV and created a Punch and Judy show for Louis when he was a little child. Then we performed "Tartuffe" for the adult Louis. With a couple of magical changes, we had a five-year-old playing the young Louis and a sixteen-year-old playing Louis at the age of 32. The kids found all of this wonderful. Why? Because the play was the children's "tale" of a servant woman who unveils the hypocrisy of the middle class bourgeois.

This summer I chose "Macbeth," because it had to do with excessive and abusive uses of power. This, too, reflects a problem in contemporary society. In doing "Macbeth," the kids said, "We had twelve Pucks; why don't we have twelve witches?" So, we had all those witches, and we had Hecate.

One of the things that we did in the summer classes — and this is terribly important not only in teaching classics but in any form of teaching — was before touching Shakespeare and before touching Greek tragedies, we touched the human themes, the content. Why would anyone bother to sit in a cave and write or get up on stage and torture themselves and dream about the kind of language that leads to the creation of literature unless there is human purpose and unless there is some deep intent? The critical thing is to come at literature through the theme, not through the technique or even less through a particular book. That is not to say that books are not important. Sometimes a book moves me very much, but the reason it moves me is because of what is in it.

I happen to be one of those people who loves books, who has always loved books. In the late 40s, my grandmother used to give me five dollars a month to buy clothes. I was supposed to go down to Hudson Street on the lower East Side of New York and buy a whole suit. Instead, I would go to a book store and buy used books. Then I would sneak the books into the house. It was not just owning the books that fascinated me, but knowing what was in them. Growing up in an all-Jewish community in the Bronx with no diversity, my books were access to the whole world. In fact, I used to hide behind my textbooks so that I could read my own paperbacks. I had to pretend I was reading in order to read! And that is frequently what happens in our schools today. You have to pretend that you are doing what you are required to do in order to get away with what you really care about doing.

Let me give you another example. My son Josh plays the trumpet in the band. He is supposed to practice at home, and we, his parents, are supposed to sign his practice sheet, once for every day he puts in. But, there's a problem. Josh has perfect pitch. Once he hears the teacher play a song, he knows it. In short, he has no reason to practice, and so he does not practice. But, he will not get a good grade in school unless we sign the practice sheets. Since both my wife and I have pretended to learn in order to protect our ability to learn, we just sign the sheets.

John Holt once said that "we are all part of the walking wounded." Yet something in us objects and says, "I will never teach like these people taught me. It took a long time for me to discover what I was going to do differently. The large change was an unwavering determination to engage students on a level that constantly shows them that life is exciting and that the world is incredibly rich. The impoverishment of life in the classroom is the major thing that causes the pretense of learning. It is the one thing you have to worry about. For instance, one of my greatest nightmares is a "reading center" consisting of workbooks, a tape recorder with plug-in earphones, and a series of comprehension drills and spelling exercises with dictionaries next to them.

My nightmare came true once. I was asked to assess a classroom which was incredibly well organized. In fact, many of the students had had behavior problems, but in the class they were all fine. The problem was that they all scored above average on phonics, yet none of them was anything less than three and one-half years behind in sixth grade comprehension. It was a great, great puzzle to everybody why these students could not do the comprehension problems.

When I went into the classroom, they were reading a book called *Crow Boy*. It's a moving book about a child who is a kind of magical loner, an orphan. It contains all the themes that rend the heart. When I entered the room, the kids were plugged into the tape recorder, and they were turning the pages every time the tape binged; most of them were looking at the ceiling. Those who wanted to read couldn't, because they had delayed auditory feedback: the tape recorder was reading at a different and much slower rate than they were reading. It is like hearing your own voice over-dubbed (which is one known way to induce schizophrenia).

When the children were finished listening, they put their books down and went to the Vocabulary Center to look up the words that they supposedly did not know. How did they know which words to look up? They were told which of the words they did not know in the text, because those were the words written on a purple ditto master. The children looked up the words, wrote down the answers, and all got 100%. They knew how to look up words and copy definitions. But, they did not know how to read the words they were looking up. They had also mastered the comprehension exercises; they were really clever kids. They figured out that a comprehension question takes a sentence from the book, tells you what page it is on, inverts it, and turns it into a question. All you have to do is reinvert it, and you have the answer to the question without reading the book. They knew at least one of Noam Chomsky's grammatical transformations, but that was all they knew. The problem in this classroom was the classroom.

Noam Chomsky has told me that it makes him ill to think about the way in which his ideas and those of thinkers like Piaget, which describe how people learn naturally, have been transformed by the commercial interests into systems which attempt to describe how to teach people to learn. It is very important to understand that ideas like transformational grammar or any of the theories of learning explain what happens physiologically and intellectually when you learn in a natural context. Piaget, in essence, is saying, "Get kids into a rich environment, and then my theories describe how they learn there." I think when teachers look at commercial products, they have to be very careful to look at the transformation of original material from the descriptive mode, how someone learns, into the prescriptive mode which says, "I'm going to teach you how to use this material."

Right now teachers have a tendency to use pre-packaged materials and turn anything into what I call "flight from content." People are afraid to have classroom talk about love, about politics, or about hypocrisy. This fear may stem from the belief that truth is not very popular in our society, because you have to face some very unpleasant facts such as the tolerance of poverty and the resurgence of racism. The fact is that truthful discussions raise all kinds of very complex and difficult issues. It is far easier to reduce learning to phonics. Learning, then, becomes the "back to basics" movement, which is an avoidance of dealing with the contradictions within our own lives and that of our society. It is a way of forcing kids to avoid expressing themselves or thinking about political and social issues in the classroom. Back to basics has nothing, so far as I can tell, to do with anything that is documented or proven. There is no proof, for instance, that phonics, as a reading method, works. In fact, this whole approach is an attempt to go back to something that has already failed. If it had not failed, we would still be using it. There would not be any reason to go back.

Since we can't find an intellectual, educational, or pedagogical reason for using an approach such as phonics, we must turn to politics. As teachers we are intimidated by the small minority of ultraconservatives and rather than risk their censure, we retreat to phonics. I think that just because ideas such as equity, racial equality, social justice, and elimination of hunger are not "popular" does not mean that they are wrong for the classroom. If you believe in them, you have an obligation to bring them up. There is a contemporary inability, for example, to talk about socialism in a fair and decent way; as a result, teachers are afraid to deal with literature that does cover the topic. Yet there is a socialist government in France; there is a socialist government in Greece; there is a socialist government in Spain. There might be a socialist government in England very soon; there have been some in the Scandinavian countries. We, however, are unable to tell our kids the difference between Socialism and Communism, because we are afraid to talk about it.

We have to rethink the whole question of our obligation in education. Our obligation is to the students and to the world they will live in as adults. Therefore, we must talk about our own social and personal obligations. We must talk about human truths in the classroom. And that is why literature exists; that is why reading exists. It exists to enrich human life.

A Janus Look
at Reading Comprehension

John D. McNeil

There is an unprecedented interest in reading comprehension. Part of the interest comes from the current work of cognitive psychologists, scholars in artificial intelligence, and students of linguistics. Researchers in these disciplines are using a constructive view of reading comprehension, holding that individuals actively construct the form and content of their own experience. Another source of interest is political. There is public concern that pupils are not learning to comprehend their textbooks and the reading materials of everyday life.

My purpose in this paper is to compare current views of the constructivists and the views of reading comprehension as expressed for many years at the Claremont Reading Conferences. An array of instructional practices consistent with the constructivist perspective is presented.

A Forward Look: The Constructivist Paradigm

According to constructivists, reading comprehension is a process by which one actively constructs meaning from among parts of the text and between the text and one's own experience. Basic to the constructivist paradigm are four assumptions:

1) What one knows affects what one will learn from reading. (Prior knowledge interacts with text in the creation of meaning.)
2) Both concept-driven and data-driven processes are necessary in comprehension. (On one hand, the reader's purposes and expectations guide one in monitoring reading; on the other hand, by attending to text new expectations are suggested.)
3) The deeper one processes text, the more it will be remembered. (Retention is greater when text is elaborated by relating it to one's own experiences and purposes and when facts within a text are connected to abstractions.)

4) Context influences what is recalled. (One's perceptions
   and interests determine what is selected from text as well
   as how statements are interpreted.)

Although these assumptions may appear commonplace, much
current teaching indicates that they are not. Conflicting practices
include using formulas which purport to assess difficulty without
regard to the learner's familiarity and interest; the presenting of
brief passages followed by multiple choices, one of which is said
to be the correct meaning; and the failure to provide for pupil
initiated questions in teachers' manuals.

Practices that follow from the constructivist paradigm call for
activating those concepts (schemata) that are related to the
reading material, predicting what will follow, engaging in mental
imagery and other elaborations, monitoring reading by confirming
one's predictions, and revising.

A Review of the Past: The Claremont Concept of Reading

What has been the perspective of reading comprehension as
expressed by presenters at the Claremont Conferences during the
past 50 years? To what extent is this perspective in agreement
with the views of today's constructivists? How has the
perspective differed from the customary and dominant view of
reading text as *reproduction* whereby meaning is assumed to be
in the text, not in an interaction between author and reader? I
sought answers to these questions by reviewing the yearbooks of
the Claremont Reading Conference from 1936 to 1982.

I was surprised. Many of the Claremont presenters were 50
years ahead of their time. Dr. Peter L. Spencer, initiator of the
conference, had ideas that are consistent with those of today's
constructionists. He saw reading and concept building as the
same process. Spencer in the 1936 yearbook defined reading as
the process of making meaningful reactions and interpreting in
light of one's own goals. Through the years, Spencer stressed that
words were not ideas — that ideas could not be extracted from
symbols because symbols are not ideas. Readers must have the
concepts which the symbols represent in order to create meaning
to go with the symbols. Accordingly, one cannot be taught to
read in isolation from content.

Content can be found in all contexts — music, math,
literature, law, and people. Indeed, the surfaces of daily life are
texts to be read. Hence reading is never learned in the sense that
it can no longer be improved. Students may be capable in reading
effectively in one field but less effectively in another. In contrast

with the dominant point of view — that reading is simply a
matter of learning to pronounce words by associating symbols
with sounds, Spencer equated reading with education itself,
admonishing that pupils needed ideas more than workbooks and
that ideas are best acquired through direct experience.

Others who addressed the Claremont Conferences reinforced
the Claremont concept of reading. In 1936 Louise Balmer
defined reading as the process of making meaningful reactions.
Louis Jacques in 1937 emphasized creating meaning from text
and pointed out how the meaning of a selection was greater than
the sum of its parts. In 1938, Beth Barry reiterated the
importance of experiential background in reading and showed
how the retelling of stories could aid in the teaching of reading.
Her words anticipated the forward view, "Reading is bringing
meaning to the page as well as getting meaning from it."
Similarly, William Burton described a good reading program as
one where pupils were not "getting meaning" but "bringing
meaning" from their own experiences.

Throughout most Claremont Conferences, Gestalt psychology
with an emphasis upon seeing the whole and not just a part in
isolation, and a theory of semantics served to remind speakers
and audience of the need to find relationships and meaning in
text.

At the 1952 Conference Edgar Dale used the acronym
COIK, clear only if known. He illustrated how one could follow
directions only if the referents were already familiar. At other
conferences speakers gave examples of how to use the known as
bridges to the unknown. Marguerite Brydegaard, for instance,
showed how primary pupils comprehended the relationship
among dividend, divisor, and quotient by first likening the
dividend to a cake (the constant quantity), the divisor to the
number of persons present, and the quotient to the amount of
cake each person would get.

John Carroll's presentation at the 1969 conference
reexamined the concept of comprehension and compared it with
the concept of inference. He said the literal sense of what is read
is *comprehension* and the inferring of deeper meanings that are
not explicitly stated is *inference.* Comprehension and inference
are necessary for the apprehension of meaning. Carroll's
recommendation that teachers try to make children aware of the
difference in the two concepts is consistent with the
constructionist view that the deriving of meaning in a paragraph
transcends understanding of the literal text. Constructivists have

acted in accordance with Carroll's recommendation and are teaching pupils how to recognize the source of information required for an answer — text explicit, text implicit, or from one's own knowledge, schema implicit. Carroll also suggested that inferences could be enhanced by teaching children to attend to linguistic clues, to "put two and two together" in arriving at a new conclusion and to draw from their own experience.

I would be remiss not to recognize Dr. Malcolm P. Douglass's contribution to the Claremont concept of reading. His leadership in organizing the conferences, his insights into the comprehension of social studies, and his persistent effort to establish a tenable theory of reading that accounts for the complexity of the process are noteworthy.

Briefly then, a Janus look at the Claremont Reading Conferences and the current views of constructivists shows a remarkable concord. Both recognize the centrality of prior experience and concepts (schemata) in the reading process. Both regard comprehension as the construction and creation of meaning rather than mere reproduction.

Practices that are consistent with the Claremont and constructivist perspectives

There are indicators that the Claremont and constructivist views are being implemented. The following abbreviated outline taken from a flowchart for the teaching of reading comprehension from a constructivist view is illustrative. The outline represents a utilization framework for teaching pupils to read narrative and exposition. The components are presented as they might occur before, during, and after reading. Each represents a strategy for teaching and reading.

In order to "read" the outline, you should be familiar with the instructional and learning strategies that go with the labels. A brief explanation may help:

In reading narrative, the concept of story grammar — setting, initiating events, plans of action, ending — is important. Assessment of the child's schema for strong grammar and other aspects of reading may occur through retelling of stories. Self-initiated questions include making predictions and reading for one's own purposes. Such questions are motivating and helpful in monitoring one's reading. Elaboration means interpreting text with existing knowledge. Mental imagery is a form of elaboration. In monitoring the reading process, one strategy calls for knowing where the answer to questions lies. Checking and debugging refer to confirming one's predictions, revising, rereading, and knowing when to read on for further clarification. In addition to assessing the child's conception of reading, story telling is a technique for revealing the meanings children derive from their reading. Questions that integrate the story are more beneficial for comprehension than questions of detail which fragmentize.

In teaching pupils to read exposition, it is important to know the reader's preconceptions, particularly those that will prevent the reader from accepting the content. Strategies for creating cognitive dissonance and dealing with it are available. These strategies expose preconceptions and offer alternative frameworks. Critical incidents and semantic mapping are cases in point. The use of analogy for bridging the known to the new, the Frayer model for developing and relating concepts within a subject matter hierarchy are also important techniques. Metacognitive strategies by which the child independently solves reading tasks are most promising. The rereading of a work from different perspectives adds to the meanings created and helps one to modify preconceptions. Teaching pupils to identify organizational patterns used in expository writing and having pupils convert a simple and less meaningful listing pattern to a more productive cause and effect on compare and contrast pattern has been found to be effective. Similarly, applying the six rules for composing a summary results in better summaries and greater comprehension of text. The revision of a semantic map after reading helps one integrate and retain new information.

On Research and the
Improvement of Reading

Kenneth Goodman

This is a historical occasion and I'm in a historical frame of mind. I feel that way everytime I come back to southern California. A lot happened to me here; I met my wife, married here, and had three children born at Kaiser Hospital in Hollywood. I always am reminded of long drives I had, as a graduate student at UCLA, over Sepulveda to the far reaches of the San Fernando Valley where we lived, late at night after evening classes. I did a lot of thinking about reading and reading research in those travels, sandwiched between the huge trucks heading out towards the grapevine and north from there, and I had some near accidents, puzzling over some things as I went.

In 1960, when I was making those trips, I began to dig at the literature on reading research which then as now was relatively copious. It is a field that has been researched probably more than any other field which educators and researchers are interested in. At the same time I was trying to puzzle through something called linguistics and trying to figure out what relevance that had for me. I really got into it mainly because I understood it was a development in English teaching (at least that was the way it came to me originally).

The more I learned about linguistics and the more I tried to dig into the reading research, the more it gnawed at me. I couldn't find much focus on reading as a language process. In fact, I found a kind of black box view! People would look at the characteristics of print on the page, and they would look at what people did as a result of reading, but what happened in the head between the page and what people did as a response was treated as a black box.

That was partly the strong influence of behavioral psychology and the philosophy of logical empiricism: "I only know what I see and anything else is speculation." It's a peculiar view that still has vestiges today.

It is very interesting to me that in the so-called hard sciences

28

for many many years there has been a strong recognition of the relationship of theory and research. In physics, for instance, theoretical physics and experimental physics are both highly respected areas, and they depend very much on each other.

There was a kind of contempt for theory that I found that pervaded reading research and in place of that a developing atheoretical technology. Americans have always been convinced that we can solve almost any kind of problem technologically.

As I dug into this a little more, I discovered that in the 20s America went through what some people had referred to as the age of scientism in educational research. We were going to find exact ways of measuring everything and on the basis of that know exactly what to do and in the right proportions. That is still around today except that it has taken on a cost accounting aspect, and it is represented in the bed sheets of behavioral objectives that I know exist in California and elsewhere.

The notion is that somehow by sequencing things and by putting them in technological appearing packages you put a scientific face on them. These technological reading programs always remind me of the cancer-curing machines where you hook somebody up to an empty box that has lights blinking, where you create the illusion of science.

I became aware that linguistic science is much more than empty technology. So essentially what I did, as I thought about how I wanted to begin to study reading, was to start where Peter Spencer started and where Edmund Huey started, trying to understand what goes on in a reader's head.

I found that that wasn't where educational research was. Shortly after I got into the field, two things happened that put a capstone on prior research; one was Jeanne Chall's famous book "Reading: The Great Debate" where she tried to put everything in a nutshell (the nutshell was much too small). The other was the series of studies that were called the First Grade Studies. When a little federal money first started to trickle into educational research, some very smart people said, "Wouldn't it be great if we could get a bunch of people to use their methods of teaching reading, and try them against each other, and then we would gather data on all of these. Then we would have the definitive view of which methodology is better or worse than which. So the First Grade Studies were funded: 30 studies of about $30,000 each, about a million dollars, all using the same tests, all feeding it into the same computer data bank at the University of Minnesota, and out of it came a single important conclusion. It turned out the teacher was the most important factor, which of course we knew before.

Something else came out of that though. If the methods that you're using don't have some kind of sound theoretical and scientific base, then you really don't know what you are doing, and why it is working, and why it isn't working. In fact then, the artistic insightful teacher who has a feeling for kids is going to make a difference, and the method is going to turn out not to be very consequential.

It seemed to me that that should have been the end of that kind of research, but it wasn't. Psychology, with educational psychology tagging behind, at that time was literally spinning its wheels. They called them memory drums then, and they were full of nonsense syllables and things like that. People were trying to study language, including reading, by using measures of seeing how long it took for someone to learn a series of nonsense syllables under highly controlled conditions.

Walter Kintsch, who became editor of *Verbal Learning and Verbal Behavior*, describes a whole period of time that psychology went through in the last several decades where they timidly moved from very small units — phonemes, letters, letter parts to, ultimately, sentences. And now they've graduated to short texts, preferably not longer than a paragraph or so, very carefully contrived. It was this preoccupation with isolating factors that philosophers of science called reductionism, reducing everything so it may be controlled.

My favorite example of what is wrong with that kind of research is the study of class size. People have claimed that they have shown that class size didn't make a difference. What they did is to isolate everything but class size so that exactly the same things were happening in all the classes regardless of how big they were. If they had asked the teachers, the teachers would have said the reason they wanted small classes was so that they could do things differently. If you don't do things differently, then it isn't going to make any difference if you have a big class or a small class.

That's reductionism: it's reducing things to the point where you lose what it is that you started to do. And that is what I found happening in language. I looked to the linguists, because I was very curious about why people weren't treating reading as a language process. I found almost nothing in the linguistic literature on reading, and it is a frightening thing for a graduate student to make a search and to discover that the stuff isn't there,

because of course you are sure it must be there, and you're just
not finding it. I found one little book by Clarence Barnhart, the
dictionary man, and Leonard Bloomfield, who had been the dean
of American linguists. It was actually published posthumously as
far as Bloomfield was concerned, as *Let's Read: A Linguistic
Approach.* Bloomfield was asked by the army during WWII for
his advice about how to train illiterate recruits to read. He
plugged in a little linguistics and developed a linguistic phonics
program. That was the only thing I could find, and it didn't
satisfy me at all, because I quickly recognized it as a kind of
linguistic phonics. Bloomfield had decided that phonics was
unscientific, so scientific phonics would do the trick.

A little while after that, Charles Fries, another very
prominent linguist, published a book, *Linguistics and Reading.*
Linguists were preoccupied with phonology at that time so that
what they thought about reading had to do with phonology and
concepts like minimal feature differences, which is the way they
went about studying phonemics. It was unfortunate, setting things
back about 10 years or so, because in teachers' minds linguistics
became associated with this kind of patterned drill phonics that
had come out of applications of Bloomfield and Fries' work.

So I started with the issue which I think has always really
been the central issue in reading research and still needs to be:
How do people make sense of print? How do they start with
written text which doesn't have any meaning (it's just ink
blotches on a page) and come away from it with a sense of
meaning and sense of text which somehow relates to the one the
author originally had in mind.

I have always had the feeling that since there isn't human
telepathy, there can't be one to one correspondence between the
author's meaning and the reader's meaning. Originally I began to
call the work I was doing linguistic and fairly quickly
psycholinguistic.

I was very lucky. At Wayne State they had a research
competition set up for assistant professors which I won. As part
of that I got funding to hold a conference to which I gave the
grandiose title, "The Psycholinguistic Nature of the Reading
Process." I searched for people who at that early age were doing
similar kinds of research with some linguistic interests. I wrote to
important people like John Carroll, Jean Chall, and Ruth
Strickland and got a few names of people.

At that conference in 1964 was a very young Bob Ruddell
who had just gotten his doctorate with Ruch Strickland at Indiana

University and an even younger Dick Venezky who defended his dissertation at Stanford and presented it the following day in Detroit. Carl Lefevre was working on a book at that time. John Bormuth had also just finished his work at Indiana. Some beginnings of things were shared there. We were certainly not all at the same point, but things were happening.

A little later NCTE and IRA, in a rare show of cooperation, had a joint committee on linguistics and reading, and I met some of the folks from the University of Chicago that ultimately led to my suggesting to Alan Robinson, when he was president of IRA, that IRA could use a committee on linguistics and reading. That's where Dick Hodges and I first met and a number of other people.

One event that sticks in my mind in that period of the late 60s is an open meeting of the linguistics and reading committee of IRA which, for some reason, was scheduled in the evening. We didn't have an agenda; we were just going to let people come and share ideas with us. One thousand people showed up. We kept running for chairs and running for chairs and wondering what we were going to talk about.

About that time, a project was funded to Harry Levin, a psychologist in Human Development at Cornell University, called Project Literacy. It lasted for a couple of years. I have to thank Jean Chall for suggesting my name to them. I was invited to spend a month there working with them. I found myself somewhat at odds with some of the things they were involved with based on some of the aspects of psychology which I didn't feel were leading very far. But I had a chance to interact with Jackie (Eleanor) Gibson, Harry Levin, and some other people.

One of the most gratuitous things was that Noam Chomsky came and spent about three days there. Chomsky, who has always been much more interested in the generation of language, talked on what he thought reading was all about. He used the term tentative information processing. That helped me to put together something I was groping for. I went home and wrote "Reading: A Psycholinguistic Guessing Game." Guessing is my term for that tentative information processing he was talking about.

The paper grew out of the miscue research that I had begun to do when I had moved to Wayne State. I said I was trying to see how people made sense of print. So it seemed what I ought to do is try and figure out what they were doing. Malcolm Douglass referred here to the advent of the tape recorder. I taped kids reading real books, not ones I had made up, or experimental texts with funny little things embedded in them. I wanted to use the kind of things they were being asked to read in school. I had them read materials they hadn't seen before, because I wanted to see what happened the first time they encountered it.

I always think of the story of Ernest Horn's wife, Madeline Horn. He was at the University of Iowa, and his wife, for her master's thesis, did a study of the vocabulary of kindergarten children with no tape recorders while she taught kindergarten. Imagine trying to keep track of kids' language, tabulate it, at the same time you're teaching kindergarten. She did a frequency count of their vocabulary. Tom Horn, their son, told me that she didn't speak to her husband for about six weeks after he casually said to her, "That could have made a pretty good doctoral dissertation."

We took tape recorders, and we went out and had kids read, and we found them making mistakes. That's not a new thing; as early as the 20s people had been studying kids' errors. But they had been studying from the view that errors are things that teachers are supposed to get kids to stop making.

Years later, in reading Flavell's work on Piaget, we discovered we had inadvertently found what Piaget found. Piaget, supposedly as a young researcher for Binet on the development of the IQ test, realized Binet was keeping the right answers and throwing away the wrong answers. Piaget began to realize that these unexpected responses, these wrong answers, were very rich in information, giving us insights into how kids think.

And that's what we found with miscues. We found them to be far from random. I have to say I was delighted to discover that in the very first tape I looked at, the kids were substituting THE for A and I said hurrah, that's linguistics; those don't look alike, but they happen to have the same grammatical function. So my hunch that kids were dealing with some linguistic information had to be right.

That began to move me in the psycholinguistic direction at the time when there was a period of exciting inter-disciplinary interaction going on between researchers in various fields. At one IRA conference in Detroit, Roger Shuy and I were on back to back. We had never met, and we discovered that we were talking about virtually the same things, from different perspectives.

Let me skip quickly from there, because I don't want to make this a history lesson entirely; I want to talk really about where I am and where the field is and what a contrast that small period of inter-disciplinary work is compared with what I think is the current very rich and exciting period of reading research. But it isn't inter-disciplinary, it's multi-disciplinary.

There are many fields interested in reading for a large variety of reasons. One of the most interesting ones is artificial intelligence. They aren't interested in reading. They don't care much about kids; they want to figure out how to teach a computer to read. Because if you could teach a computer to read, you could feed in a text, and the computer could do the comprehending for you. That has all kinds of potential applications.

The problem is that computers aren't nearly as smart as 5- and 6-year-olds, and if you don't give them the right programming information, they can't make head or tail out of texts. So the AI people have gotten into reading, and they have a very pragmatic way of going about it. They keep trying new algorithms until one works.

Cognitive psychology has suddenly shed its behavioral roots, though there are lots of closet behaviorists who now are coming out as cognitive psychologists. They moved away from their preoccupation with very small units and become interested in comprehension and what they have been calling higher mental processes.

A whole group in anthropology is using an ethnographic methodology, essentially developed through studying cultural aspects in little known cultures, to study things like how people learn to read in classrooms in the U.S. They're coming up with some very interesting kinds of things.

The field of literature, after an era of the New Criticism that lasted some several decades, has returned to where Louise Rosenblatt was in 1938 when she wrote *Literature As Exploration* at the request of the Progressive Education Association. She used a transactional view based on Dewey's concept. And a whole school is now calling itself Reader Response Theory: how the reader responds to literature. I have to admit that Louise Rosenblatt anticipated at least by 30 years many of the ideas I was developing and that I didn't read Edmond Huey until Paul Kolers, who was responsible for his republication by MIT Press, made him available to me. And then again I saw the roots of my ideas and my work and my research.

What I see happening in the field now is that the model and theory developing, so important to my research and to the research of others, has now become fashionable. Psychologists are still rather reluctant to deal with things beyond micro levels, while linguists are still very much operating on totally theoretical bases.

We've resurrected terms like schema, which is one Piaget and Dewey used extensively, and dusted them off. We rediscovered that what the reader brings to the text is certainly as important as what the reader takes away from it.

I think what is emerging from all this, if we could only get people to read each other's work in different fields, is a kind of knowledge of how reading works which I'm very pleased with. In some cases I'm a little impatient, wishing that they would not have to go through two or three decades of work and get to the point where they were interested in some of the things I think are important. At least it is better than spinning the memory drums.

In my own work I find myself going in several directions. We have a gold mine of data in the miscue data base that we have produced from several studies, and we are remining it. We have been looking at readers and the reading process, and now we are looking at the text from the reader's perspective.

There is a great deal of interest among researchers in text and propositional analysis. We have very powerful data, because we can look at the text from the point of view of what a number of readers did in producing miscues and then say what is going on with the text that is involved in such miscues.

Another thing that I have linked up with is Michael Halliday's systemic view of language. Halliday is one of the few linguists who has been interested in very practical pragmatic aspects of linguistic theory and who has kept everything whole and together. It makes his stuff very complicated. Most of it is still in Michael Halliday's head, and you only get bits and glimpses of it in the articles he publishes. But I think it is very productive in terms of putting language into a social context. And in my own work I am looking more at the intention of readers, the purposes, how that affects what they do; that relates of course to the schema.

Inference is something I have always been interested in, but it has become more important to me now, because it seems clear that a general strategy readers use is inferring on the basis of what they do know and what they don't yet know. So reading is a kind of Piagetian process.

I think where the field is, and where I am, is that we're moving back to the notion of getting everything together. And the goals of reading research are still to understand how readers make sense of print, to understand how they learn to make sense, and to then understand how to support that learning with teaching.

The Concept of Structure and Learning To Spell

Richard E. Hodges

Around the turn of the present century, a New Orleans policeman was walking his beat when he came upon a dead horse lying in a Tchoupitoulis Street gutter. According to local lore, the policeman briefly pondered the situation, then dragged the horse two blocks to Camp Street in order to write up his report.

While it is doubtful that many of us would find it necessary to drag a dead horse two blocks in order to avoid spelling a difficult word, the fact remains that the larger society expects correct spelling, and we often find other means to get around spelling troublesome words. Thus, we write illegibly, or we substitute a word whose spelling we know for the one that we don't (a less strenuous form of dead-horse dragging).

Largely because of a widespread belief that the English writing system is at best an onerous chore to master, correct spelling through the centuries has come to symbolize scholarly habits of study. As a result, spelling instruction has long enjoyed a solid place in the curriculum as a subject in which achievement is gained by diligence and hard work, usually by means of rote memorization (Hodges, 1977).

When one examines closely the content and method of any school subject, underlying beliefs are revealed about both the nature of the subject and about learning and the learner. With respect to spelling, the fact that the subject still continues to be taught largely by means of studying word lists and taking weekly tests is a reminder that traditional views of English spelling and its acquisition have changed very little.

In recent years, however, renewed attention to the structure of English orthography by linguists and others with interests in spelling has resulted in detailed descriptions of the writing system which, in conjunction with a growing understanding of how knowledge of that system is acquired, challenge traditional beliefs and pose some basic questions for curriculum makers and teachers. What I should like to do, then, is to share with you a changing view of learning to spell based on recent and current research, a view in which spelling development necessitates intellectual activity on the part of the learner, not merely rote memory in spelling words.

The common assumption that English orthography is an unreliable writing system is based on an apparent lack of correspondence between alphabet letters and the sounds of speech. Were English orthography truly alphabetic, its detractors contend, each speech sound would have its own distinct letter representation. That is obviously not the situation in our writing system. As a result, spelling reformers and educators alike have responded to the seeming vagaries of English spelling by pointing to the excessive costs involved in time and effort to master the written code, with reformers seeking to change or simplify the orthography and educators concluding that, in the absence of generalizable rules, the spellings of words must be individually memorized (Hodges, 1972).

Such beliefs have run deep in the culture, and it was not until the mid-twentieth century that serious attempts were made to determine the actual nature of English spelling, attempts which incorporated the research tools of linguistic science and the concept of *phoneme* which provided a valuable construct to examine the relationship between spoken and written language. Within this framework a number of studies were carried out, including that of the linguist Robert Hall, Jr. (Hall, 1961) and a Stanford University group (Hanna, 1966). The results of these and other studies described a more cohesive writing system than commonly had been held to be the case. But, these studies were not without conceptual limitations, particularly in focusing on sound-letter correspondences *within* words rather than on the spelling patterns of words themselves.

Other researchers redressed this shortcoming, however, most notably Richard Venezky (Venezky, 1967) and Noam Chomsky and Morris Halle (Chomsky and Halle, 1968). Venezky's detailed analysis of about 20,000 words clarified the complex structure of English spelling in showing how both phonology and word structure are related, while Chomsky and Halle, within the framework of transformational grammar, asserted that English orthography was nearly optimal for its purposes when lexical relationships are taken into consideration.

What has become clearer from these studies, then, is a picture of a complexly structured orthography, not simply an erratic, unreliable alphabetic code. Yet, while these findings may have theoretical interest to linguists, the more important question concerns whether these structural properties have practical consequence for the speller. Here as well, important differences in conventional views of how spelling ability is achieved are occurring, primarily in a realization that young learners at the outset seem intuitively to search for structure in the orthography and over time develop an awareness of many of its complex structural features.

We are indebted to developmental psychologists and other researchers for these insights who are demonstrating anew that intellectual growth is not simply an outcome of a passive reaction to objects and events in the environment, but stems from learners' active involvement in the world around them. As the American psychologist William James, whom I paraphrase, once remarked, each of us is born into a "kaleidoscopic flux of confusion" of which we strive to make sense, a euphonious way of pointing out that as we grow we must try to determine relationships among the objects and events which we experience — that is, to determine structure.

Perhaps in no other area of human growth and development is this insight so vividly illustrated than in the process of acquiring a first language. Surely, we must marvel at how young learners in a very short portion of the normal life span universally gain linguistic fluency on the basis of language interactions among others and themselves from which they elicit the basic structural properties of their native tongues.

Our interests here, however, concern written language development and learning to spell in particular. Is learning to spell developmentally governed also? Or, is spelling ability essentially only a consequence of memorizing words? Happily, attention has also been turned to the development of spelling ability using many of the constructs about general language development. When spelling development is viewed in this context, a number of important observations become apparent.

Several studies over the past decade which were designed to investigate how children naturally learn to spell (as distinct from direct instruction) provide compelling evidence that spelling ability also develops over time in accordance with a biological timetable and experience. The seminal work which precipitated a wide range of studies of children's spelling development was that of Charles Read, now at the University of Wisconsin (Read, 1975). Read's research into preschoolers' knowledge of English phonetic structure involved their attempting to spell and revealed that, even at an early age, children are able to draw upon a knowledge of phonetic features of speech by using a "letter-name" strategy in which articulatory features are used to determine the choice of letter to represent a sound (e.g., GAT=GATE; LADE=LADY). Most revealing was Read's observation that while his subjects' spelling was usually incorrect according to standard orthography, their invented spellings were, with minor variation, remarkably alike, thus indicating that the children were independently arriving at similar generalizations about spoken and written code relationships.

Subsequent studies have been undertaken to look more deeply into children's spelling abilities in order to determine the developmental stages which learners go through enroute to a functional knowledge of the orthography. Among the more important studies have been those of Edmund Henderson and his associates at the University of Virginia (Henderson and Beers, 1980). Their research clearly describes how children progress from an initial global awareness of writing as another language system toward competence in writing words in standard orthography and in which a letter-name strategy plays a significant role. Parenthetically, it seems to me of more than incidental interest that many children's word games and puzzles are based on the letter-name principle. My eight-year-old son recently tried the following examples on me.

"Hey, Dad, stick out your neck and spell I MET."

"Dad, make a circle around your head with your arms and spell IMAGE and then say LIGHTBULB."

The humor that children (and some adults) find in such linguistic pleasantries lies in a recognition that the letters and their names do double-duty by representing both speech sounds and words. The young speller's use of the letter-name strategy indicates a growing awareness of the concept of *word*, a pivotal concept in the growth of spelling ability.

What we are describing, of course, is the learner's developing knowledge of word structure and the application of this knowledge in beginning spelling. The evidence we have of this process is more secure for younger spellers than for those in later developmental stages because of researchers' initial interests in the beginning speller. Yet evidence is beginning to mount about the course of later spelling development, also, and it is to that line of inquiry to which we will briefly turn.

Glenda Bissex followed the progress of her son, Paul, from inventive to conventional speller over a four-year period (age five to age nine) and observed how he proceeded from an initial letter-name strategy toward the use of meaning and affixation as spelling aids (Bissex, 1980). Rebecca Rule followed the progress of a single subject, Brian, through third and fourth grades and found that his spelling process paralleled that of Bissex's son (Rule, 1982). An Australian research group has been examining how children through the elementary school years generalize knowledge of words they know to words they don't know when attempting to spell (Elliott, 1982; Thomas, 1982). Their findings to-date describe students' early attempts to relate sound-letter correspondences in known words to unknown ones and beginning, but less successful, attempts to use morphological cues such as compounding and affixation in their spelling.

Shane Templeton's studies of older students (sixth, eighth, and tenth graders) provides additional evidence of how maturing spellers use word structure principles in attempting to spell unfamiliar words (Templeton, 1979). In addition, I have been observing during the past few years contestants in regional spelling bees from which winners are sent to the national finals in Washington, D.C. The "super" spellers, with rare exception, draw heavily on word meaning and word structure when spelling words they are not sure of, falling back on phonological strategies as a last resort.

What, then, are some conclusions that can be drawn from this brief accounting of the current state of knowledge about the development of spelling ability? First, spelling is not an "innocent" activity, an exercise in which the speller brings little more than a rote memory of words to the spelling situation. Rather, learning to spell is a complex intellectual accomplishment. The available evidence potently demonstrates that a rich linguistic environment is not only essential in the development of oral language but in the development of written language competence as well. Every interaction with written language both in and out of the school setting affords an opportunity to gain new information about the structure and uses of the written code. Only in a very limited sense is knowledge of the writing system learned as the outgrowth of words that are individually memorized in spelling class.

Related to this first point is a second — that the growth of spelling ability emerges in concert with written language growth in general. Like oral language, the rate of growth in written language may vary among learners because of biological and experiential factors, but there is little variation in the sequence of this growth. Learning to spell is a developmental process.

Third, spelling ability rests upon a base of *word* knowledge — about meaning, structure, and sound. Learning to spell involves learning about words in many guises and how they function in written communication. The form of spelling study that we advocate (Hodges, 1981; 1982) goes far beyond learning the correct order of letters in words; it places spelling in the context of the study of language itself. Thus, while spelling may continue to be taught as a separate subject, effective instruction about the written code can occur wherever an opportunity is afforded during the school day — in the special vocabularies of other subjects, in daily writing, and in informal explorations of our written language, among numerous possibilities. Spelling study should not (for learning to spell does not) be kept independent of the uses of written language in a literate society.

Fourth, spelling errors and spelling growth are handmaidens in the developmental process. Children's spelling errors, like their oral language errors, can provide the discerning observer with important information about their level of understanding of the orthography. There are few, if any, random spelling errors in an individual's writing.

Fifth, the studies we have cited offer vivid illustrations of perhaps the most fundamental insight of all — that children are not miniature adults who make deviant mistakes from an adult standard. The evidence at hand clearly demonstrates that children make qualitatively different judgments than adults do about oral and written language relationships. Spelling study, as written language study should in general, needs to be carefully orchestrated in tune with the student's developmental progress and should take place within a rich experiential environment in which numerous and varied learning opportunities are available.

John Dewey, of course, set forth this proposition nearly ninety years ago when he noted that ". . . the child's own instincts and powers furnish the material and give the starting-point in all education . . . Without insight into the psychological structure and activities of the individual, the educative process will therefore be haphazard and arbitrary" (Dewey, 1897).

The studies we have reviewed enable us to glimpse, if only in part, children's developing psychological structures of English orthography and, in doing so, provides us with fundamental considerations for spelling instruction. At the least, we should be constantly mindful of students' contributions to their own learning and move spelling instruction toward a more active exploration of the written code, as we have seen that children do naturally.

REFERENCES

Bissex, Glenda L. *Gnys at Wrk: A Child Learns to Read and Write.* Cambridge, Massachusetts: Harvard University Press, 1980.

Chomsky, Noam and Halle, Morris. *The Sound Pattern of English.* New York: Harper and Row, 1968.

Dewey, John. "My Pedagogic Creed," *The School Journal,* 54 (January 16, 1897), 77-80.

Elliott, Irene. *Learning to Spell: Children's Development of Phoneme-Grapheme Relationships.* Research Project 4/82, Curriculum Services Unit, Education Department of Victoria, Carlton, Victoria, 1982.

Hall, Robert A., Jr. *Sound and Spelling in English.* Philadelphia: Chilton Company, 1961.

Hanna, Paul R.; Hanna, Jean S.; Hodges, Richard E.; and Rudorf, Erwin H., Jr. *Phoneme-Grapheme Correspondences as Cues to Spelling Improvement.* Washington, D.C.: U.S. Government Printing Office, U.S. Office of Education, 1966.

Henderson, Edmund H. and Beers, James W. (eds.). *Developmental and Cognitive Aspects of Learning to Spell: A reflection of Word Knowledge.* Newark, Delaware: International Reading Association, 1980.

Hodges, Richard E. "Theoretical Frameworks of English Orthography," *Elementary English,* 49(November, 1972), 1089-1097.

Hodges, Richard E. "In Adam's Fall: A Brief History of Spelling Instruction in the United States." In *Reading and Writing in the United States: Historical Trends,* H. Alan Robinson (ed.). Urbana, Illinois and Newark, Delaware: ERIC Clearinghouse on Reading and Communication Skills and International Reading Association, 1977. pp. 1-16.

Hodges, Richard E. *Learning to Spell.* Urbana, Illinois: ERIC Clearinghouse on Reading and Communication Skills and National Council of Teachers of English, 1981.

Hodges, Richard E. *Improving Spelling and Vocabulary in the Secondary School.* Urbana, Illinois: ERIC Clearinghouse on Reading and Communication Skills and National Council of Teachers of English, 1982.

Read, Charles. *Children's Categorizations of Speech Sounds in English.* National Council of Teachers of English Research Report No. 17. Urbana, Illinois: National Council of Teachers of English, 1975.

Rule, Rebecca, "The Spelling Process: A Look at Strategies," *Language Arts,* 59(April, 1982), 379-384.

Templeton, Shane, "Spelling First, Sound Later: The Relationship Between Orthography and High Order Phonological Knowledge in Older Students," *Research in the Teaching of English,* 13(October, 1979), 255-264.

Thomas, Valerie. *Learning to Spell: The Way Children Make Use of Morphemic Information.* Research Project 1/82, Curriculum Services Unit, Education Department of Victoria, Carlton, Victoria, 1982.

Venezky, Richard L., "English Orthography: Its Graphical Structure and Its Relation to Sound," *Reading Research Quarterly,* 2(Spring, 1967), 75-107.

The Alternative to Progressive Education and Mastery Learning Practices*

Jeannette Veatch

With no little trepidation, I must question the concept of Open Education, or Progressive Education, as it has been interpreted. Perhaps I am the one who can do this, since my credentials as an Open Educator are, I think, unassailable. The problem, as I see it, with the awful condition of teaching in our nation's schools, is that the teachings of John Dewey are not being followed. He was clear, but those who have come since are decidedly mixed up. For example, take the play and movie, "Auntie Mame," in which her nephew goes to a progressive school where they learn about the birds and the bees by taking their clothes off. Audiences laughed, but, I suspect, said to themselves, "No child of mine will go through that kind of nonsense."

And nonsense it was. It has come to mean that, to learn in a progressive school, one needs no discipline, no systematic organization, no planning. You can do as you please. Through these past decades, Progressivism, and its later counterpart, Open Education, has been identified as one extreme end of a continuum at the other end of which is Authoritarianism. That is, there is laissez faire at one pole that is all choice of doing-as-one-pleases, with no rhyme, reason, rigor, or system. While at the other pole there is planning, rigor and organization, and NO choice. In fact, at that pole, choice is to be prevented.

So we are saddled at present with the extremes of behavioral objective writings, of cognitive domains, of prescriptive teachings, and the like, which destructively, I think, insist that children master one tiny item after another, in succession, as alleged to be logical by authorities who have established that that is the way learning develops. They have, I submit, loosed the dogs of war

---

*Presented during a panel discussion.

on little children. Such sequences may be logical, but to impose them without using the internal experience and personal interest of the learner is grossly ineffective.

In the 50s I was supervising student teachers from New York University. I had several placed in private schools of that city which had national reputations. Whatever may have been their original claims to fame, by the time my students arrived, the problem that still plagues us, which I noted to begin with, was in full bloom. These schools did not know the difference between laissez faire, all choice (and chaos) and no choice (mandates). In one school whose name would be recognizable, every year, the same middle grade "did" the post office, and another the store, regardless of the desires, interests, or inner motivations of the pupils concerned. Yet in those same classrooms, there was the wildest of activity, with accidental learning coming from spontaneous occurrences. The sterility, the low-man-on-the-totem pole of my students, the confusion about what was teaching, what was instruction, even what was education, was such that I pulled my students out, for all of our sakes.

Frank Jennings tells the story of his first days in the fifth grade of another one of those schools. He found the kids wild, uncontrolled, with no respect for order of any kind. One boy, in defiance against Frank, stood on the window sill, which was five floors above the street. Frank TOOK him down, turned him over his knee and paddled him. "There goes my job," he told his wife that night. The next day, as expected, the father arrived, but to Frank's amazement, rushed over to him, threw his arms around Frank and said, "At last!" Thus began a fruitful year for all concerned. At the end of the term Frank, alone, took the entire group on an overnight trip to the State Capitol.

These show that parameters are necessary. Parameters can promote, not prevent, education. Yet if the parameters are too restrictive, following a series of adult-developed objectives, the seeds of destruction of a democratic society will find fertile soil. For this is what democracy is all about. The organized, systematic process, by which children become creative, productive individuals, not programmed robots. I am suggesting that there is a middle, or at least another, ground between the ends of laissez faire and those of authoritarianism. Somewhere in this middle we have left out something important. I think it has to do with the meaning of the word STRUCTURE. But the structure I am concerned about is the structure of *process,* not, as Benjamin Bloom and others would have it, the structure of *content.*

As a classroom example, there is none better than that of Sylvia Ashton Warner's Key Vocabulary. It is as structured as you can get in terms of process. If you don't do certain things right, you don't elicit a useable vocabulary from the child. The learning situation must be so structured that the child will dredge up, so to speak, from the middle of himself, those words, unexpected to the teacher. Such dynamic, vital, "special" words: Ghosts, Lightning, Monsters, and the like, are widely reported, in all languages, around the world. It would be impossible to get such words by means of a list in a set of behavioral objectives.

This is the structure of process to which I refer. Without a firm concept of the child's inner resources of living experience, you are stuck for learning. A teacher must figure out how to get such ideas from within the given child. From these ideas come words which can be turned into writing, and on into reading. If you teach a child something that has no relation to his OWN living, breathing, experience, you might just as well get out of teaching. For these living experiences are the major source of the structure of education.

I knew a teacher once who used to tell her pupils, "When you are in bed tonight, think of something you can write tomorrow." They would come to school the next day brimming with contributions, for the paper, for wide black spaces of the chalk board, for the typewriter. They were "just dying" to contribute. Their inventiveness then gave the teacher what she needed to teach them. She took those words, and taught spelling and punctuation and all of those things that make a literate mind. She checked off what she had taught, and later, when she saw some item had been missed, she taught that! But she developed a set of authors who were excited about writing. It was no chore in that classroom.

I don't think you need to charm children in order to get them to learn. In itself, education, learning, are exciting and stimulating and wonderful. It is not entertainment, but it is as exciting as if it were entertainment. When you are in such a learning situation, it is almost like falling in love (I nearly got fired, and did NOT get hired, once for saying just that, but it is true).

So there does have to be structure in the learning process. When it is present, there is rigor in the acquisition of skills and knowledge. Open Education has not been good at that. Those who claim allegiance to Open Education have allowed the stigma of the Auntie Mames to make that word an anathema. Discipline and parameters are essential. Certainly there is a time to say,

"Stop," or "Sit down!", but children will accept such orders when they are excited about what they are doing, what they are learning. And when that learning is based upon their inner sources, you won't have much need for discipline imposed from without.

Another example of misunderstanding appeared, in of all places, the Christian Science Monitor, in an article castigating Piaget as producing a generation of "me-ism" in the schools. Nothing, indeed, could be further from the intent of Piaget. I was outraged and wrote to the editor in complaint. Of all the authorities who advocated the structure of process it was Piaget. As you well know, manipulating objects and the recognition of what such means is a process of maturation. Impose certain manipulations on a child and you get nothing, because the "good Lord hasn't yet growed him up enough." I was gratified to get a personal response from their recently retired editor, Cynthia Parsons, who had watched helplessly and who saw such things more clearly than many professors I have known.

Similarly, I might talk about the concept of "invented spelling." At age five, that kind of spelling, which is really the internalization of the alphabet, is what you want. Why? Because it gets the writing going. But at the fifth grade level, to allow continued such phoneticisms, seems to me, to be an abdication of teaching. The child of ten has already developed his capacity for invention using the letters of the alphabet and recognition of sound patterns. Now he needs to learn how to spell correctly, based on such a solid foundation.

So, to me, structure of process is the important thing. It occupies a different area from the laissez faire lack of controls, to the rigidities imposed by authoritarian controls. That area comes from the inner experience of the pupil. Once it is elicited, children are going to learn. They will find it hard, perhaps, but it will be more than fun. It will be "glorious!"

A Cultural Perspective
on the Teaching of Reading

Bruce R. Joyce

It was a great privilege to be invited to share in the fiftieth Claremont Reading Conference. The extraordinary quality of Malcolm Douglass' paper that opened the conference extends the privilege, for I have not heard such a powerful paper on the history and structure of instruction in reading or such a clear enunciation of the issues attendant to curriculum and reading for a good twenty years. It was intimidating to follow his presentation and the obligation of the privilege was considerable also.

My personal scholarship is not on reading. It is on the identification of alternative models of teaching and curriculum and the processes by which teachers can expand their teaching repertoires and curriculum changes can be implemented. To prepare myself, I dug through recent textbooks on the teaching of reading, then explored what little literature there is on the reading of film and the relationship between the reading of traditional print material and the reading of transmission through the electronic media. I looked at the reading programs of a number of schools and reacquainted myself with the work of "Hooked on Books" by Dan Fader of Michigan and Jim Duggans and Tom Finn from San Francisco State University. Duggans and Finn introduced me to the reading-immersion programs in some of the San Francisco area high schools.

The literature was disappointing. Few new techniques have been developed since the days when I taught courses in curriculum and instruction in reading and the language arts. I was struck by the rhetorical nature of much of the literature and how many articles about the current state of reading instruction appeared to have been written by Jeremiah himself. Essentially, the literature did not guide this presentation. I decided to focus on the reading of books and my personal belief that reading should be an integral, moving part of everyone's life and to stay away from the issues as currently defined. Like Malcolm

Douglass, I simply cannot get excited about whether we use a "whole-word" or "part-word" approach. The "great debate" appears trivial to me when compared with the question whether reading and literature are taught vigorously and powerfully and whether the environment of the school is suffused with the development of literacy through the study of literature. Therefore, I am going to present you a series of "if-I-could-run-the-world" statements that come from my observation of education over the years, my intuition about what makes vigorous reading instruction, and my perspective that reading should be seen as a cultural activity. Through instruction in reading and literature, we both pass on the culture and are trying to change it. I am not satisfied with the level of literate attainment in contemporary society but wish to transform it and bring it to a far more central place in the lives of most people.

Proposition 1: All teachers should be omnivorous readers

Partly, I believe this because much of teaching is accomplished through modeling. The omnivorous reader radiates devotion to reading and continuously shares with colleagues and students perspectives and tidbits from the content of what is read. If we are all readers, everyone knows how important reading is to us.

Also, much of the craft of the teaching of reading comes from insight into our own reading processes. As we read and read well, we develop an understanding of what it takes to read, and we develop teaching methods from "inside" the process, as it were.

With my colleagues Michael McKibbin and Robert Bush I have recently conducted a set of studies into what we call the "states of growth" of teachers. Our focus is on the extent of teachers' cultural interchange, the process by which they reach into the cultural opportunities around them and grow from that contact, and incorporate from that growth information, ideas, opinions, and techniques into the teaching process. Our original focus was on teachers' utilization of the formal systems that provide staff development opportunities to them: workshops, university courses, professional organizations, etc. We added a concern with informal interchange with other teachers in an attempt to learn the content and quality of those interchanges and the effects on the content and process of classroom practice. We have extended our inquiry into personal activity, probing especially the extent to which teachers read, attend and discuss films, explore the wilderness, engage in athletic activity, participate in or consume products from the performing and visual arts, and so on. We attempted to get as complete a map of these kinds of activities as we can.

We currently classify teachers in five levels of growth. The terms of our classifications are reminiscent of Maslow's descriptions of psychological stages and manifest his considerable influence on our thinking. In colloquial terms, they are:

— omnivores

— active consumers

— passive consumers

— entrenched

— withdrawn

We describe activities in each of the following domains: the formal system of staff development, the informal system of interchange within the school district, and personal activities initiated in their private lives. Few people maintain the same growth state across all three domains, although some do. However, few behave in widely discrepant states across the domains. I'll pause here to describe just two of the categories.

The omnivores

These people actively use every available aspect of the formal and informal system available to them. Their lives are rich with books, the performing arts, travel, sports, university courses, and the offerings of teacher centers and districts. They have found professional colleagues with whom they are close and can exchange ideas. They are active in the attempt to improve the state of the schools in which they work. They simply will not be denied. They seem able to overcome obstacles and they do not allow dysfunctional emotions to isolate them from a great variety of activities. They do not spend much energy complaining about colleagues, administration, poor presenters at workshops, etc.; they simply take what they can where they can get it. This does not mean that they are undiscriminating — their energy is simply oriented toward growth rather than possible impediments to growth. They tend to be happy and self-actualizing people. Teaching has not jaded them, nor has the rest of life. Some teachers behave omnivorously over one or two domains of activity and some manage several.

The passive consumer

Another state is exemplified by persons who are *there* when opportunity presents itself but who rarely seek or initiate new activities. Thus if the formal system becomes active, it will tend to draw them to greater activity. If they are a member of a family which engages in much reading and theater going, they will tend to go along, and they may be pulled into workshops or other activities by peers or supervisors. However, they are dependent on the activity levels around them to draw them into the activity. If they are in a low-energy informal system, they will tend to interact relatively little. If their district maintains a strong formal system, they will engage in its offerings.

The importance of consort has become increasingly apparent to us in these investigations. It is particularly important for persons whose natural level of interaction with the culture is at the passive level. If they live and work with omnivores and active consumers, they are drawn in to the higher levels of activity generated by those persons. If they live and work with other passive consumers, they tend to stay at the passive level.

We currently estimate that more than half of the teachers that we have interviewed are passive consumers. Occasionally, as we have studied whole school faculties, we have found high concentrations of relatively inactive people.

In one elementary school where I have conducted all of the interviews, eighteen of the twenty faculty members do not have a well-developed personal interest that has provided them with extensive reading habits. Only two of the faculty members are regular readers, either of fiction or of nonfiction. Nearly everyone in that school is being taught to read by teachers who do not, themselves, have well-developed reading habits.

It is extremely important to me that we change that situation. Hence, the first proposition, that teachers of reading should be omnivorous readers.

Proposition 2: Read what children read — become expert in children's and adolescent literature.

Part of our reading needs to be the best that is available for our students. The quality of literature for young people, especially literature for adolescents, has increased markedly in the last fifteen years. The current smorgasbord is far above the level of Nancy Drew, and it promises to continue to get better. For one thing, the quality now enriches us. For another, it helps

us to understand the feelings and ideas the students are being
exposed to and to anticipate their reactions and how we can
capitalize on their interests and the content and styles that they
are reading.

*Proposition 3: Teach as a lover of reading and
as lovers of reading want to be taught*

I have always been partial to the "experience" and "self
selection" approaches, because they enable readers to soar, to
stretch themselves, and because those methods so directly teach
students to select what they read and so clearly integrate reading
and writing experiences. I'm not adamantly against textbooks in
reading; in fact there are some very nice anthologies. I am
concerned that they are often used to put a ceiling on the amount
and quality of reading that is encountered in school. I remember
from my own childhood my first day in the third grade. The
teacher passed out the first reading book I had seen that had
some really good stories in it. She admonished us never to take
that book home or to read ahead. Ordinarily a shy and dutiful
child, I schemed all day to conceal that book and get it home
with me. That evening I sat in front of the fire with my parents
and consumed the entire reader. The next day the establishment
fell upon me and, like so many childish omnivorous readers, I
decided that if I must be a closet reader, then so be it, but I was
not going to be limited by what anyone else needed for
instruction or was thought to need.

I never observe the "read aloud around the circle"
technique without shuddering. I don't think lovers of reading
want to wait while others read aloud. If you want to read, you
want to *read* and to be unfettered. If you are slowed down below
the level of your natural inclinations, you become frustrated.
Essentially I think the "read around the circle" practice is a very
effective aversive conditioning program. It drives the omnivorous
readers crazy by frustrating them. It drives the slow readers
crazy, because they receive attention primarily for errors made
rather than for achievement. Whatever other instructional needs
we feel we have to satisfy, our reading method should be tuned to
the lover of reading, and we should be sensitive to the nature of
that lover.

On that subject I have another personal story. Just before
they went to school, I taught each of my children to read, not to
accelerate them but because I did not want to take a chance that

someone would foul it up. If the initial reading experience is not successful, many bad things happen, and I wanted to ensure that they would not happen for my kids. When my son Brendan went to school, he had a reading habit that included about twenty books a week. In October of that first year of his schooling I went by his classroom to deliver a pair of sneakers or something that he had forgotten to take to school. (For some reason in that school, if you didn't have the right shoes, you couldn't go out to play.) As I arrived at the classroom and chatted with the teacher, Brendan was sitting in the back of the room reading *Where the Wild Things Are* to a group of other children. The teacher chatted with me for a while and then looked over at Brendan and remarked, "Isn't he cute. He thinks he can read." The instructional tasks she had given him had not yet demanded reading activity and nothing had happened, including his reading for hours in the back of the classroom, that had convinced her that, not having been instructed, he was in fact an accomplished reader. When I helped her discover his actual competence, she was somewhat upset. "What am I going to do for the rest of the year?" she asked.

"Let him read," I said, "and don't worry about it. Have him read to the reading groups you are not working with."

"But he might have missed something that's in the program," she said.

I don't think I need to elaborate what I was thinking. If we teach as the competent and loving readers read, we need not worry. They can help us create an environment that surrounds the other students with readers.

Proposition 4: Pervade the environment with reading and writing activities

Learning to read is part of the process of socialization. We *enculturate* people to read. The environment in the school needs to be a statement of the value of reading as a major part of social life. Its manifest importance as the normative activity needs to be demonstrated in all ways. I find myself attracted to the "Hooked on Books" approach, because it surrounds the student with books, provides time for reading and sharing what is read. Reading should simply be an inescapable facet of life during much of the school day.

Proposition 5: Surround each subject with relevant literature

It is a truism to say that every subject needs to be taught as reading, at least in part. However, what I am referring to here is not simply the instructional facet but the provision of material that stretches whatever area is being studied and transforms it metaphorically. Think of secondary school science, for example, and the literature that is available to enable us to see the scientific endeavor in ways that is not encountered in the physics textbook. Imagine the different treatments of the same subject in James Michener's book *Space*, Norman Mailer's *Of a Fire on the Moon*, and Thomas Wolfe's *The Right Stuff*. In all of these we have the story of our adventure with NASA. Michener, less eloquent than the other writers, covers the subject thoroughly and asks us to become fascinated with his richness of detail. Mailer treats the subject as part of his own contemporary odyssey in which the effort to conquer space is fascinating, frightening, transporting. The impact on a reflective human being is documented for us all to see. And Wolfe takes us to the world of high adventure and bravery and helps us live for awhile in the incredible world where our adventurers are treading. That is the kinds of experience I think we should provide, where literary treatments not only increase perspective but stretch the ways in which the substance can be perceived by the human mind.

Proposition 6: We should concentrate on teaching people to read rather than teaching them about reading

As I watch classes in literature, reading, and foreign languages, I am frequently surprised at the amount of attention that is paid to the rules of phonetic and structural analysis and grammar. Somehow, I cannot swallow the notion that the definition of the past-pluperfect or past-imperfect is important. What is important is to internalize the variety in the language and take command of it, to be able to extract the meaning rather than to know the rule by which the meaning is embedded in the written word.

That rules are necessary, I do not deny, but I think *our* rule of thumb should be that every minute spent in formal analysis is a minute not spent in reading itself, and we should be constantly balancing the potential benefits of the formal analysis against benefits of the reading activity.

Proposition 7: Be absolutely determined to bring about
the best possible conditions for the learner

Determination and *joi de vivre* are the keys to an atmosphere
that literally pull the learner into reading activity. I don't think
that we teach reading so much by instruction or by motivational
techniques as by the social climate that simply says everyone
can, everyone *must*, and *it's a lovely thing*, and we never need to
utter those statements to make them true. We often need to be
quite brave and able to reach out and change the conditions
under which students learn.

A friend of mine from Denmark was at the house the other
day and told me of an experiment that they are currently
conducting in some school districts there. They are operating on
a number of principles that make eminently good sense to me. I
put them forth to you not so much because I think we should
follow them, but because I think that they illustrate how bold we
can be when we choose to and if we have clear principles on
which to operate. The first principle is that the initial transition
from nonreading to reading occurs during a relatively short
period. It is only about six to ten weeks between the time when a
learner moves from that place where simply not enough words
are known and not enough decoding ability is operable to that
point where a book can be brought off a shelf and read.

However, this short transition period occurs only when
instruction coincides with the point of readiness; that is, when the
learner has the language development to permit the instruction to
have considerable effect. Teaching before that time can be
disastrous, because if initial instruction is not successful, the
learner can become very frustrated and develop feelings about
self and the reading process that make it very difficult to
overcome the early failure.

The other principle is to use the best of us to facilitate the
transition to reading. Under our current system every primary
teacher is a teacher of reading, whereas we know that some of us
are better at it than others. Based on these simple principles the
experiment is as follows:

As students reach school their readiness to read is assessed.
It is expected that perhaps two-thirds, or perhaps somewhat
fewer, of the students will be deemed to be ready to read. Those
most ready to read are put in the charge of those teachers who
appear to be the most effective teachers of reading. They enter
what is essentially a reading immersion program. From the
beginning of the day to the end, every activity is turned in some

way or other to language development and the promotion of reading and writing skills. They expect that they will have success with a high proportion of those students who are deemed ready to read within, say, eight or ten weeks. Then the group of students next most ready to read enters the reading immersion program. Students are not introduced to reading until there is clear evidence that the readiness stage has been thoroughly entered.

Last week when I discussed this program with school and university educators, the first question was, "What will you do with those students who are not ready to read?"

I think the answer is easy. Currently we frustrate them and maim them spiritually. What the Danes are attempting to do is recognize that we are not fully successful with a fairly good proportion of our students, perhaps as many as a third, and that bold measures are needed to bring about a change so that we can become more effective. They have developed principles for such an experiment and they are doing it publicly. They have been brave in that they have acknowledged that the current system is not completely successful. They have been brave in that they acknowledge that children are hurt when taught too early and that they wish to discontinue that practice. They are brave when they acknowledge that not all of us are equally skilled in taking children across that initial threshold. And they are bold in being willing to explain to parents and others that it may be some time before the optimal moment has come for *their* child. What we need to borrow from them is their determination to do a fine job and their willingness to reach out and try something that will be criticized, because they believe it is the right thing to do at this time. As I said earlier, I am not suggesting that we do what they are doing, but I am suggesting that we have the will and the determination to do what we think is right.

A Study of Teaching Effectiveness Variables of Influential Teachers

Robert B. Ruddell*

An extensive body of research has been compiled on teaching effectiveness. Various factors, ranging from clarity of directions and task-oriented behavior to praise and structuring comments through summary, have been identified as contributing to instructional performance (Ornstein and Levine, 1981). The Beginning Teacher Evaluation Study (Fisher, 1980), by the California Commission for Teacher Preparation and Licensing, concluded that learning time was the most important variable in influencing the academic achievement of students. Medley (1977) supports this conclusion based on his examination of approximately 300 studies by noting that the more effective teacher emphasizes academic activities and devotes more class time to academic skill areas than does the less effective teacher. Research is also present which has examined the relationship between student achievement and teacher characteristics such as experience, age, and salaries. These factors have been shown to contribute approximately five percent of the variance in achievement variation (Ornstein and Levine, 1981). In brief, research on teaching effectiveness has focused heavily on variables related to achievement product and provides minimal insight into the nature of teacher effectiveness.

Bloom (1982) suggests that the teaching process and the learning environment should represent the major focus of future research on teacher effectiveness. Support for this emphasis is also found in Dunkin and Biddle's (1974) extensive summary of work on teacher interaction with students. This viewpoint demands that greater emphasis be placed on the study of the teaching process rather than the teaching product and that greater concern be given to interactive learning in the classroom rather than the achievement product. The relationship between teaching style and the learning process, as it occurs in the classroom, must

*The author wishes to recognize the support provided by Marilyn Draheim who served as research assistant for this project.

be given higher priority if the nature of teaching effectiveness is to be better understood.

Hypothesis of the study

The research by Ruddell (1980, 1981) and Ruddell and Haggard (1982) offers a unique approach to study of teaching effectiveness and the teaching process. This longitudinal research has identified influential teachers and has examined characteristics of these teachers based on student perception and teacher self-perception. An influential teacher is defined as a teacher who has had a significant impact on the academic achievement or personal adjustment of a former student, as perceived by the student. This research identifies five influential teacher descriptors consisting of personal characteristics, understanding of learner potential, positive attitude toward subject, concern for student life adjustment, and quality of instruction.

While high and low achievers perceive their influential teachers in much the same manner, the high achievers have approximately twice as many influential teachers as their low achieving counterparts during their elementary and secondary school careers. A marked difference was also found in the way students place priorities on the characteristics of good teaching when contrasted with those expressed by their influential teachers. Both high and low achieving students view quality of instruction and life adjustment as most important to good teaching, characteristics which were ranked lowest by their influential teachers. Conversely, personal characteristics of teachers and understanding of learner potential were ranked lowest by both types of students but highest by the influential teachers.

Using a teaching effectiveness scale based on the work of Fisher *et al.*, (1980) it was concluded on the basis of teacher observations that the influential teachers were substantially alike in meeting individual needs of students, although these needs were met in different ways. The most recent work of Ruddell (1982) and Haggard (1982) recommends that four key instructional variables, i.e., classroom communication, view of self, management style, and problem solution approach, be used in the study of the teaching effectiveness of influential teachers, in order to better understand the nature of the instructional process.

Because of the complex nature of the teaching process, a conceptual model of this process must reflect the interactive influence of a wide range of variables. Such a model must account for background factors which influence teacher and student expectations and performance, instructional features of the learning episode, and outcomes of the teacher-student interaction, all of which influence cognitive, affective, and meta-cognitive changes of both teacher and student.

The discussion which follows will first present an interactive model of the instructional process, and second, report findings from a study contrasting the teaching effectiveness of influential teachers with other teachers by examining specific features of a controlled learning episode based on the model. Specific hypotheses used in guiding the study are:

1. Influential teachers will rate significantly higher than other teachers in instructional effectiveness for the controlled learning episode, based on the California Scale of Teaching Effectiveness.

2. Influential teachers will demonstrate more effective use of higher level questions and questioning strategies than other teachers during guided discussion in the controlled learning episode.

An interactive model of the instructional process

An extensive review of research literature in the fields of education, linguistics, sociolinguistics, and psychology lead to the formulation of an interactive model to account for three major sets of variables which influence the instructional process. As noted in Figure 1, An Interactive Model of the Instructional Process, these variable sets are 1) factors influencing expectations and performance of teachers and students, 2) features of the learning episode, and 3) outcomes of the teacher-student interaction. Each of these three variable sets is depicted to influence the cognitive, affective, and meta-cognitive schemata of both teacher and students, identified at the center of the model. The process of assimilating and accommodating new concepts will result in schemata which enable the student and teacher to interact in a different way, either more or less effectively, with experiences encountered in the school or in the extra-school setting.

The work of Erickson (1982), Coulthard and Sinclair (1974), and Au and Mason (1981) illustrates the impact of extra-school factors which influence expectation and performance in first area of the model. These researchers examine the impact of family, cultural background, and peer group on children. In

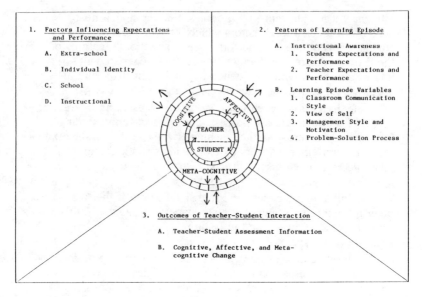

Figure 1. An Interactive Model of the Instructional Process

particular, they emphasize the mismatch between teachers and learners of different cultural backgrounds and the influence of this mismatch on expectations, communicative speech, and non-verbal responses. This mismatch can lead to communication breaks and over time result in severely impaired learning. Furthermore, cultural background can influence students' expectations for literacy use in the classroom and expectations for the future use of literacy. Peer influence is particularly instrumental, as a child matures, in determining the effectiveness of classroom interaction with the teacher.

Individual identity factors in the model define the characteristics of the individual learner. These include such things as learning style, accommodational and adaptational ability, prior knowledge, acceptance of the school's demands, and familiarity with the nature of instruction as carried on in the formal school setting. Learners possess varying degrees of ability in accommodating new information in the environment to their already acquired mental structures or in changing their structures in response to the environment. Students' ability to function successfully in the learning episode is often related to their acceptance or tolerance of the classroom rules and policies of the school. Depending on their respective learning styles and prior knowledge, students can thus be relatively capable or incapable of functioning within the demands of the lesson episode.

While the extra-school and identity factors may shape students and teachers, the school and instructional factors in the first part of the model are, for the most part, unique to teachers. School is recognized as the purveyor of a monoculture where a specific language, e.g., standard English, specific behaviors, e.g., turn-taking mechanisms such as floor-holding and question-answer routines, and specific socio-economic values, e.g., middle class, coalesce to represent a uniform social phenomenon unlike any other social institution (Sacks, Schegloff, and Jefferson, 1974). Considering one of these features, socio-economic values, researchers have found that such values can prompt teachers to unconsciously stereotype children in ways detrimental to their achievement. Rist (1970) noted that arbitrary grouping based on social factors, such as appearance, hygiene, and language, persisted from grade one into subsequent grades resulting in a "fulfillment of prophecy" effect and in turn poor performance on literacy tests. Rosenthal and Jacobson (1968) report on this phenomenon of inaccurate stereotyping from perceptions of ability.

Instructional factors include those variables directly related to the act of teaching. Advocates of mastery learning, for example, specify the importance of presentation of a lesson, monitoring ability, skill in giving feedback, and assessment (Bloom, 1982; Rosenshine, 1976; Levin and Long, 1981). These factors are considered to be essential to the successful planning and execution of a lesson.

The second part of the model, features of the learning episode, consists of instructional awareness of student and teacher and learning episode variables. Learning awareness is accessed from the affective, cognitive, and meta-cognitive components of teacher and student as noted in the center of the model. These components have been formulated from student and teacher experiences as defined in the first part of the model. The match between the student and teacher expectations is critical if the learning episode is to be successful. As discussed earlier, a match or mismatch between student and teacher will be influenced by extra-school factors, individual identity factors, school factors, and instructional factors.

The learning episode occurs within the time span devoted to instruction. Based on Jacobson's discussion (1960) the episode is defined by the interaction between the addresser, i.e., teacher, and the addressee, i.e., student, using a code, i.e., verbal or nonverbal, and making contact, i.e., oral, visual, or print, to convey a message, i.e., content, within the context of the classroom. In the interactive model the learning episode is conceptualized as consisting of four features which are highly interrelated, process oriented, and closely parallel to those of Jacobson. The first feature, classroom communication style, accounts for the nature of teacher-student interactions, the way in which student responses are received, the degree of clarification and resolution present in the interaction, and awareness of student intent. The second feature, view of self, includes self-concept, shared control, and locus of control. The third feature, management style and motivation, is defined as purpose and goal orientation of the lesson, timing and pacing, and flexibility or rigidity of the presentation. The final feature is problem-solution process and learning attitude and embodies intellectual curiosity, attitude toward learning, and questioning strategies leading to resolution. Operationally, the successful learning episode will develop for a close fit between teacher and student expectations through such features as clear goal orientation, sensitivity to the teacher-student interaction process, shared control, and effective use of questioning strategies.

The third part of the model, outcomes of the teacher-student interaction, will in many instances be an integral part of the learning episode. For example, the teacher will frequently have a clear idea of a student's story comprehension as the learning episode concludes. Frequently, however, end-of-discussion questions will be used to assess the learning episode. Assessment of some form is essential to determine the success of the learning episode. This assessment in the model provides feedback to the student reflecting the degree of success in achieving the cognitive, affective, or meta-cognitive goals of the episode. In addition, this feedback is also of vital importance to the teacher, as the learning episode itself is reevaluated in light of student outcomes. Student self-evaluation, a form of meta-cognitive awareness, should be encouraged as the learner reflects on the mental operations used during the learning episode. Such awareness is also important as the learner decides how to approach an instructional task. The assessment of teacher and student performance in the instructional episode should provide insight into cognitive, affective, and meta-cognitive change.

The interactive model thus makes provision for school and extra-school factors which influence expectations and performance for both student and teacher. Features of the learning episode account for classroom instructional expectations and performance and critical instructional variables in the episode itself. Outcomes of the teacher-student interaction provide for assessment of student and teacher performance and expected cognitive, affective, and meta-cognitive change. Each of the three parts of the interactive model constantly and directly influence the cognitive, affective, and meta-cognitive components for both teacher and student. These components, in turn, directly influence teacher and student expectations and performance in the learning episode.

Design of the study

The study is longitudinal in nature and follows a series of studies described below. The sample was drawn from teachers who participated in an extensive research project conducted in a primary grade school in a Northern California School District in the 1970-71 academic year (Ruddell and Williams, 1972). At that time 24 teachers and 522 students participated in the project. A detailed examination of school district records nine years later indicated that of the original population, 20 teachers and 132 students remained in the district.

A detailed questionnaire and interview schedule were formulated to study the characteristics of the influential teachers and to identify the way in which students used literacy skills both in and out of school. In addition, the students were asked to identify teachers who had greatly influenced their academic and personal lives throughout their academic careers. An analysis of student responses and district records revealed that 79 teachers were designated as influential teachers and still remained in the school district. Of this number, 15 elementary and 25 secondary teachers were willing to cooperate in the research study. Results of this research are reported elsewhere (Ruddell, 1980, 1981, 1982; Ruddell and Haggard, 1982; Haggard, 1982).

Of the 79 influential teachers identified, four teachers were found to be present in the original study population of 24 teachers. Each of these teachers had been identified by more than one student as an influential teacher. Influential teacher characteristics present in student descriptions included personal characteristics of the teachers, understanding of learner potential, attitude toward subject, attention to life adjustment, and quality of instruction.

In addition to the four influential teachers, identified by their students, four teachers were randomly selected from the original population of teachers for purposes of the study. Thus, the study population consisted of eight teachers, four influential teachers, and four randomly selected teachers identified in this discussion as other teachers.

The classroom performance data used for learning episode analysis consisted of controlled videotaped lessons which had been presented by the eight teachers in the original study (Ruddell and Williams, 1972). Each presentation was based on the book, *Alexander and the Wind-Up Mouse* (Lionni, 1968). Six children were randomly selected from their own primary grade classroom for the presentation. Each teacher was asked to use the book as they would normally use it in their classroom.

The learning episodes were analyzed using the California Teaching Effectiveness Scale. This observation scale assesses four elements of the learning episode on a seven-point scale. The elements are: *classroom communication system*, ranging from nature of interaction to awareness of student intent; *view of self*, ranging from sense of self to degree of shared control; *management style and motivation*, ranging from sense of purpose and goal oriented to flexibility vs. rigidity; and *problem-solution process and learning attitude*, ranging from intellectually curious to use of questioning strategies and resolution. The viewing and evaluation of the eight videotaped learning episodes were completed independently by two raters and resulted in an interrater reliability of .95.

The analysis of question levels and questioning strategies was based on a comprehension taxonomy developed by Ruddell (1978). Three levels of questions were analyzed. These consisted of: *factual*, defined as a question requiring student response to be based explicitly on statements in the text; *interpretive*, requiring student response to be based on the text but which must be reached through inference; and *applicative*, which requires student response to be reached through inference but demonstrating ability to apply this inference to a novel situation outside of the text. Teacher-student interactions were analyzed for two types of questioning strategies which are most frequently used to further understanding of higher level questions. These are: *extending*, in which a question is asked on the same comprehension level of the previous question and is designed to provide more information on the original question, e.g., "Can you tell me more about that?"; and *clarifying*, in which a question is asked at the same comprehension level or on a level below that of the previous question with the intent of correcting a misinterpretation or building further understanding in relation to

the original question, e.g., "What was Alexander really like?"
"Why do you say that?"

Data related to the first hypothesis contrasting teaching
effectiveness of influential teachers and other teachers were
analyzed using the Fisher Exact Test which assumes
independence between and within subjects. Data related to the
second hypothesis on use of questioning strategies in learning
episodes were treated by observation and descriptive analysis.

Findings of the study

The first hypothesis of the study predicted that influential
teachers (IT) would rate significantly higher than other teachers
(OT) on instructional effectiveness for the controlled learning
episode. Findings related to this hypothesis are shown in Figure
2. Significant differences were found for the variables identified
as View of Self (IT, 5.25; OT, 2.70), Problem-Solution Process
and Learning Attitude (IT, 4.75; OT, 2.25), and for overall
Teaching Effectiveness (IT, 5.0; OT, 2.7). While trend directions
are clearly present, no significant differences were found between
the two groups on the variables of Classroom Communication
(IT, 5.2; OT, 3.2) and Management Style and Motivation (IT,
4.6; OT, 2.8).

The View of Self variable is based on four descriptors: sense
of self (strong-weak), enthusiasm (high-low), shared control, i.e.,
turn-taking, wait-time for response (high-low), and locus of
control (internal-external). These factors appear to combine to
reflect a high degree of self confidence on the part of the
influential teacher and lead to greater sensitivity to student

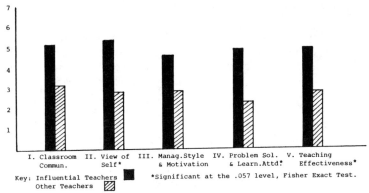

Figure 2. Influential Teacher and Other Teacher Effectiveness Factors as Rated
on the California Teaching Effectiveness Scale.

response. This sensitivity may also account for the reason these teachers were selected by their former students as influential teachers.

The Problem-Solution Process and Learning Attitude variable is based on the following descriptors: intellectually curious (high, low), attitude toward learning (positive, negative), develops teachable movement (frequent, seldom), and questioning strategies lead to resolution (frequent, seldom). Based on observations of the videotaped learning episodes, the influential teacher is highly effective in developing a higher level of interaction, and in turn interest on the part of the student, than is the case with the other teacher. This is accomplished in large part through the questioning strategies used, particularly in the more effective use of the clarifying strategy which will be discussed below.

While the variables of Classroom Communication and Management Style did not differ sufficiently between the influential and other teachers to reach statistical significance, there is a strong trend difference in favor of the influential teachers.

The second hypothesis predicted that the influential teachers would demonstrate more effective use of higher level questions and questioning strategies than other teachers. Data related to the first part of this hypothesis are shown in Table 1. An inspection of these data reveal that influential teachers and other teachers ask factual level questions at about the same degree of frequency. While influential teachers ask slightly fewer questions at the interpretive level than other teachers, they ask slightly more questions than other teachers at the applicative level. These findings show very little difference in levels of questions asked by the two groups of teachers.

More significant, however, is the way in which the two groups of teachers use questions within a given comprehension level as shown in Table 2. While there is very little variation in the use of the extending type strategy across the three levels of questions for influential and other teachers, i.e., factual, 43 vs. 50; interpretive, 43 vs. 42; applicative, 7 vs. 8; there is a marked difference in the way in which the two groups use the clarifying strategy. The relative difference increases between the two groups as questions move from simple recall, factual questions to high level inference applicative questions. Influential teachers use the clarifying strategy very little at the factual level, 2 percent, in contrast to the other teachers, 46 percent. At the interpretive level, influential teachers use this strategy substantially more, 64

Comprehension Level

	Factual	Interpretive	Applicative
Influential Teachers	42	44	14
Other Teachers	41	48	11

Table 1.   Percent of Questions by Comprehension Level Used by Influential Teachers and Other Teachers

Questioning Strategy by Comprehension Level

	Factual		Interpretive		Applicative	
	Extend	Clarify	Extend	Clarify	Extend	Clarify
Influential Teachers	43	2	43	64	7	34
Other Teachers	50	46	42	46	8	8

Table 2.   Percent of Extending and Clarifying Strategies by Comprehension Level Used by Influential Teachers and Other Teachers.

Note: Percent shown represents only those questions of the extending and clarifying type at a given comprehension level.

percent, than do the other teachers, 46 percent. At the applicative level a similar observation can be made, 34 percent vs. 8 percent, in favor of the influential teachers.

These findings suggest that the influential teacher group is much more effective in the use of the clarifying strategy than is the other teacher group. The significance of markedly different performance in the use of the clarifying strategy is found in teacher sensitivity to student response and in providing cognitive guidance to correct a misinterpretation or to build further understanding in relation to the original question. This finding also lends support to the significant difference favoring the influential teacher group over the other teacher group for the Problem-Solution Process and Learning Attitude variable.

Conclusions and implications

The teaching process is indeed a complex phenomenon. The Interactive Model of the Instructional Process clearly demonstrates that a wide range of factors influences teacher and student expectations and performance. Features of the learning episode also directly influence learning outcomes. Outcomes of teacher-student interaction are of great import in influencing student and teacher cognitive, affective, and meta-cognitive change. While the three major areas of the model have been discussed separately, the central core of the model, i.e., cognitive, affective, and meta-cognitive abilities of the student and teacher, constantly interact with each of the three areas.

The focus of this study is found in features of the learning episode. Based on the contrast of influential teacher and other teacher performance, in the learning episode studied, the following conclusions are reached.

First, the performance of influential teachers differs significantly from other teachers on the variables of View of Self, Problem-Solution Process and Learning Attitude, and overall Teaching Effectiveness. Strong trend differences also favor the influential teacher in Classroom Communication and Management Style and Motivation.

Second, influential teachers differ in a substantial way from other teachers in the use of the clarifying type questioning strategy. The relative frequency of clarifying questions asked by the influential teacher increased in direct relationship to the abstractness of questions asked. This was not the case with the other teacher group. This conclusion supports the significant difference which was found to favor the influential teacher on the Problem-Solution Process and Learning Attitude variable.

Implications from the study reinforce the importance of teacher self concept and the problem-solution process and learning attitude as key variables in the teaching process. While some aspects of self concept may be altered, e.g., shared control, other features may be relatively fixed, e.g., locus of control, in teacher performance. In contrast, most features of the problem-solution process, e.g., use of questioning strategies, would appear to hold excellent potential for change. Direct implications would suggest that variables which have high change potential be included in the development of preservice and inservice teacher education programs.

Finally, there is great need for research which will lead to an improved understanding of those school and extra-school variables which directly influence student and teacher performance in the learning episode. This effort can best be conceptualized through an interdisciplinary approach and must focus on the teaching process and interactive learning in the classroom, if the nature of teaching effectiveness is to be better understood.

REFERENCES

Au, K. and Mason, J.M. Social organizational factors in learning to read. *Reading Research Quarterly*, 1981, 17: 115-152.

Bagford, J. Evaluating teachers on reading instruction. *Reading Teacher*, 1967, 34: 400-404.

Bloom, B. *Human characteristics and school learning.* New York: McGraw-Hill. 1982.

Brophy, J.E. and Good, T.L. Teachers' communication of differential expectation for children's classroom performance: some behavioral data. *Journal of Educational Psychology*, 1970, 61: 365-374.

Coulthard, R.M. and Sinclair, J.M. *Towards an analysis of discourse: the English used by teachers and pupils.* London: Oxford University Press, 1975.

Dunkin, M. and Biddle, B. *The study of teaching.* New York: Holt, Rinehart, and Winston, 1974.

Durkin, D. What classroom observations reveal about reading comprehension instruction. *Reading Research Quarterly*, 1978, 4, 481-533.

Erickson, F. Talking down: some cultural sources of miscommunication in inter-racial interviews. In A. Wolfgang (ed.) *Research in non-verbal communication.* New York: Academic Press (in press).

Fisher, C.W., Berliner, D.C., Filby, N.N., Marhave, R., Cahen, L.S. and Dishaw, M.M. Teaching behaviors, academic learning time, and student achievement: an overview. In C. Denham and A. Lieberman, *Time to learn.* Washington, D.C.: National Institute of Education, 1980, 7-32.

Flanders, N. *Teacher influence, pupil attitudes, and achievement.* Washington, D.C.: U.S. Department of Health, Education, and Welfare, 1965.

Haggard, M.R. Pre-teacher and influential teacher perceptions of the teacher's role. Paper presented at National Reading Conference: Clearwater Beach, Florida, December, 1982.

Haslett, B.J. Dimensions of teaching effectiveness: a student perspective. *Journal of Experimental Education,* 1976, 44: 4-10.

Jakobson, R. Closing statement: linguistics and poetics. In T.A. Sebeok, (ed.) *Style in language.* Cambridge, Mass.: M.I.T. Press, 1960.

Levin, T. and Long, R. *Effective instruction.* Alexandria, Virginia: Association for Supervision and Curriculum Development, 1981.

Medley, D. Teacher competence and teacher effectiveness: a review of process-product research. Washington, D.C.: AACTE, 1977.

Mehan, H. *Learning lessons: social organization in the classroom.* Cambridge, Mass.: Harvard University Press, 1979.

Ornstein, A.C. and Levine, D.V. Teacher behavior research: overview and outlook. *Phi Delta Kappan,* 1981, 62: 592-596.

Pederson, E., Faucher, T.A. and Eaton, W. New perspective on the effects of first grade teachers on children's subsequent adult status. *Harvard Educational Review,* 1978, 48: 1-31.

Rist, R.C. Student social class and teacher expectations. *Harvard Educational Review,* 1970, 39: 411-415.

Ruddell, R. and Williams, A. *A research investigation of a literacy teaching model.* Washington, D.C.: U.S. Department of Health, Education, and Welfare, EPDA Project No. 005262, 1972.

Ruddell, R. Developing comprehension abilities: implications from research for an instructional framework. In S.J. Samuels, (ed.), *What research has to say about reading instruction.* Newark, Delaware: IRA Press, 1978, 109-120.

Ruddell, R. Literacy achievement profiles and literacy use — high and low achievers. In M.L. Kamil and A.J. Moe (eds.) *Perspectives on reading research and instruction, twenty-ninth yearbook of NRC.* Washington, D.C.: National Reading Conference, 1980, 292-300.

Ruddell R. Significant teachers: characteristics and influence on high and low achievers. Paper presented at National Reading Conference: Dallas, Texas, December, 1981.

Ruddell, R. An analysis of the development and performance of influential teachers. Paper presented at National Reading Conference: Clearwater Beach, Florida, December, 1982.

Ruddell, R. and Haggard, M. Influential teachers: characteristics and classroom performance. In J.A. Niles and L.A. Harris (eds.), *New inquiries in reading research and instruction, thirty-first yearbook of NRC,* Rochester, New York: National Reading Conference, 1982, 227-231.

Rosenthal, R. and Jacobsen, L. *Pygmalion in the classroom: teacher expectation and pupils' intellectual development.* New York: Holt, Rinehart, and Winston, 1968.

Rosenshine, B. Recent research on teaching behaviors and student achievement. *Journal of Teacher Education,* 1976, 27: 61-64.

Sacks, H., Schegloff, E. and Jefferson, G. A simplist systematics for the organization of turn-taking for conversation. *Language,* 1974, *50,* 4, 696-735.

Weinstein, R. Reading group membership in first grade: teacher behaviors and pupil experience over time. *Journal of Educational Psychology,* 1976, 68: 103-116.

On Learning To Write and To Read

Sam Sebesta

One of the best speeches I ever heard was in 1972 at the
Claremont Reading Conference. It was given by Gail Haley, who
had just won the Caldecott Medal for the best American picture
book of the year. Ms. Haley told of her great alarm over what she
termed "fatal damage . . . done to the culture of childhood" by
"arrogant technology," "mass culture," and "passive
consumption." In her Caldecott acceptance speech, given at about
the same time, she put the matter this way:

> The first generation of TV-reared children has now
> reached maturity. It may not be too far-fetched to attribute
> the loneliness of many and the drug habits of some to the
> hypodermic injections of a pacifying culture. (1)

I believe that Gail Haley's alarm was well-founded. She spoke
at a time when, with few exceptions, television ignored children. It
was also a time when the post-Sputnik era in education had
brought confusion. In the confusion, the "hard" diciplines —
mathematics, the natural sciences, linguistics, and classical literary
analysis — had taken center stage in determining curriculum, and
sometimes the manner of instruction, for childhood. Behavioral
psychology in its most simplistic form threatened to dominate,
with a learning model comprised mostly of operant conditioning.
Gail Haley's warning was powerful and timely.

Not surprisingly, the serious children's books of the decade
that preceded Ms. Haley's speech often reflected the "damage to
the culture of childhood" of which she spoke. Taboos were lifted
so that books for children and young people could speak of drugs,
premarital sex, and abuse from adults — "pot, pregnancy, and the
pill" as one critic remarked. A lot of these contemporary novels
were "downers"; they ended pessimistically. The optimistic ones
were set in the past — nostalgia tinted rose through the
dissonance reduction of memory.

I believe that Gail Haley's speech and the protests of others
who warned of damage to the culture of childhood helped to
change things. Americans are afflicted with self-analysis. We
listen and read evidence or opinion about what we are doing

71

wrong, and then we go home and try to shape up. We start jogging, eating differently, training our dog with a choke collar — or reading to our children more, or hugging our child daily. Perhaps that's the reason we get so much advertising. It works on us! The "mass culture" that Gail Haley was so concerned about may also be our salvation; it can be the communication that makes us aware of a problem and helps us respond. We are a "challenge and response" culture.

Reasons for optimism about what Gail Haley called "the culture of childhood" spring from many places, some of them quite unexpected. When she spoke of "arrogant technology" and "mass culture," many of us immediately identified the main culprit: TV. There was evidence then, as now, that television could damage the culture of childhood. Courtney Cazden was finding that TV failed to promote language development because it lessened language interaction. Dolores Durkin had found in her New York sample that children who learned to read early were those from homes where TV-watching was at a minimum. Nancy Larrick was pointing to the particularly insidious promotion of "passive consumption" by advertisers on children's Saturday morning cartoon shows.

These charges are still true. Nevertheless, there are hopeful developments. TV viewing, the great impetus to "mass culture," began to decline two years ago. There began to be evidence that Americans had other things to do than to become a "pacifying culture." Some observations revealed that children are not always glued to the TV simply because the set is turned on. Given opportunity, they, too, do not choose to be passive.

Then, too, there are signs of improved programming, despite the persistent drivel. This Christmas children and adults all over the country could hear and see an opera "Hansel and Gretel" live from the Met, the American Ballet production of "The Nutcracker," and the great Leontyne Price at Kennedy Center. The opportunity to hear great music and to see passably good drama has greatly expanded over the past ten years. It is hard to call TV an "arrogant technology" when we really study the benefits that selective viewing can bring.

It would be naive to say that improved programming leads automatically to selective viewing that takes advantage of such opportunities. But such programming does give us options. It permits concerned adults — parents and teachers — to help children benefit from mass media, to avoid the dangers of a "pacifying culture."

I mention this matter as a preamble to a discussion of reading and writing, because these skills cannot be separated from the wider environment of communication. They cannot be separated from the development of taste. To attempt to improve the teaching of reading and writing without a concomitant attempt to improve reception and production in all the communicative arts is not likely to give us what we want. What we want is to aid the sensibilities and taste of those who comprise the culture of childhood.

Our penchant for self-analysis, for self-criticism, has been heaviest in the field of education. When I began teaching in the 1950s and when I went to Stanford to do graduate work in the 1960s, the names of John Dewey and Progressive Education were linked as a common enemy which scientific educators must attack or from which they must flee. The post-Sputnik revision in educational goals and the entrenchment of behavioral objectives pre-determined to establish curriculum and instruction were seen as the final defeat of Dewey and the Progressive Education movement.

The teaching of reading was a particular case. In the late 1950s many people believed that most children could not read because they had been haphazardly taught, especially because they had not been taught phonics. Then, in the 1960s, the structural linguists, notably followers of Bloomfield and Fries, promised salvation. They simplified the task. They argued that reading meant decoding, and decoding meant matching letter patterns with sound patterns — accomplished by concentrated drill on the patterns, the "fat cat at bat" procedure.

That was, indeed, quite a switch from the 1950s. It might also be viewed as a defeat for the culture of childhood, since it ignored children's interests, their meaningful language, and what Dewey believed to be their intrinsic right and desire to participate in figuring out how to learn. In fact, the solution was simplistic. It worked only up to a point. Then it reached a level which phonics critics used to call "exceptions" but which later linguists called morphological level.

There followed a decade of study. First there were the studies of the "utility" of the old phonics generalizations. Then there were studies of how a morphological level of language might help the learner modify and make sense out of the letter-sound connections. And, more recently, there is better effort to see how sentence context and broader cohesion contribute to decoding.

So what began as a doomed-to-fail movement to reduce reading to barking on cue has, in my opinion, helped bring us to a more solid understanding of decoding and how to teach it. And — not by accident — we learned, along the route of its development, that we could not ignore the culture of children in the process. To study or teach decoding, we must do more than look at how spoken language patterns are represented by orthography; we must also look at how children developmentally become aware of these patterns and their representation in print. Nowhere has this been shown more clearly to me than in the work of Eleanor Gibson. In her early studies she patiently *told* children the rules for decoding print into sounds. Her research soon led her to this discovery: that she must help children figure out those rules for themselves before they would be able to apply them. That's part of what John Dewey had been saying all along!

A similar case can be made of the recent movement to improve how we teach reading comprehension. Intensive criticism, notably by Durkin in her two studies reported in *Reading Research Quarterly* (2) and by David Pearson in his speeches, is leveled at how comprehension is taught — or, rather, *not* taught. Characteristically, researchers responded to this alarm not by studying the problem head-on but by studying text. Many examined expository writing to see how its message might be organized for better communication. From such research, we might expect more explicit, more consistent top level structure, and clearer statements of macropropositions. Eventually, as researchers and practitioners try this improved expository writing in the classroom, we might expect comprehension to improve.

It is a slow process. Like so many movements in education, it sometimes seems to begin far away from children. It seems to begin simplistically, with the behaviorist's penchant for neatness and control and for manipulating one variable at a time. No one seems to be asking, for instance, whether *all* information a child wants can fit well into the five top-level structures that the researchers seem to have found — or whether children's cognitive abilities are really accommodated by the prose-reforming strategies. But the pressures are there. The alarm has been sounded. Researchers who are also practitioners, teachers themselves, and cognitivists in general will, I believe, refine and apply these ideas for improving comprehension. Eventually, they will assist, not ignore, the "culture of childhood."

To be effective, an innovation to improve literacy must have two characteristics. First, it needs to integrate the communication skills. This includes production as well as reception. Second, it needs to focus on child development, the culture of childhood — not just on the discipline to be taught.

If these things are true, then the recent movement to improve written communication of children and young people is right on target. It is based solidly on ethnographic study of children, as evidenced by the work of Donald H. Graves and his followers. These researcher/teachers have worked hand-in-hand or pencil-in-pencil with children to find better ways to encourage pre-writing, conferencing, drafting, and revising.

There are also signs that this movement to improve the composing process will help integrate the language arts. James Squire has pointed out that, before a child can comprehend a reading assignment such as a story problem or a set of directions, he or she must have had experience in composing such a message through written composition. My colleague Phillip Gonzales is presently experimenting with story grammars not, at the outset, as a means of measuring or teaching reading comprehension, as others have done, but as a way of helping children compose stories in speech and writing.

If my two premises are true — that integration of the communicative arts is essential and that innovations for teaching them must begin with study of child development, a cognitivist view rather than a behaviorist view — then the attempt to improve written composition is likely to be our most successful achievement in education in this decade.

And what of literature? There have already been attempts to integrate the teaching of language arts through literature, notably through the government-sponsored Project English centers at the University of Nebraska, University of Oregon, and others during the 1960s. They attempted to teach "literature, language, and composition" through a core curriculum of selected literary works. At the University of Nebraska, where I worked, the lessons presented large helpings of literary analysis: the identification of literary elements such as plot devices, characterization, point of view, and theme. They aimed at genre and motif identification, mostly according to the gospel of Northrop Frye.

Such an attempt to integrate language arts through literature cannot be said to have failed. But it had one serious limitation. It virtually ignored the "culture of childhood." It taught children to talk about and write about literature in a more sophisticated manner, but I doubt that it got to the heart of their response. It may have developed their taste, but I doubt whether it improved their interest.

Ostensibly, a more child-centered approach appeared in the 1970s, when Alan Purves and his followers studied the response to literature of children and adolescents. Now the focus was upon how you responded to what you read and how to broaden and deepen that response.

At present, this movement, too, seems lacking. The results of literary study with its attempts to measure response have not shown improvement, according to the most recent National Assessment of Educational Progress. Perhaps the trouble is that response to literature is still mainly verbal. Purves measured it that way, and even the open questions on literature designed to elicit Purves' categories of response are seeking engagement-involvement, perception, interpretation, and evaluation through vocal or written discussion.

A more productive enticement to respond to literature is through the arts themselves: music and movement; new techniques of drama including story theatre, readers theatre, and oral interpretation; and visual arts including sculpture and design. Beyond retell, a child's response to a story or poem may often be encouraged best through the arts.

Such techniques are not well taught through books or lists of suggested activities. To learn to handle a role-playing session or a session in which oral interpretation gets to the heart of a literary work requires training for teachers. I say this at a time when my own university has decided to curtail its courses in child drama, music education, and art education. The result, if we lose these means to responding, will indeed do damage to the culture of childhood.

I would like to offer a few implications for teaching based on these remarks. After a third of a century spent in and near classrooms, I feel compelled to do so. I only wish I knew as much now as I thought I did when I started in this profession 33 years ago.

1. First, I think we teachers have a responsibility to teach children and parents about selective viewing and listening — not just in regard to TV but in all encounters with mass media. The first National Assessment, in about 1970, surprised us by showing that fourth-graders were not very good at interpreting the *TV Guide*. But there's more at stake; it isn't just a matter of

reading mass media schedules but of determining what one should hear and see. We should not under-rate our influence in this matter. I've known a teacher near Palo Alto who played Wagner and Chopin records in the classroom simply as background a bit each day until, by the end of the month, third-graders were asking, "Could we have a little Chopin during spelling?" In Minneapolis, where schools attend the symphony, parents were amazed to find that their children identify instruments and background themes at the movies. "They stole that from Wagner!" a fourth-grade friend of mine told his mom when the music announced the arrival of war planes in a recent film.

2. Second, I think we teachers must be experimentalists. If the researchers on reading comprehension are going to take so long in exploring the mysteries of schema training, story grammar, top-level structure, key lexical items, and all the rest, then I really don't see any danger in going ahead and trying those ideas in the classroom. *I've* done so. As soon as I learned to do a passable story grammar designed by a wiser mind than mine (Arthur Applebee's), I took it out and used it in teaching literature to fifth graders. When it didn't work very well, I told them all about it and asked them what went wrong. And they told me. The study I'm doing now is on historical fiction. I'm trying to find out why so many fifth and sixth graders don't like historical fiction and why they can't seem to understand it. I didn't get very far until I explained the whole study to them and asked them for help. Now I'm getting some answers. Also, I'm beginning to wonder: Have we been missing the boat all along by trying to understand the culture of childhood without asking children themselves to help us figure it out?

3. Third, I think we teachers can dare to move beyond questions and a mere list of suggested activities when we work with literature, whether the literature is an excerpt in a basal reader or a whole trade book. A literature session that begins and ends with everyone seated and talking or writing answers to questions or drawing a picture is probably not going to foster active involvement. Even if we are not skilled in oral interpretation, the plastic arts, or mime, we may still open up avenues of response that will heighten taste and develop lifetime readers. Without such involvement, our growing success in teaching how to read and how to learn from text is incomplete.

Over the winter holidays I began to read a very long children's book about four illegitimate children whose mother had been taken away to an institution for the insane. Amazingly, the story was warm, happy, and optimistic. The children cared for each other and for the embittered grandmother who took them in. They formed mutual protection that withstood troubles, including one child's inability to learn and another's inability to cope with his own excessive anger. I read how the children managed with too little clothing in cold weather and how they gave each other sustaining comfort when their mother died. Over-all, the book achieved a tone of genuine happiness and optimism and a fine, genuine regard for the dignity of childhood.

By midway in this long novel, I decided that it had to be nostalgic, had to be set in the past, perhaps in the author's own childhood. People simply haven't been writing so happily and optimistically about deprived disadvantaged children in our own "troubled" times. So it was a shock to find, three-fourths through the book, that one character referred to President Johnson and another told him that President Johnson "isn't President any more." The book's setting is *now*. The optimism is not forced — nor are the "troubled times" minimized.

When, in January of 1983, that book — *Dicey's Song* by Cynthia Voight — won the Newbery Medal for best children's book of the year, I wanted to say to Gail Haley and others who have been so worried: "Take heart. Some of your hopes have been fulfilled, some of the damage averted. Here we are — almost to the once-dreaded 1984 — and the 'culture of childhood' is still alive."

REFERENCES

1   Haley, Gail. "Caldecott Acceptance Speech," *The Horn Book Magazine,* XLVII, *4*, (August 1971), pp. 363-368. p. 366.
2   Durkin, Dolores. "Reading Comprehension Instruction in Five Basal Reader Series," *Reading Research Quarterly*, XVI, *4* (1981), pp. 515-544; "What Classroom Observations Reveal About Reading Comprehension Instruction," *Reading Research Quarterly*, XIV, *4* (1978-1979), pp. 481-533.

Reading the Newberys

Doty Doherty-Hale

The Newbery Award is especially pertinent for us today for
two reasons. One is that its history roughly parallels that of the
Claremont Reading Conference. The oldest reading conference is
celebrating its fiftieth anniversary this year; the oldest continuing
book award, established in 1922, started just a decade earlier.

Another, very different reason for re-examining some of the
Newbery winners is recent articles with titles like:

"Victim of Success? A Closer Look at the Newbery Award"
(1972)

"The Newberys: Getting them read (it isn't easy)" (1974)

"Who Reads the Newbery Winners?" (1977)

Even the more positive "Newbery Medal Books Are Alive
and Well at Court Street School" (1981) implies that elsewhere
their health could be more in doubt. Norma Schlager's 1975
Claremont Reading Conference address, "The Significance of
Children's Choices in Literature: New Insights Based Upon a
Developmental Viewpoint," has a less obvious title, but contains
the results of one of the more influential studies on the Newbery
Award books and their popularity with young readers. Based on
a 1974 Claremont Graduate School dissertation, and published
in a slightly altered form in 1978, Schlager's findings were cited
by Betty Brett and Charlotte Huck in their 1982 "Research
Update" for children's literature:

> The criticism classified as *child-centered* is small in
> quantity, rather general in nature, but thought-
> provoking in substance. It seeks to establish a
> relationship between the disciplines of literature and
> psychology, a relationship which is reinforced by the
> findings of both formal research and empirical
> observation. Schlager (1978), for example,
> emphasizes the need for "cross-pollination" between
> the two disciplines in an attempt to relate knowledge
> of child development to children's literary
> inclinations. Based on her study of the five most
> popular Newbery award-winning books and the five

79

> least popular ones, she concluded that literary quality
> alone will not ensure child interest in books. Books
> which are to appeal to childhood must have the
> developmental perceptions of childhood.(1)

Norma Schlager certainly did her share in the "cross-pollination," especially in the areas of empirical data and their relationship to findings in child development. Her original study surveyed 100% of the regional libraries in the Los Angeles County system and 25% of the branch libraries to determine how often the first fifty-one Newbery Award books had been checked out between 1971 and 1973. Then, drawing "upon the developmental concepts of Piaget, [Anna] Freud, and Erikson," she analyzed the most circulated books and the least circulated books "for their congruence with what these theorists suggest typifies child thought during the ages of approximately seven to twelve." (2)

I hope here to continue the exchange between the disciplines by using both literary criticism and Schlager's studies in child development to look at the Newbery Award and to compare the most circulated book on her list, *Island of the Blue Dolphins*, with the least circulated, *Dobry*.

First, though, we have to admit that some aspects of children's book preferences are outside both our disciplines. Newbery Award books like *Mrs. Frisby and the Rats of NIMH* and *The Voyages of Doctor Dolittle* experienced a surge of popularity when movies were made from them. Time is also an important, although not a determining, factor. Of Schlager's ten least circulated books, one came from the 1960s, *I, Juan de Pareja*, and one from the 1950s, *Amos Fortune, Free Man*, but all the rest were from the 1920s and 1930s. Of her ten most circulated, two were from the late 1940s, *King of the Wind* and *The Twenty-One Balloons*, but the rest were published within fifteen years of her study.

But other areas of popularity can benefit from cooperation between the disciplines of child development and literary analysis. A first step would be to look more closely at the Newbery Awards. Schlager says that since these books "are all considered to be of high literary quality, this characteristic [winning the Newbery] is held as a constant, an unvarying element within the sample against which the effect of changes in others may be investigated."(3) Like many artistic awards, however, the Newbery books are chosen by a committee, and also like other awards, the results can vary. In questioning if the

awards are a "Victim of Success," Peggy Sullivan suggests that
there "is something ingenuous in the attitude that once a book
has won the Newbery Award, it demands the allegiance and
attention of all who are concerned about children's literature . . .
We should accept the fact that the committee is not always right,
but that does not allow us to question their motives or their
morals."(4) The Newbery winners are usually good books, but
they are not an "unvarying element" with consistent "high
literary quality." They are not even necessarily the best
children's book published that year. For example, *Charlotte's
Web* was a runner-up, or Honor Book, in 1953, but the largely
forgotten *Secret of the Andes* received the award itself. Groups of
children that were most successful at "getting them read,"
including the one at Court Street School, admitted that the books
varied in quality and let the children themselves debate which
books deserved an award and which did not.

Another assumption that might bear further investigation is
Schlager's choice of the seven to twelve age group as the primary
audience for the Newberys. One study of the winners from 1940
to 1973 found that a little over a third were at the junior high
reading level, and the rest were heavily weighted at the upper
elementary grades. This researcher, Paul J. Schafer, also adds
that the data provided by readability formulas do not consider
subjective factors like content, organization, and the child's
interest and motivation. "In short, judgments concerning the
readability of a book should be based on sound knowledge of
stylistic elements of difficulty, tempered with a common sense
understanding of the interests of young readers."(5)

One of the common sense understandings of the interests of
young readers — and some not so young — is that, given a
choice, most would be more likely to check out a book if its
opening paragraphs provoke interest and involvement. In this
context, compare the first two paragraphs of the most circulated
book in Norma Schlager's study with the least circulated.

> I remember the day the Aleut ship came to our
> island. At first it seemed like a small shell afloat on
> the sea. Then it grew larger and was a gull with
> folded wings. At last in the rising sun it became what
> it really was — a red ship with two red sails.
> My brother and I had gone to the head of a canyon
> that winds down to a little harbor which is called
> Coral Cove. We had to gather roots that grow there
> in the spring.(6)

82   CLAREMONT READING CONFERENCE/1983

Island of the Blue Dolphins, in the best storytelling tradition, quickly sets up character and situation, and in this case also creates the historical tone in a language that is nevertheless easily understood by twentieth century readers. The one unusual word, "Aleut," instead of distracting, only adds to the mysterious atmosphere of the strange ship.

> Dobry ran to a window, slid back its window-panel carved with buffalo heads. "Snow! Why, it's snowing, Grandfather! The courtyard is white already." Snow was never rare in a mountain village of Bulgaria, but nobody, not even Dobry's grandfather, had seen snow coming down to hide red apples on the tree, late corn on the stalk, ripe peppers in the field, grapes on the vine. The golden-leaved poplar tree in the courtyard of Dobry's peasant home was completely hushed with snow. Wool, too, from the autumn shearing was hanging out to dry. The wool grew thicker, the thickest wool imaginable as more and more snow came down. Without making a sound, the sky itself seemed to be coming down bit by bit.
>
> "Nobody has ever seen a happening like this one," Dobry's grandfather said, and followed the little boy to the window. "Snow already, even before the gypsy bear gets here! My back, my legs complain of getting in the grass and the early corn. They wanted a good rubbing before snow set in. Snow? To the devil with gypsies! They should be here with the massaging bear!"(7)

Dobry, also a historical novel, sets its time and place with a burst of repetitious, insistent dialogue, augmented by a long list of descriptive details. One cliche, "hushed with snow," seems particularly inappropriate when applied to a taciturn object like a tree. In the second paragraph, grandfather at first seems like the stock European *pere*, huffing and grumping away, but his words soon degenerate into unintelligibility — "the massaging bear"? The next paragraph turns to other local scenes, and even if one does read on after this inauspicious start, the massaging bear is not really explained until the middle of the book. (The gypsies have a bear that massages people by shuffling back and forth over them as the people lie on the ground. Intelligibility does not greatly improve even with explanation.)

In short, the opening of *Island of the Blue Dolphins* promotes involvement and suspense, while *Dobry* only provides tedium and puzzlement.

Similar arguments could be made for the opening of Schlager's second most circulated book, *The Witch of Blackbird Pond*, in which we sail briskly into Connecticut Colony with newcomer Kit Tyler. The second least circulated book, *The Trumpeter of Krakow*, starts more intelligibly than *Dobry*, but no more interestingly. With no evidence of characters or dialogue, its first paragraphs read like a slanted, pretentious history lesson on the invasion of the Tartars: "Brave they were as lions, courageous they were as great dogs, but they had hearts of stone and knew not mercy, nor pity, nor tenderness, nor God."(8)

Norma Schlager's study briefly notes matters of style and tone, but her major emphasis is on character and content, and it is probably in these areas where our two disciplines can most usefully share knowledge. She notes, for example, that when Karana of *Island of the Blue Dolphins* has to tackle the problems of survival on an abandoned island without adult help, Karana provides the young readers with a gratifying example of Erikson's "reality orientation," or in Schlager's words, "the phenomenon whereby the seven- to twelve-year-old simultaneously gains a keen desire to handle reality situations independently and to assess his or her own ability to cope and succeed in reality situations." Karana also appeals to a child's mind with her developing ability at what Piaget calls "syllogistic reasoning," or the "ability to plan logically or build from a hypothesis to a logical conclusion." This, in turn, appeals to "cognitive conceit, . . . the child's perception of a situation that allows him or her to feel the ability to handle any reality situation beautifully without any adult assistance."(9) I would agree with this but use different terminology (each discipline has its own, and one goal should be to better understand each other's). Throughout the book, Karana exhibits believable character development, one that a child can recognize and feel a kinship with. I do not think I would even limit it there. Abandonment brings out the child in all of us, and Scott O'Dell's story arouses these emotions so powerfully that I myself identify with Karana's struggle, and it is also my conceit that really I would be able to cope as well as she.

In her articles and in her original dissertation, Schlager praised *Dobry* for a section like this:

> "Why do you always follow me around?" Dobry asked the moon. "Everywhere I go there you come looking, looking, looking . . . you say nothing. Just follow me about staring! How do you expect me to

> sleep? Nobody could sleep while you stare the way
> you do and say nothing."(10)

Unlike his comments about snow in the opening paragraphs,
Dobry's words here are a convincing portrayal of a child's speech
patterns and mode of thought. Schlager's understanding of the
development patterns of childhood is helpful in explaining just
how this mode of thought works. Dobry is a child in the
"preconcrete stage," believing in Animism (the moon is alive)
and Artificialism (it exists for the "sole purpose of helping
men").(11) But Schlager's other example of Dobry's Animism
and Artificialism poses some problems for the literary critic:

> The light chaff blew away on the wind. But Dobry
> thought this happened only because they sang to the
> wind.
>> "Wind, wind, take these sheaves
>> golden beards and golden leaves.
>> Take the chaff. Oh blow it far!
>> Let the grains fall where we are."(12)

We can intellectually see Dobry's belief that the wind is alive
and responsive to his bidding, but leaden, unmusical lines of his
song diminish the emotional appeal of the rite.

Schlager is again helpful when she notes a major defect:
Dobry's middle childhood is skipped altogether. Between
chapters the author jumps four years, and Dobry is suddenly an
accomplished artist, betrothed to his childhood chum. As
Schlager notes, *Dobry* therefore provides little for readers of
middle childhood to relate to.(13) It also poses a literary
problem. The readers can guess how his feeling for Neda
changed from friend to fiance, but we do not see it happening,
and guessing is not our job. Similarly, we see his young interest
in carving, and later see him sculpting an entire nativity scene as
an adult, but we never see how he got from one to the other. In
short (or, in literary terms), the development of his emotional and
artistic character is inadequate.

Content and character of the number two books on
Schlager's list again provide grounds for accord; Kit Tyler's
"reality orientation" and "cognitive conceit" are indeed
convincing as she slowly learns to cope with the habits and
prejudices of colonial New England. On the other hand, the
intricate maze of adult activity in *The Trumpeter of Krakow*
inexplicably abandons the children who are supposed to be the
main characters.

I hope that these remarks can be part of a mutually profitable exchange between the child development specialists and the literary critics. The popularity of a book is not the sole indicator of its literary quality, but critics have long insisted that all literature must entertain as well as inform, and that delight is as important as increased understanding. John Newbery is famous today because he overtly offered "amusement" in addition to the usual "instruction" in his eighteenth century children's books. The twentieth century Newbery Award winners, with their relatively long history and national prominence, provide the ideal forum for adults in various disciplines to learn not only more about what amuses children, but also why.

(Note: This talk was in association with a retrospective exhibit of all the Newbery award winners at the George G. Stone Center for Children's Books.)

FOOTNOTES

1 Brett, Betty M. and Huck, Charlotte S., "Research Update: Children's Literature — The Search for Excellence," *Language Arts*, (1982), p. 879.

2 Schlager, Norma, "The Significance of Children's Choices in Literature: New Insights Based Upon a Developmental Viewpoint," *Claremont Reading Conference 39th Yearbook*, Malcolm P. Douglass (ed.). (Claremont: The Claremont Reading Conference, 1975), p. 65.

3 _____, "Predicting Children's Choices in Literature: A Developmental Approach," *Children's Literature in Education 9* (1978), p. 137.

4 Sullivan, Peggy, "Victim of Success? A Closer Look at the Newbery Award," *School Library Journal*, (May, 1972), p. 41.

5 Schafer, Paul J., "The Readability of the Newbery Medal Books," *Language Arts*, (1976), p. 559.

6 O'Dell, Scott, *Island of the Blue Dolphins*, (New York: Dell, 1960), p. 1.

7 Shannon, Monica, *Dobry*, (New York: Viking, 1934), p. 5.

8 Kelly, Eric P., *The Trumpeter of Krakow*, (New York: Macmillan, 1929), p. 1.

9 Schlager, Norma, "Predicting," p. 138.

10 _____, "Developmental Factors Influencing Children's Responses to Literature," Diss. Claremont Graduate School, (1974), p. 95.

11 _____, "Predicting," p. 140.

12 _____, "Developmental Factors," p. 95.

12 _____, "Predicting," p. 141.

A Recognition of Merit Presented to

beverly cleary

honoring

her body of work

For their power to please and to heighten the awareness of children and teachers as they have shared the books in their classrooms

presented by the george g. stone center for children's books of the claremont graduate school, at the 50th annual claremont reading conference 1983

Presentation of the Recognition of Merit Award to Beverly Cleary

Nancy Roozen

In this day of the competitive entertainment of television and electronic games, it needs to be remembered that books are still the most desirable and important media to provide children with aesthetic encounters with an art form. Authors of fine literature have something to say — special messages, ideas, thoughts, feelings, and information gathered along their road of life. As Charlotte Huck said in *Children and Books*, (pg. 18) "Children's literature should provide enjoyment and lead to a deeper understanding of life."

This year the George G. Stone Center for Children's Books is happy to honor an author whose stories for young people are full of humor and provide both recreation and wholesome personality development, resulting from the natural telling of a story.

Beverly Cleary has created over 20 books for children in the middle and upper elementary grades. Her personal knowledge of children of these ages is very evident as she describes their adventures, problems, and often improbable, but very natural, hilarious activities.

Happy group experiences, all very realistic, are presented in her books about children, as *Mitch and Amy*, typical fourth grade twins; *Otis Spofford*, who stirs up trouble at his school; Jimmy who puts *The Real Hole* to good use; *Ellen Tibbits*, who struggles with ballet, braces, and long woolen underwear; *Henry Huggins*, who has several books of experiences with his self-confidence, his dog, his friends, and his nemesis, Ramona Quimby, who in the kindergarten book is a pest, in the first grade story brave, in subsequent books 'special' to both mother and father, and finally unforgettable at age 8.

Popular animal stories include *Socks*, the cat who tells how his family status is threatened by a new baby; *Ribsy*, Henry's four-legged 'best friend'; and most recently a series about the delightful, intelligent, talking *Ralph S. Mouse*.

A few young adolescent novels, sprinkled in between, are the warm stories of a first young love for a *Fifteen*-year-old girl; of the excitement and confusion in a family preparing for a wedding as seen by the *Sister of the Bride;* and of *Emily's Runaway Imagination* that helps to get a library for a small Oregon town in the 1920s.

These stories, and the ones not mentioned here, have consistently been reprinted and have been read by millions of children over many years. We are happy to present Beverly Cleary with a Recognition of Merit for her entire Body of Work.

Illustration by Alan Tiergreen from *Ramona Quimby, Age 8* by Beverly Cleary. Copyright 1981. Permission to reprint graciously given by William Morrow and Company, Inc.

Acceptance Statement

Beverly Cleary

The writer of books for children is often asked, "Why do you write for children?" The inflection sometimes suggests the writer is spending time on inferior work when he or she might be writing for adults. My answer to the question, no matter what the inflection, is: I write for children because reading meant so much to me when I was growing up. I am grateful to the men and women who wrote the books that captured my imagination and to the librarians who held to high standards in the libraries available to me in childhood.

In the thirty-four years that I have been writing, I have received thousands of letters from children, more than I can possibly answer, who tell me what they want from a book. First of all, they tell me, they want to be the person in the book. They want to read about problems children can solve themselves. They reject the book that overtly teaches, but they appreciate the book in which they find what they want or need. They want books written in language they can understand, but they object to books that are written down, or as they say, "babyish."

Unfortunately, today many children are unhappy about reading. They say they hate reading, they are bored by the books they find in the library, or they can't understand what the author is trying to say. Some tell me the teacher is making them read a book, and they have to write to the author. If the author answers, they get an A. Why, I wonder, should a child's grades be the responsibility of an author? Two girls wrote of an elaborate project based on one of my books and concluded their letter with "and we even read the book."

Fortunately, not all children are unhappy about reading. Many say they love reading and can't get enough of it. They tell of sharing books with friends. They write about parents or teachers who sparked their interest in reading by reading aloud.

However, in the past eight or ten years, more and more children have told of turning to books for comfort. Their parents are divorced, they live in mobile homes or apartments, they have had to give away their pets, they have no place to play, they are lonely, and some are frightened. They grieve for fathers they no longer see or worry because their fathers are out of work. One sad letter said, "My Dad is the kind of man who doesn't like to be around kids."

Such children, if they have been helped by adults to enjoy reading, turn to books and tell me of reading favorites over and over, because the stories make them feel better. One child wrote wistfully, "I wish the whole world would be like it says in your books." These children have made me realize that I, too, read for comfort in childhood — and still do. However, writing to offer children solace never once entered my mind. I write the books I wanted to read as a child, books set in the neighborhood of my childhood which to me was, and still is, real but not ideal. I count myself exceptionally fortunate that the books that have come out of my childhood emotions give pleasure and comfort to children in today's frightening world. Books cannot solve children's problems, but they can offer relief and hope.

I accept with pride and pleasure the 18th Recognition of Merit for my work. Thank you.

The Case for the Language Experience Approach and Individualized Reading

Jeannette Veatch

When the roll is called up yonder many years hence, when distant, and presumably objective, observers evaluate the current reading scene, they could hardly fail to notice the overriding concern for the use of commercial material in the teaching of reading. It is curious that the prominence of major figures in the field of psycholinguistics, such as Frank Smith, Kenneth Goodman, among others, have not appreciably broken the stranglehold of commercial publishers upon the school market. Not that such individuals have not had a major impact, *philosophically* upon reading, for they have justifiably earned recognition on a world wide basis. Yet with all that, the sales of readers, even more restrictively on a one text, one company basis, as opposed to multi-text adoptions, goes inexorably and exceedingly profitably onward.

It is true, I think, that the language experience approach is in greater favor than previously. It is hard to see why there is any argument about its effectiveness in early reading. But individualized reading, on the other hand, the only systematic instructional program based upon the use of trade books, has indeed been throttled by various forces in the educational world.

Teaching reading without a reader, or teaching writing without a text, arouses terror in the hearts of many teachers. It is unfortunate that this is so, as teaching literacy without a text is not difficult. It is just different. There are two approaches that are frequently used to describe such strategies: 1) the language experience approach and 2) "self-selection," personalized reading or individualized reading. The widespread adoption of these practices would effectively doom the existence of the textbook industry, which would strike terror in *their* hearts. The Catch 22 situation is that commercial companies respond to the marketplace, but, in this case, they are the ones who, through their sales force, and authors, *make* the marketplace. Should

91

teachers, for example, learn how to induce literacy in all pupils
without the use of texts, the sale of such profitable items would
be substantially lowered. The problem is that the practice of
language experience and individualized reading is not the most
widely understood methodology in the panoply of education. This
paper is an offering to correct this situation.

To accomplish this task, may I suggest that the key, the
crucial, the fundamental principle is that each teacher, no matter
the grade, the subject, or the age, must utilize some aspect of the
internal world of the pupil. There must be some kind of personal
choice, some kind of individual input into the task of learning the
given matter in hand. The act of instruction must be predicated
upon a process that guarantees such personal choices. This might
be called structure of process, as a teacher must work in a
prescribed way, or be unsuccessful. To cite a structure of process
is to cite a total, polar opposite of a structure of content.

There have been many who have been responsible for the
imposition of content upon hapless children. But the one who has
produced the most seismic effect in this direction has been Bloom
(1956) with his various domains, cognitive, effective, and psycho-
motor. By his monumental analysis of the nature of what children
learn, he has itemized, yea, atomized, step by step, the progress
of a student in the acquisition of knowledge. As these are
addressed to *what* children learn, they are of minimal utility in
the understanding of the *how* children learn. Thus he has
provided the behaviorists, the behavioral objective people, the
mastery learning folk, the machine programmers, with a field day
of program development that allows adults to prescribe and
impose content to be learned. Never mind that the learner must
be psyched up, must be persuaded, must be "motivated," to learn
said content. Each pupil must be convinced by his teacher that
he should commit himself to such structured material. The point
is that, lacking the spark of the internal world of the child, the
"lived world" as Blakey describes it, instructional practice is
based on highly authoritarian principles. All system, all lock step,
all planned sequential work, and no choice: all organizational
patterns to *prevent* personal intellectual development.

But what is the alternative? Most teachers, in fright that they
will "miss" something, salve their consciences by following, to
the letter, the "domains," or the behavioral objectives mandated
by their given school system. For, to most, the idea of basing
instruction on pupils' choices is an invitation to mayhem, to
disorganization, and to chaos. And indeed it could be so! To
have a classroom situation in which there is *no* system, *no*

organization, no planned structure of how to control idea output, is to provide an invitation to disaster. Of course, this is the decades old cry against Progressive Education. "Let-the-little-darlings-do-what-they-please." Dewey was not confused on this matter, but a lot of others were. We wish to present, therefore, a methodology that is highly structured, and, indeed, very systematic, but one which allows teachers to teach without texts.

A recent study by the Department of Education in the State of California (1980) is instructive. Taking all of the statewide reading test achievement results on a continuum, from those showing increasing scores, to those showing decreasing scores, they randomized a set of schools from the upper and lower 20 percent ends of the scale. Sending in evaluators to ascertain the reasons for the differences, they found, surprisingly perhaps, that ethnic and economic conditions were not prime. What was crucial was that, in those schools with increasing reading achievement, the teachers had had an input into the selection of the reading program to be used. Further, in those schools, teachers were not rigorously restricted to the manual of the given program. They were able to use their own judgment in their teaching. Contrariwise, those schools with decreasing reading achievement scores were found not to have involved teachers in the selection of the reading program. The evaluators found complaints on this matter, as well as complaints about the requirement of undeviating following of manual directions. In addition, many of those schools had an hour of mandated phonics, usually of the worksheet type of activity. The evaluators also reported marked differences in morale between these two sets of schools. Those on the top of the achievement ladder revealed far more positive attitudes in all human relationships.

With this introduction as a backdrop to our main presentation that embodies these elements of structured process, i.e., pupil choice with orderly procedures, let us begin with the first of our approaches, that of "language experience."

The language experience approach

The language experience approach is not a thing. It is a multiple, variegated set of activities designed to serve one purpose, namely, the instructional use of pupils' own language. It is profoundly psycholinguistic in that the language that is used is drawn directly from the persons involved, i.e., from their own psyches and experiences. Psycholinguistics is, as Frank Smith noted (1973), a field of study that lies at the intersection of two broader disciplines, psychology and linguistics. The content, the instructional material, that derives from the processes and strategies used, is as different as the pupils themselves. Perhaps it is understandable that such variety strikes fear in the hearts of teachers. One is scared of what one does not know. What, then, are the strategies of the language experience approach?

There are five interrelated aspects that weave in and out of daily classroom practice. The first is the Alphabet, which is learned usually long before the school years as a rote piece of memory. In school, the alphabet should be large enough, with appropriate pictures, and low enough on the classroom wall to be easily seen by all. The usefulness of the alphabet lies in its letter names. The alphabetic principle (Veatch 1978) or letter name strategy (Chomsky 1970; Clay 1977) is exceedingly useful. With the exception of the short vowels, with hard "g", "h", "w", and "y", the letter names trigger off, when mouthed, recognition from their sounds, i.e., "boy" must start with a "b," as "lake" starts with an "l." The letter name is there to be heard. Read (1975) found that very young children in kindergarten were able to spell remarkably well phonetically because of the letter names. Contrary to all commercial phonics programs, Clay (1977) and others have established that the evidence in children's writing shows that they proceeded from letter names to letter sounds, especially where vowels are concerned.

This leads us to another aspect of the language experience approach, that of Writing. I refer here to writing that is original to the pupil writer, which includes evidence of what is known as "invented spelling." It is important to describe "invented spelling," which has come to refer to that spelling having a semblance to "phonetic spelling" but which is derived from more profound origins. Piaget pointed out that counting, or number sense, came when rote counting was succeeded by one-to-one correspondence to the numbers, as "8" was 8 beans, or marbles, or something tangible, and "14" was 14 things. Similarly, invented spelling represents progress from rote parroting of the alphabet to the concept of "l" is "l" and not part of the phrase "elemeno," i.e., l, m, n, and o, the bugaboo "letter" of first grade teachers. What must happen is that the alphabet becomes internalized, hence, "invented" just as counting becomes internalized. The breakdown of the rote recital of the alphabet into its component letters allows the words to be spelled on a letter name basis, which eventually should, at least, lead in later grades, into formal, accurate, and correct spelling.

The breakdown of the rote into one-to-one correspondence

brings us to the third aspect of the language experience approach, that of the Key Vocabulary, in its classic presentation by Sylvia Ashton-Warner. It is unfortunate that the reading segment of the educational establishment has not recognized the exceptional and unique value of Ashton-Warner's activity. It is a highly structured process in which the teacher elicits a personal word from each pupil in a specified, organized way. But, be it noted, the word is unknown until given *by* the child. It is, perhaps, the best example we have of structured process as opposed to structured content.

Once the word is elicited, the teacher proceeds to print the word on a 4 x 7 card, as the child says each letter as it is written. Should the teacher doubt whether or not the child knows the letter, the alphabet on the wall is referred to. In this way the "elemeno" problem is met and resolved. Blakey (1980) established that the rote breakdown occurred at this point. These potent key words were also found supportive of Fernald's (1943) activity of letter tracing in words. The research shows that after tracing, copying, and other similar activities, children rarely forget their own words. Veatch (1978) uses the tracing activity to inculcate proper directional patterns leading into later easing of problems involved in changing from manuscript to cursive. Nor is that all. All reports of key vocabulary studies indicate, beginning letters are written first, initial sounds are easily taught using those words beginning: 1) with lip sounds, 2) with sibilant sounds, and 3) with dental sounds. For example, if a child gives the word "bike," then all children can be urged to purse their lips as with the "b" sound, thence coming forth with other words having the same beginning sound, such as "ball," "boo," "bottle." "Sun," can lead to "sea," "soap." "Dog" can lead to "daddy;" "top" to "teeth," etc. It can be seen, then, that the key vocabulary is rich in instructional possibilities relating to learning to read and to write.

The fourth aspect of the language experience approach, though not necessarily in this order, is that of the well-known and respected "experience chart." Despite massive and gross misunderstandings, this activity of pupil-teacher dictation has the greatest potential for teaching reading of any of the preceding elements. These charts see the possibilities and deserve some of our space for attention.

This activity is, in my opinion, in contrast to the preceding, best for whole-class instruction. It admirably lends itself to beginning the school day. All children are gathered to focus on the teacher who starts out with a statement or question, such as "What shall we put in our newspaper today?" or, "What has happened since yesterday that is important enough to write down?"

Thus, the teacher elicits ideas from the several children who respond to the invitation to contribute. After five or six ideas have been offered, the teacher makes a judgment as to which one is the most interesting, stimulating, or provocative. This is important as the purpose of seeking ideas is to provide vital and dynamic material from which instruction can ensue. There is no vote needed. No one is rewarded (at least openly) for an idea. The teacher decides.

Going back to the pupil who offered the idea selected, the teacher probes for more details, especially colorful details, that would give sparkle to the language. In so doing, the teacher is *changing* spoken language into written language. The teacher transmogrifies the talking modality into the writing modality, which is, after all, the type of language children *must* use in order to read. This is a sore subject with some who are considered language experience experts and who insist that the child's language be recorded verbatim by the teacher. Oral language is not the same as book language. All the reader need do to be convinced of this fact is to read an unedited transcript of a speech. It is easily distinguished from a speech that is "read," not "said!"

Thus, from the pupil idea, the teacher writes on the chalkboard or easel, for all to see, these transmogrified ideas, repeating each word as it is written. One after another, ideas are so transcribed for all to see until four or five are recorded. As a result, a chart of approximately 60-70 words is available as the finest instructional material possible. What is so good about it is that the teacher, in an organized, non-chaotic, systematic way, has turned some of the "lived world" of pupils into prose from which all manner of literary skills can be developed.

What, for example, is possible? Some questions that might be asked follow:

1. Who can find a word that begins like their name?
2. Whose idea was this line? This line? This line?
   Can you read your own line?
   Can you read someone else's line?
3. Who can find some words that are exactly alike? How many? Can you read one of the lines they are in?

4. Who can find a word that rhymes with one you can think of? (Wood ryhmes with good, etc.)
5. Who can read the whole chart?
6. Go some place where you like to write. If you get stuck, the word you want is on this chart (or perhaps on one the other day).
7. Let us all read it aloud and see how your voice goes when you come to a period. Click that period with your tongue.
8. Think of a story all your own. If you get stuck, see if the word you want is up here.
9. Copy all the words you like best.

With these and a myriad of other suggestions, it can be seen that such examples of teacher-pupil dictation are loaded with opportunities for learning. They are, as might be said, hot off the griddle. They are certainly highly personal, which is what provides the incentive to acquisition without "motivation" in the psyched-up, hyped-up sense.

The final aspect or element to be presented here relates to both the language experience approach and to self-selection or individualized reading. I refer to the use of trade or library books as the basic instructional materials for the teaching of reading. These are books that deal with only one idea or concept in some kind of a plot. They are usually written by creative artists rather than professorial educationists. No one *has* to read them. They have a point of view, take it or leave it. They sink or swim on their charm. They are often beloved for their own sake, and most assuredly, force feeding, *a la* written book reports, makes them hated.

It might be asked, "What is the personal commitment in such material published by commercial companies? The answer is that they are *chosen* by the reader. Through a set of clearly organized steps beginning with "the Rule of Thumb," a pupil selects a book that is just right for him, and which he likes. The book is read, recorded, and then brought, on a frequent basis, every day or two, to the teacher for an individual instructional conference. The questions used in these conferences zero in on the personal reactions of the pupil to the chosen book. Skills and abilities to divine meaning, to read aloud, to analyze words, all are involved in these sessions, which are, according to most investigators, highly prized by both teachers and pupils. Space prohibits detailed description of procedures, but the reader is referred to Veatch (1978) in that regard.

Specifically, though, in reference to the language experience approach, these books are among the best materials available when read aloud by the teacher. As they are replete with the best and the most readable English, they provide an admirable language model for children whose home language is not standard, or is not English at all. Hearing a teacher, theoretically the best oral reader in the class, read a charming story book gives children an incomparable idea of what books *are!* For enjoyment, for knowledge, for escape, and for drama and thrills. Not, as more than one first grader said when asked what reading was, "To keep the place." Trade books put spice in school life. While they can be used as entertainment, they are not necessarily used to entertain. By bringing up the matter of entertainment as opposed to education, we can close this paper by suggesting that all of the preceding is clearly on the side of education, so stimulating, so provocative, so fascinating that it might as well be called entertaining. We have shown how to use the alphabet and how to weave letters into word recognition, into writing skills of penmanship and spelling, how to derive skill needs from dictation provided by the teacher from ideas of friends, how to use libarary books all alone, all by one's self. No one ever needs to read the same book as someone else, unless there is a goal of appreciation to be sought.

In sum, teaching and learning, based on these principles, is firmly grounded on order, on rigor of knowledge acquisition, on system, and on a high degree of personal commitment that comes from one's own world of thought, ideas, and language. With such activities in our schools, a child cannot help but feel that his world is his oyster, and his mind is a glorious instrument that makes his living vital, dramatic, and worthwhile.

REFERENCES

Ashton-Warner, Sylvia. Teacher. New York: Simon and Schuster. 1963.

Blakey, Janis. An investigation of the relationship between children's Key Vocabulary responses and certain Piagetian concepts. Ed. D. diss. University of British Columbia. 1981.

Bloom, Benjamin S., ed. Taxonomy of educational objectives. Handbook I: Cognitive domain. New York: David McKay, 1956.

Chomsky, Carol. Reading, writing, and phonology. HARVARD EDUCATIONAL REVIEW. 1970. 40. (2) 287-309.

Clay, Marie M. Write now, read later: an evaluation. Auckland, New Zealand. New Zealand Council of the International Reading Association. 1977.

Daro, Philip, ed. Report on the special studies of selected E.C.E. schools with increasing and decreasing reading scores. Department of Education. State of California. Sacramento, Cal. 1980.

Read, Charles. Children's categorization of speech sounds in English. Urbana, Ill.: National Council of Teachers of English. 1975.

Smith, Frank. Psycholinguistics and reading. New York: Holt, Rinehart, and Winston. 1973.

Veatch, Jeannette. How to teach reading with children's books. 2nd ed. New York: Scholastic Magazines. 1968.

Veatch, Jeannette. Reading in the elementary school. 2nd edition. New York: John Wiley. 1978.

The Effects of a Single-task vs. a Multi-task Approach to Literacy: a Sociological View

Janet Kierstead

Most discussions of the relative merit of various approaches to literacy take up the question from a psychological point of view. The discussion usually focuses on which approach is appropriate given the way children learn. I am going to take up the question from a sociological perspective, considering instead, 1) what kind of a classroom situation the approach establishes and 2) what effect that situation is likely to have on the way individuals interact and the perceptions they form of themselves and others. I will begin by describing recent research on the topic of Task Structures, relating that research to two basic approaches to literacy, the traditional basal reader/workbook and the naturalistic language experience/project approach. Then, I will describe related research, and finally, discuss implications for classroom practice.

Research on task structures

Stephen Bossert (1) has conducted some interesting research on the organizational patterns established by different types of tasks children perform in classrooms. He did not concern himself with any curriculum area, yet his findings have implications for those considering the relative merit of different approaches to teaching reading and other language arts.

Bossert made a distinction between the nature of instructional tasks which will be referred to here as "single-task," and "multi-task," and looked to see what behaviors and perceptions were related to each. *Single-task* is defined as group recitation and seatwork requiring the same performance of all students, including cases where individuals are working independently at different levels in a text or workbook. *Multi-task* is defined as numerous individual or small group projects in which children are encouraged to select and organize their own tasks. *Note that the traditional basal reader approach, which relies heavily on sets of "readers," workbooks or ditto sheets to determine the student's activity, tends to establish a single-task structure. The language experience approach, which relies heavily on self-created projects which integrate oral, written and visual forms of communication, tends to establish a multi-task structure.*

Also notice that there are two major differences between the settings established by the two types of task structures: 1) who/what is in control of (and thus responsible for) the pace and sequence and the content of activities and 2) whether interactions are public or relatively private. Specifically, in a single-task setting, the teacher and/or materials maintain tight control over the content and process of activities. To maintain that control, the teacher must see what is happening at every moment, so behavior must be public. In other words, what each child is doing must be similar enough so that the teacher (and everyone else) can see at a glance that each child is behaving exactly as the teacher intends.

In a multi-task setting, the student and teacher mutually agree on content and process, and skills are developed in the sequence needed to carry out that process. Materials are used as a resource rather than as a means of control. The teacher maintains control over long-term goals but encourages the child to exercise some choice in the selection of the content and process of his daily work. Along with that choice the child assumes responsibility for achieving what is expected of him on a daily basis.

In handing over some of the control and responsibility to the student, the teacher has relinquished the possibility and lessened the need to see exactly what is happening at every moment, and so behavior in the classroom is relatively private. In other words, the manner in which each child decides to select and organize materials and activities will probably not be similar enough so that the teacher (or anyone else) can always see at a glance exactly what each child is doing.

These two factors, who is at the center of control and the relatively public or private nature of activities, have an impact of their own on the interactions between participants and the perceptions they form within the situation. Bossert's research revealed that this impact is independent of the teacher's philosophy and teaching style and independent of the children's personality. That is, when looking at the same teacher and group of students in a single-task and then in a multi-task setting, he noted very different behaviors from one setting to another. Further, when looking at classrooms which were predominantly either single- or multi-task, Bossert also discovered striking differences. These differences are described below.

The pace and sequence of activities and student opportunity to participate

Bossert found that the point of reference used to determine the pace and sequence of activities was quite different in the two task settings and that this affected the opportunity of various types of students to receive instruction and participate in activities. Specifically, in the single-task setting, the pace and sequence of activities was matched to a segment of the class which was somewhere in the middle. Those able to go faster had to wait or receive other assignments, and those who needed more time often did not have the opportunity to grasp the material. Bossert found that teachers varied in their treatment of the faster and slower students. Sometimes teachers used top performers as models for the group, giving them more time to recite and display their information and skills. At other times, teachers gave these students extra assignments to keep them busy and spent additional time with them to explain those assignments.

Whatever means was used to deal with these faster children, the end result was that they received more time, attention and reinforcement than the slower students. It seems reasonable to assume that in the case where the task is of the same type day after day, as with the single-task basal reader approach, the same students would continue to be the top performers. Thus, it would be the same individuals who would receive more attention and reinforcement over time, which would eventually result in a widening of the gap between the slow and fast performers.

In contrast, in the multi-task settings, the pace and sequence of activities were geared to the individual student's performance. Bossert found that the teacher allowed those who were doing well with their task to continue and gave more attention to those having difficulty. It also seems reasonable to assume that in this case, where the activity is mutually agreed upon by the teacher and student, the tendency would be to modify the task when it proved to be too difficult for that student. As a result, the same children would not continue to have difficulty day after day. Thus the teacher would be less likely to be giving more attention and reinforcement to the same individuals over time.

Sanctioning of behavior

Bossert found that teachers in the different settings used different means for controlling student behavior. In the single-task setting, the teacher tended to rely on equitable, impersonal sanctions, i.e., "desists." Bossert recorded an average of 19.2 desists/100 minutes in group recitation and 12.6/100 minutes when students were working individually in workbooks as compared with 9/100 minutes in the multi-task setting. In addition, teachers and students in the single-task setting reported feeling socially more distant than those in the multi-task setting.

It would seem that the use of a quick, impersonal means of control in the single-task setting is due to two factors. First, in this public setting where everyone can see and hear the exchange, the teacher needs to appear to be applying the rules equitably. But more importantly, once established as the center of attention and control, there is an urgent need for the teacher to remain free in order to keep things going. The teacher must not take time out to deal in depth with a student, for fear that the rest of the class may get out of control.

By contrast, in the multi-task setting, Bossert found that the teacher tended to covertly "bend the rules" to fit the particular situation and needs of the individual. Students and teachers reported experiencing a strong sense of rapport.

It appears that a multi-task setting allows for this in two ways. First, few will observe the exchange, as the setting is relatively private. So the question of equity is not such a problem. Second, there is not the same urgent need to stay in control, to keep things moving, because the teacher has shared some of the control and responsibility with the students. So it is possible to take more time and thus be in a better position to observe and judge what is actually occurring and to make adjustments accordingly.

Evaluation of performance and social status

Individuals used a different reference for evaluation of performance in the two settings. Bossert reports that in the single-task setting, evaluation was group referenced and based on the few skills required in the single task. In multi-task settings, evaluation tended to be referenced to individual growth and based on a greater variety of skills.

It appears that this difference is due to the relatively public versus private nature of the settings as well as the difference in complexity of the tasks. For example, in the public, single-task setting, it is relatively easy to see and thus to rank students on common criteria and establish a status hierarchy accordingly. Conversely, in the multi-task setting, where performance is relatively private, it is more difficult to see and thus to judge how each student measures against the others. In addition, with tasks involving many kinds of materials and skills there are more facets of behavior to evaluate and thus more ways to measure and achieve success. For example, compare a spelling test or work sheet to designing and producing an art or science exhibit accompanied by a piece of writing. So it is less likely that one student will be rated "top performer" over all the others and treated accordingly.

Bossert found that the ways students evaluated one another and chose friends were linked to the task structure predominant in their classrooms. In classrooms which were usually single-task, there was a tendency for students to compete with one another to establish performance status and then form cliques with others of similar status to win special privileges. There was solidarity within these cliques but a high degree of between-group competition on the playground as well as in the classroom. The result was the development of a competitive status system within the classroom and a decrease in overall group cohesion.

In contrast, in multi-task settings children were much more cooperative. They formed friendships based on mutual interests and worked well with alternative subgroups even when friendships were not involved. Perhaps when there is so much going on simultaneously in a classroom, so that evaluation and thus status are not based on comparison with the group, it is simply not as possible, or necessary, for students to join together to compete with others for status and rewards. Instead, it is possible for a feeling of cooperation to develop. (This effect of the task structure, more than the use of special materials, might account for a phenomenon that Montessori repeatedly witnessed. She has reported that in her classrooms, which were multi-task, a feeling of cooperation and group spirit spontaneously emerged.) (2)

Generalization to other settings

What is particularly important to note here is that Bossert found that these characteristics appeared to generalize to other settings. For instance, art and science teachers who dealt with these students outside of their regular classrooms reported similar

differences in behavior between the students from the different
task settings. They noted that the children from the multi-task
settings were more self-directed, more cooperative while working
on group projects and more open to exploring new forms of
expression. In contrast, the single-task students were quieter,
easier to control and showed less initiative.

When looking at individual students from one year to the
next, Bossert found that students who remained in the same type
of task setting (even though they had all changed teachers)
displayed the same behaviors. He also found that the behavior of
students who moved from one type of setting to another changed
accordingly. Students, parents, teachers outside the regular
classroom and the school counselor all reported changes in
attitude and behavior from one year to the next in cases where
students were assigned the second year to a different task setting.
They noted, in particular, that students who had been in multi-
task classrooms developed a competitive feeling and began to
select friends based on performance status when moved to a
single-task setting. They also reported that the reverse was true.
So it did not appear that these attitudes were a result of the
child's personality, but rather, were related to the task setting in
which he operated.

Similar research

Interest in the issue of control is not new in educational
research. For example, in 1943 Lippitt and White (3) published
the results of experimental studies they and Lewin conducted to
explore children's reactions to the different types of control
exercised by adult leaders. Of particular interest here is the
difference in response they found between authoritarian and
democratic settings.

In the authoritarian setting, the leader dictated the task and
working companion and informed the children of the activity one
step at a time, so that future steps were always uncertain to a
large degree. In the democratic setting students and leader shared
in the establishment of goals and general steps toward reaching
those goals. The leader provided technical advice along the way
by posing alternative procedures from which a choice
could be made.

The findings in these studies are compatible with and expand
on what Bossert found. Specifically, when compared with the
authoritarian setting, these behaviors were found in the
democratic setting:

Greater spontaneous group cohesion formed. Children
worked together for common goals and showed more
friendliness and less hostility. They exhibited less ego-
centered, competitive behavior and were more inclined to
recognize with approval the work of others. This
"cohesion" was a result of attitudes which the group
formed, rather than those induced by the leader and were
not dependent upon his presence in the group.

Fewer expressions of discontent. Children made an
average of 1.6 remarks expressing discontent with the
situation during each 1-hour meeting in the democratic
setting as compared with an average of 9.8/1 hour in
the authoritarian setting.

*Less change in the quantity of time spent on serious
work when leader left the room.* The quantity of time on
task remained virtually unchanged when the leader left the
democratic setting. Work related behaviors dropped by
approximately two thirds in the authoritarian setting when
the leader left the room.

Lower quantity/higher quality of work. Children in the
authoritarian setting produced a greater quantity of work.
Children in the democratic setting took greater care for
detail, and there was less "slopping of paint" in their
approach to their work.

More recently, other researchers have made a distinction
between task structures similar to those made by Bossert. They
refer to them as "unidimensional" and "multidimensional." Their
findings are also compatible with his. For example, Carl Simpson
(4) reported that when compared with unidimensional
classrooms, multidimensional classrooms differed as follows:

Fewer students rated "below average" in reading.
Teachers in unidimensional classrooms rated 50% of their
students "below average"; teachers in multidimensional
classrooms rated 25% of their students in that category.

*Less inequity between teachers' perceptions of minority
and non minority students.* Teachers in unidimensional
classrooms rated 15% of the minority students in the
bottom ability category, while teachers in the
multidimensional situation rated 3% of their minority
students in that category.

*Lower degree of peer consensus of individual students'
ability.* When students were asked to select who is "best"
in math (reading and social studies) and who is "worst,"
there was greater agreement in unidimensional classrooms.

Rosenholtz (5) also found that a higher percentage of students were judged to be average or above in multidimensional classrooms. In addition, she found a higher polarity of social power between individual students (as reported by the students) in unidimensional classrooms and a significant relationship between perceived reading ability and social power in those classrooms.

Finally, these researchers also report that students in multidimensional classrooms had a higher self concept of ability. Specifically, Simpson found that 74% of students in multidimensional classrooms rated themselves as "about in the middle or above" as compared with 58% in the unidimensional classrooms. Rosenholtz found 83.2% and 72.8% respectively.

Implications for classroom practice

Viewing the issue in light of these research findings, it becomes obvious that there is more to the question of the relative merit of the traditional versus naturalistic approach to literacy than is generally recognized. The usual discussion of which is more appropriate, considering the way children learn, addresses only part of the issue. What must also be considered is how the behaviors, perceptions and attitudes of individuals might be affected by the classroom situation related to the approach.

Clearly, the findings presented here add to the argument supporting a naturalistic, multi-task approach to literacy. Now, it is important to add a few notes of caution and encouragement to those who set out to establish such an approach.

First, I am not suggesting that teachers never bring children together for large group activities, to sing, be read to, take part in planning sessions, etc. What I am suggesting is that this should not be the predominant situation and that when it is appropriate to pull students together for large group activities, the teacher should be aware of the probable effects and do whatever possible to guard against them.

Second, group size is not the key factor. The function of materials is also critical. That is, the alternative to large group activity should not be taking students lock-step through sets of materials, either individually or as part of a small group. Instead, materials should be used as a resource by students as they select and organize their own activities and make decisions about the management of their time. This is as they do, for example, when they plan, write, illustrate and act out their own stories, select their own reading materials according to their interests and share their creations with others.

Further, neither of these two factors, group size or function of materials is the central issue here. Responsibility and control are the critical factors.

When establishing a multi-task setting, the teacher must be absolutely clear on the issue of responsibility and control. Recall that in the single-task setting the teacher and/or materials are in tight control of the content, pace and sequence of activities. When this control is shared with the students, as it is in the multi-task setting, the teacher must not make the mistake of relinquishing all responsibility and control. The teacher must maintain control over and responsibility for the ultimate outcome, saying, for example, "These children can become literate, and it is my responsibility to see that they do." The teacher must also maintain control over the mutually agreed upon outcome of each day's work, saying to the student, for example, "This is about what you and I have agreed that you will have accomplished by the end of this day in school. I hold you responsible for it." Having retained control over and responsibility for the long-term goal and established a mutually agreed upon daily (short term) goal, the teacher can then allow the student to assume control over and responsibility for the minute-by-minute decisions which lead to the realization of that daily goal.

To accomplish this balance of shared responsibility and control, the teacher must build into the situation a structure which will make it possible to monitor and guide the student as he operates within the mutually understood parameters. A discussion of this structure, which I have described elsewhere in detail (6) is beyond the scope of this paper. What it is vital to emphasize here, however, is that an effective multi-task approach to literacy does not "just happen," but is well planned and carefully orchestrated so that each child receives the support and guidance he needs to help himself become literate.

Finally, we must keep in mind what attributes we need to develop in children who are being socialized to take their place in a democratic society. We must recognize that experience within a carefully structured multi-task setting can empower the child with more than the ability to read and write. By assuming responsibility within that structure, the child has the opportunity to develop, in addition to literacy skills, the ability to make responsible decisions regarding the use of time, to plan and organize activities which lead toward a preestablished goal and to work with others with an attitude of mutual concern and cooperation. These are attributes which we would surely all agree are vital to the maintenance of our democratic society and thus essential to consider as we address the question of the relative merit of the traditional and naturalistic approaches to literacy.

NOTES

1 Bossert, Stephen, *Tasks and Social Relationships in Classrooms: A Study of Classroom Organization and Its Consequences.* New York: Cambridge University Press, 1979.

2 The argument over how to develop a cooperative group spirit within the child accounts for much of the difference between the practice devised by Maria Montessori and John Dewey. Dewey contended that this would best be accomplished by having children work as members of a group and Montessori insisted that by encouraging them to work on individually paced tasks she was allowing a group spirit to spontaneously emerge. See: Kierstead, Janet, "Montessori and Dewey: The Best From Both," in M. Douglass (Ed.) *The Claremont Reading Conference Forty-Fifth Yearbook.* Claremont, CA: 1981.

3 Lippitt, R. and R. White, "The 'Social Climate' of Children's Groups," in R. Barker, J. Kounin and H. Wright (Eds.), *Child Behavior and Development.* New York: McGraw-Hill, 1943.

4 Simpson, C., "Classroom Structure and the Organization of Ability," *Sociology of Education* 54:120-32, 1981.

5 Rosenholtz, S, "Organizational Determinants of Classroom Social Power," *Journal of Experimental Education,* 54:2, 83-87, Winter 1981-1982. See also: S. Rosenholtz and B. Wilson, "The Effect of Classroom Structure on Shared Perceptions of Ability," *American Educational Research Journal* 17:75-82, 1980.

6 Kierstead, Janet, "Recommendations for Structuring Effective Classrooms: How to Organize and Manage the Classroom to Promote Literacy for All Students." This paper appears as an integral part of the training materials for Workshop #5 of *The Effective Classrooms Training,* California State Department of Education, 1982.

Chinese Education: Reading, Rote, and Regimentation?

Arthur Lewis Rosenbaum

Most outside observers agree that the Chinese educational system is very traditional in its emphasis on basic skills, rote learning, and a disciplined, regimented student body. While the specific content of the curriculum is modern, the basic teaching approach and educational philosophy draws heavily on two thousand years of Confucian tradition. Confucian insistence that moral example and mastery of basic texts and skills takes precedence over self-expression is reinforced by many elements of Chinese Communism. However, both the traditional Confucian approach and the contemporary methods employed in the People's Republic also reflect a pragmatic acknowledgement that a substantial degree of rote memorization is required to learn to read.

The following observations were derived from a six-month stay in Beijing, China, in 1982, a period during which our six-year-old daughter was enrolled in the second semester of the first grade at Fucheng Primary School. We were not able to formally observe the classroom — Chinese parents also were not involved in school visits or school operations — but we did have the privilege of a brief visit. Additionally, we spent long hours talking to neighbors and their children about education.

The classroom environment

Fucheng Primary School is a reasonably large neighborhood school, and its student body comes from a variety of socio-economic backgrounds, ranging from children of college faculty and scientific researchers to common workers and former peasants whose farms were swallowed up by urban growth. The school has a good reputation in the neighborhood, but it is not one of China's elite key-point schools which select students through competitive examinations and get special equipment (those are the schools usually shown to foreigners). Facilities were spartan — essentially blackboards and desks.

In comparison to the United States, the class size was quite large, with over forty students in a class taught by a single teacher. There were no teacher aides, assistants, or parent volunteers, nor any audio-visual equipment. Discipline was very strict. Students sat rigidly at their desks with hands placed behind their backs, raised hands to answer questions, and stood to answer questions. There was more misbehavior in the classroom than we had expected from published reports of foreign visitors to Chinese schools, especially if the teacher left the room. However, the teacher had little difficulty controlling the class, which meant that the classroom atmosphere was conducive to learning, despite its size.

Chinese teachers probably have an easier job in handling students than their counterparts in public schools in the United States. Chinese culture always has esteemed teaching, and from the first day in class, students are taught to "love," and fear, the teacher. The final line from one song taught to students ran, "Mother, father, rest assured. The school is my home." Additionally, there is much greater stability and organization bonding within the student body and between students and teachers. Because job transfers are relatively rare, and people live in housing assigned to them by their work units, almost all students remain in the same school through graduation. Additionally, Fucheng Primary School kept each class together from one grade to the next, and teachers stayed with "their class" for a minimum of three years and frequently through graduation. While this potentially increased the likelihood of a pecking order being established prematurely, the teachers felt this allowed them to "know" their students and improved classroom solidarity.

Students were given more responsibility than they are in the United States. In addition to a rotating series of job assignments, such as sweeping floors, the students elected their own class "leaders," who wore arm bands with markings equivalent to those of privates, corporals, and sergeants. Leaders assisted the teacher in organizing the class for certain activities and frequently helped instruct students who were having difficulty completing classroom assignments. According to friends, some schools even used the leaders to grade papers for the teachers.

Chinese students spend more time at school than do American students. The school day began before 8:00, ending at 4:30 in the winter and 5:00 in the fall and spring, with approximately a two-hour lunch recess during which students return home for lunch and a nap. Classes were scheduled from Monday to Saturday, with half-days on Tuesday and Saturday. Summer vacation lasts for only six weeks, and during this vacation students are given exercise books to review material. This undoubtedly reduces the loss of knowledge, which predictably occurs during the long summer vacation in the United States.

The most striking difference between Chinese and California schools was the amount of homework assigned. Even in the first grade, students completed almost an hour of homework a day; by the second grade, the assignments required close to two hours of work. Such a heavy emphasis on homework had many negative features. Tired by the long school day and anxious to play, many students worked inefficiently, so that an assignment that should take one hour could end up requiring two hours for completion. In our apartment building, it seemed that eighty to ninety percent of all arguments between parents and students began when parents tried to get their children to do their homework. On the positive side, children learned at an early age that school work took precedence over all other activities. Of course, there were fewer distractions in China, where television programming is limited in duration, organized activities are few, and parents assign a high priority to school success.

Ideographic languages and teaching methodology

The fact that Chinese is an ideographic, rather than a phonetic language with an alphabet, places many constraints on the types of teaching methods which can be employed. Minimal literacy requires mastery of two to three thousand characters, while a college student will need between five and seven thousand characters. Languages with a phonetic alphabet allow even a first grade student just beginning to read to make educated guesses when confronted with new vocabulary. With an ideographic language there is no way to determine the word; the student must have learned the character. Only when the student has acquired a sufficient vocabulary to use a dictionary is it possible to break free from total dependence on a teacher or parent when reading materials contain characters not previously learned. The only exception is texts with a romanized pronunciation placed under each word.

Recognition of characters is a difficult process, and the ability to write them from memory is even more taxing. Two months prior to our departure to China, I began tutoring my daughter (already bilingual) to recognize the two hundred characters used in the text for the first semester. Although she has a phenomenal memory, it was necessary to display a character close to eight or ten times before she could identify it, and constant review was essential for retention.

As has been suggested above, rote memorization is the only practical means to acquire the basic vocabulary. In imperial times, students began their reading lessons by memorizing a rhyming primer of Neo-Confucian thought. Not only did this provide them with a basic vocabulary essential for a classical education, it also exposed them to fundamental philosophic concepts, the full significance of which would be apparent as their education progressed. Memorization hence was valued not only as a means to acquire vocabulary, but also because it was an essential prerequisite to the mastery of classical texts. Self-expression, interpretation, and questioning were not valued until the student had demonstrated full mastery of the basic texts and the relevant commentaries on them.

Today the Chinese educational system uses teaching materials which are more appropriate for the age level of the student and offer shortcuts to the acquisition of basic vocabulary. Beginners start by learning the *pinyin* system of romanization, so that texts can use a romanized spelling for new words when they first appear. Students then are taught the strokes used to write the characters and fifty-eight characters (plus ten numerical characters) which have their own meaning, but then part of more complex characters are used to classify words in a dictionary. By the end of the first year, a student will have learned almost seven hundred characters, many of which look similar or have identical pronunciation. They also have been exposed to a much greater number of compound words formed by two or more characters.

This formidable feat is facilitated by several devices. In the 1950s the government introduced a system of simplified characters which reduced the number of strokes in many characters and in some cases changed half of a character to a component that would better indicate its pronunciation. The former meant that some ideographs which once had twenty strokes now have only seven; the latter permits the students to memorize word lists in which characters are grouped together by a common component with identical or similar pronunciation. Still other word lists in the text consist of opposite meaning or characters which bear a strong resemblance to one another.

The heart of the learning process is constant repetition. An average lesson in the first grade is normally less than one hundred words of text with perhaps ten new words to be learned; the very first lessons may be a single sentence or just a set of words. After several readings out loud, either singly or in unison, pupils write the word and its romanization in a vocabulary book and then copy it eight more times as part of their classwork or homework. The process continues the second day, with the teacher calling on students to read the word. Typically the student recites the word two times, states its tone, and then repeats it a third time (e.g., li, li, third tone li). By the end of a lesson, a substantial portion of the students have memorized verbatim not only the new characters but also the entire text of the lesson and a standard interpretation of its significance. It is not unknown for a student to be able to recite from memory the entire text book without missing a word.

Students also must write out compounds used in the text; some homework assignments require the parent to read the text while the student writes out the words from memory. Other teaching devices are not dissimilar to those employed in the United States: writing the characters on the basis of romanized spelling, making compound words using a character, and filling in the blanks in sentences taken from the text. Throughout the school year, the class will go back to review previous lessons by copying out once again the vocabulary. The only respite from this almost numbing repetition and memorization is a few lessons in which the entire text is accompanied by romanization and no vocabulary is to be learned. For the most part, however, the main objective is to introduce as much new vocabulary as is possible in the shortest time.

While the entire process seems tedious and unimaginative this system, which is also used to some extent in other Chinese-speaking areas, accomplishes its basic objectives. By the third or fourth grade, students have sufficient vocabulary — over two thousand characters — so that they have access to a reasonable variety of reading materials. One obvious weakness in the Chinese approach is the absence of supplementary texts that would enable students to review vocabulary while reading new stories. Additionally, there are a few children's magazines and story books which are geared to the reading ability of children in the lower grades, but they are limited in number. Nonetheless, the fact remains that the Chinese have succeeded in imparting basic literacy despite the difficulty of the language and very limited resources. They have done this by insisting that children work hard and are relatively unconcerned by the fact that the learning process is not always fun.

Implications of rote memorization

The Chinese educational system provides little room for individual self-expression, creativity, or different levels of ability — at least at the lower grades. While much of this derives from the evident imperatives, need to memorize in order to read, other features of Chinese society and culture also point towards a regimented curriculum. The Chinese firmly believe that the task of education is to teach students to conform to correct standards and master basic skills. School regulations establish the proper position for reading and writing, the sharpness of the pencil point, and what is expected in an answer. Even in art classes, first grade children turn out astonishingly professional pictures. They are taught to use certain steps in drawing and to follow the proportions of the subject matter. The objective is to duplicate the pictures in the art books as closely as possible without actually tracing the outlines.

These tendencies are reinforced by a highly centralized educational system which determines not only the texts and rate of progress but also requires students to take standardized tests. Even the regular classroom examinations, not just finals, are drawn up by committees selected from more than one school. This, plus the existence of competitive entrance examinations to junior and senior high school, make it almost impossible for a teacher or student to experiment with alternative ways of dealing with material. The consequences of such policies might well be considered by those in the United States who would place undue stress on proficiency examinations. On the positive side, Chinese students display a remarkable mastery of basic reading and mathematical skills. The first grade students at Fucheng had completed the rough equivalent of second grade mathematics in California and were extremely proficient in doing calculations in their heads. They also had an astonishing capacity for memorization, which they used to great effect. On the negative side, students were content to remain within the parameters of the text, rarely stating their own views, and never questioning the material. It is not unusual for students in a college English course to answer the instructor's question by reciting verbatim several paragraphs from the assigned readings. Unfortunately, many could not answer the question in their own words or do more than they had been asked to do in the text. It might be added

parenthetically that they also were outraged when the instructor
proposed to test them by using materials they had never
seen previously.

Socialization and didacticism

No discussion of Chinese educational practices can ignore the
content of the texts. In Confucian times, education was designed
to enable students to pass civil service examinations based on
Confucian classics which would guarantee entrance into the
scholar-official elite. It also presumed that education should
provide students with role models of proper decorum, appropriate
values, and an appreciation of morality and education. These
cultural biases continue in the People's Republic of China, with
appropriate modifications for a modern socialist country. Almost
all stories in textbooks — and in children's books — make some
moralistic point about appropriate human behavior. Major
themes emphasize that good people are those who serve the
people, respect for teachers, reverence for education, the need for
sanitation, discipline and physical exercise, and the value of hard
work. Overt political indoctrination has been sharply reduced
since the death of Mao in 1976, but there remains a strong
nationalistic orientation. Revolutionary heroes are presented
doing good deeds, much as earlier generations of American
students learned about honesty and public service from the
exploits of George Washington and Abraham Lincoln. Finally,
one sees in the texts a great stress on the importance of science
and technology. What is missing are stories which deal with
fantasy and imagination, to be read simply for the pure pleasure
of reading.

Conclusions

The true test of a school system comes when its products
graduate and assume roles in society and the economy. The
current Chinese system is very much a "back to basics" system
with some similarities to nineteenth century American
educational philosophies. It assumes there are fundamental truths
which students must learn and a basic corpus of knowledge to be
imparted by the teacher. It stresses character traits of social
responsibility, frugality, self-reliance, hard work, and love of

country. These are not ignoble objectives and may be appropriate for a developing country such as China.

To the outsider who believes in self-expression, creativity, spontaneity, and a radically inquiring mind, the Chinese system will seem excessively regimented. However, Chinese culture never has been comfortable with the idea of pure individualism. Instead, the individual finds individuality and fulfillment by working within society and the group.

China undoubtedly would benefit, as some of their own commentators have suggested, from a reduction of one-sided emphasis on memorization and homework. They also might want to consider giving more priority to non-academic objectives and simply allowing children more leisure time to play. On the other hand, Americans might take more seriously the Chinese contention that the key to educational success lies in making education the chief priority of the student. Rote memorization, regular homework assignments, and an insistence on rapid progress from all students seem to work in China.

Help Your Child Learn To Read

William P.J. Costello

Since the now-outdated *Why Johnny Can't Read* was published in 1955, the relatively-new field of Psycholinguistics has provided a great deal of information relevant to the reading process. This article will draw upon this new information, with particular reference to how the mind plays with language, and present suggestions for parents about how to foster the emergence of reading behavior in their children.

The reading activities that will be described are based on the following assumptions about how human beings learn to read:

- *Reading is not a subject that we can teach to children, but rather a natural process that will unfold with the proper nourishment.*
- *The best way to learn to read is to "do reading."*
- *"Informal" instruction is as effective as "Formal" instruction in fostering reading behavior.*
- *The mind makes sense of the world primarily by recognizing patterns.*
- *Reading is a process of generating meaning in which the mind makes sense of print on the basis of the patterns it recognizes in the language.*
- *The mind becomes aware of patterns in the language not by trying to consciously memorize them but by playing with them.*
- *Just as the speaking process naturally unfolds after the listening process, the reading process naturally emerges after speaking.*
- *Fluent reading occurs when the reader's mind successfully guesses the meaning that is coming in the next chunk of text.*
- *The emergence of reading behavior requires a language-rich environment in which the mind is informally exposed to language patterns.*
- *Before attempting to read print, children should first understand that what they read is supposed to make sense.*

- *Reading should be drawn out of children, not stuffed in.*
- *Getting the meaning from print is more important than precise pronunciation.*
- *Because they last a long time, attitudes toward reading are as important as reading skills.*
- *The emergence of reading is enhanced greatly when the child discovers that what he says can be "turned into reading."*

To insure that the relationship between theory and practice is clear, let's dwell on three of these assumptions.

A process, not a subject

In most schools, reading is presented to children as a subject: students "take" Reading along with courses in disciplines such as Science, Math, and History. Thus is the reading process broken down into small, isolated parts, which are then exercised, memorized, and tested. But reading is not a subject, it is a process that naturally emerges in a language-rich environment. Schools would be more effective in promoting reading behavior if they provided more informal opportunities for children's minds to play with the language so that they can actively experience language patterns and focus on the primary purpose of reading: making meaning from print.

"Do reading"

When we say that the best way to learn to read is to "do reading," we mean that the unfolding of reading behavior is more akin to other learning processes, like learning to ride a bike. If we were to be foolish enough to try to make the riding process a subject in school, we would break it down into its component parts and study the wheels, the spokes, the chain, etc. Then we might study the concept of equilibration and perhaps include a few lessons on leg muscles. But, of course, we have discovered that it is far more effective to put the child on the bike, grab hold of the seat, and say "Start pedaling!" Experience has taught us that the best way to learn the process of riding is to jump onto the bike and, with some assistance, to start riding! So it is with many other processes — including the reading process. The best way to learn to read is to jump into the print and, with some assistance, start reading!

Another way to look at this idea is to consider that the best way to understand the relationship of the *parts* of something is to first experience the *whole* something. For example, if we gave the same jigsaw puzzle to six people, but gave the cover to only three of them, it would take the group without the cover much longer to do the puzzle. Why? Because the picture of the whole puzzle allows a person to easily recognize how all the parts fit into the whole. And so when we help children to read, we must first show them the whole process by letting them "do reading" the way that fluent readers do it. Certainly, children will stumble over individual words, but from the very start, they will have a sense of the whole process.

Formal vs. Informal instruction

Many parents today are dissatisfied with the Reading instruction provided by schools. Most of what goes on in schools in Reading class is "formal" instruction, which means that the child is subjected to lessons, exercises, and drills on isolated parts of the reading process. And while it could be argued that this approach is successful, since many children leave school able to read, it makes just as much sense to suggest that they learned to read *in spite of* these systematic attempts to confuse and misinform them, and that they might have learned to read more effectively by means of an "informal" approach to instruction. The point here is not to settle the "Formal/Informal" controversy, but rather to emphasize the major role that informal instruction can play in the learning-to-read process and to show how parents can employ the informal approach by engaging in reading activities with their children at home.

Because attitudes last a long time, one thing should be foremost in the parents' mind when they use informal instructional methods: the reading activities at home should not be an extension of the direct instruction in school, but enjoyable experiences that put the emphasis on playing with the language. Our goal is not "Reading home-work," but "reading home-*play*." The whole effort will turn into a disaster if parents, in their anxiety to rush things along, develop in their child a negative attitude toward reading. If the informal approach is used correctly, the child should learn not only to read, but also learn that reading is enjoyable.

Talk to the child

We want to expose the child's mind to the *patterns* of the language as soon as possible. While we shouldn't be foolish enough to try to *formally* teach speaking or reading to an infant, we can take advantage of the infant's ability to hear the patterns of the language. So talk to your infant. Avoid "baby talk." That is, you don't have to break the language down into simpler form (individual sounds or words) for the child. Speak to the child in whole sentences — the same sentences that you would speak to someone who can already read. The idea here is to let the infant hear the language as it is naturally spoken so that he can model normal speech patterns. Then, when you run out of things to say, try the following:

- Provide a running commentary of what you are doing for the infant. For example, if you are cooking: "Now I'm chopping the mushrooms and onions. Then I'll put them in the pan and . . ."
- While you are reading the newspaper, read it aloud to the infant. You'll get to read your paper, and the child will benefit from hearing the sound patterns in the articles.
- If you are all talked out, turn on the radio and tune in a talk show, an all-news station, or a baseball game.
- Play children's stories that are available on records and tapes, or if you have time, record a few yourself.

Read to the child (as soon as the child begins to speak sentences)

My informal survey of people who learned to read early shows that they all remember being read to frequently. Reading to children has always been considered a "nice thing," but the activity has rarely been equated with learning to read. But if reading is a process of generating meaning on the basis of pattern recognition, we can see how reading to a child promotes that process. Here are some things to keep in mind when reading to a child:

- Be sure that the *child* chooses the book. Take the child to the bookstore or library and let him pick out some books.
- While you are reading, have the child sit right next to you, so he has a clear view of the page. Be sure to run your finger along the line of print as you read. Do *not* insist that the child follow your finger; given a little time, he will do it quite naturally.
- Do not stop to ask questions of the child during the story.
- If the child becomes disinterested in the story (as many younger ones will), do not insist that you "finish the story." If he is still interested in doing more reading, let him choose a new book. If he's tired of reading, discontinue the activity.

- Let the child "read" a story to you. Children will spontaneously volunteer to "read" a story to you that you've read to them before. Terrific! Let the child do whatever he can. He'll fumble around with words and the plot, and the story won't be exactly the one that you read to him, but so what? The important thing is that he's trying out his reading behavior: going from the front of the book to the back, from the top of the page to the bottom, from left to right on the line of print. Also, you'll notice how he is already learning to tell a story, which shows an awareness of characters and plot.
- When you are reading a story that is continued from a previous day (usually with older children), ask the child to describe what has happened so far in the story and ask him to guess what he thinks might happen in the next part of the story. This gives the child some practice in *predicting meaning.*

Listen to the child and write what he says (toddlers to adults)

This is called the "Language-Experience Approach" in the field of Reading. Simply stated, you will ask your child to tell you a story (or a riddle, joke, etc.), and then you will write it down. Then, with some help from you, he will read it back. Since it is very important that early reading materials be of interest to the child, it makes sense to start with the things that make up his life. Here are the steps to follow:

- Ask the child to tell you a story, a riddle, or joke; anything that the child wants to talk about is fine.
- Write it down for him. Be sure to *print* it, since we want it to resemble print in books.
- When the whole piece has been said, ask that it be read back. When the reader stumbles on a word, don't make a big deal out of it or start to "sound it out." Just say the word and keep the reading process moving.
- Most kids like to illustrate their stories, so encourage this activity.
- Many children like to see their story typed so it looks like a "real book." If the child can handle it (no matter how long it takes), let him type his story. Otherwise, ask him to read it to you while you type it.
- All the stories and other writings and illustrations should be saved. He will want to go back and re-read his stories and share them with his friends.

Play with the child and the language

There are some commercially available games that give the child's mind an opportunity to experiment with and manipulate the language so that he can start to recognize the patterns of the letters, words, and meanings in the language. Here are some examples:

- Letter cubes
- Word cubes
- Scrabble and Scrabble Jr.
- Noun phrase cards (*The Shuffle Book* and *The Animal Shuffle Book* by Hefter and Moskof)

If parents stay relaxed and remember that "reading home-*play*" is for enjoyment, they will find that these informal activities will significantly foster the emergence of reading behavior in their children.

REFERENCES

Flesch, Rudolph, *Why Johnny Can't Read* (Harper & Brothers, 1955).

Smith, Frank, *Reading Without Nonsense* (Teachers College Press, Columbia University, 1978).

Douglass, Malcolm P., "Writing and Reading in a Balanced Curriculum," Keynote Address, Claremont Reading Conference, January 14, 1982.

Hart, Leslie, *Human Brain and Human Learning* (Longman, Inc., 1983).

Costello, William P.J., "The Emergence of Reading Behavior" (Claremont Reading Conference Yearbook, 1982), p. 58.

Lee, Doris, and Allen, R.V., *Learning To Read Through Experience* (Appleton-Century Crofts, 1963).

Reading, Thinking, and Play:
A Child's Search for Meaning

Robert G. Collier

At first glance, play seems an unlikely bedfellow for the likes of reading and thinking. After all, reading and thinking are highly valued cognitive processes with social and academic respectability, while play is generally accepted as a frivolous activity with little purpose. However, play is the predominant activity of childhood. One researcher has estimated that children may spend as much as 15,000 hours at play prior to beginning school. (1) Research in child development tells us that during this same period, a substantial degree of one's intellectual capacities develop and that children master the basic fundamentals of one of our most complex human functions, language. Such prominent theorists as Piaget (2), Bruner (3) and Vygotsky (4) have linked children's play with these aspects of cognitive development.

Play

The work of Jerome Singer (5) and other noted researchers, has made children's play not only respectable, but worthy of intense and rigorous scientific study. Currently we are experiencing an escalation of interest and research in children's play as noted by the increasing number of scholarly articles and books in this area. (6)

The researcher encounters difficulties, however, when attempting to investigate child play and its effects. Michael Ellis (7) called play a "plastic construct," in that a mutually acceptable definition of play may not be possible. Paul Chance described play in other terms: "Play is like love; everybody knows what it is but nobody can define it." (8) The difficulty in defining play is that play is not a specific behavior and, therefore, resists the confines of a single definition. Nor is play the domain of one developmental area, but rather spans all areas of human growth.

However, play can be described in terms of its social context and the child's actions. The social descriptors of children's play, according to Mildred Parten, include onlooking, solitary, parallel, associative and cooperative play. (9) In terms of children's actions, the following taxonomy of play is most widely accepted: physical, manipulative, symbolic and games with rules. (10)

While all the above aspects of play are closely related with the child's development, it is through the growth of symbolic play that the most direct connection with reading and thought is displayed. Symbolic play includes the simple and complex uses of imagination through manipulation of the child's reality and a transformation of the here and now. This type of play takes place during the preoperational period, beginning at the age of about two years, with children using real objects in a make-believe way. (11)

Sociodramatic play is the most complex form of symbolic play and is observed at its onset sometime between the ages of three and one half and four years. Smilansky characterized sociodramatic play by the following six aspects: 1) assumption of an imitative role, 2) use of make-believe in regard to objects, 3) use of make-believe in regard to actions and situations, 4) interaction with one or more other children, 5) verbal communication in play and 6) persistence in role play. Using these six characteristics, Smilansky developed the following rating scale for sociodramatic play: no dramatic play, dramatic play, poor sociodramatic play and good sociodramatic play. (12)

Thought and reading

Before examining the relationship of play to reading and thinking, the commonalities between reading and thought need to be established. This connection can best be viewed from a Piagetian perspective in which thought is seen as an adaptive process representing the interaction and equilibrium between assimilation and accommodation. Other possible outcomes of this interactive process could be imitative behavior, a prevalence of accommodation, or playful behavior, the dominance of assimilation. For Piaget, behavior reflects the structure of the child's cognitive processes, and thinking reflects the interaction between these cognitive structures through the child's action upon the environment. (13)

Walter Loban bridged reading and thought by describing the "bedrock" of reading as the child's search for order, meaning and equilibrium. Loban saw the child's need to find meaning from what he/she encountered in the environment as the key to learning to read. In noting the inseparability of a child's past experience and growth from reading, Loban touched on a second aspect common to both, that they are interactive. (14) A child's ability to read or think is dependent upon and reflective of his/her growth and all acquired experiences.

Furth and Wachs (15) suggest a third possible relationship between reading and thought, that both are integrative processes. Such a relationship denotes the interdependence of these processes with all developmental aspects of the child, i.e., physical, emotional, sensory and intellectual. Reading and thought are then interactive and integrated processes with a common goal of searching for meaning and equilibrium.

Play and reading

The link between play and reading rests in the development of representation, as both use symbols or indicators. (16) In play, the child uses symbols to define, interpret and represent reality in his/her own terms. In the development of symbolic play the child manipulates the reality of objects and their uses through language and/or actions.

To read, it is necessary for the child to evoke meaning from a series of signs or indicators. Using Piaget and Vygotsky as a theoretical base, the relationship between reading and play can be explained in that play uses symbols while reading requires signs. (17) The distinguishing features between symbols and signs, according to this argument, are that the former is an external representation of a child's internal ideas or concepts while the latter, in the case of reading, is a written word or indicator used to convey a mutually agreed upon idea or concept.

The development of representational abilities, such as the use of signs or indicators in reading, is dependent upon the quantity and quality of the child's internally represented meanings or concepts, which are developed through symbolic play. If such is the case, then the symbolic play of children is both an indicator and facilitator of representational ability. As the child develops his/her sociodramatic play abilities, representational skills are being advanced toward a point where children can make the switch from relying predominantly on symbols in their search for meaning to signs. (18) Supporting such a relationship is the research done by Pelligrini who found children's symbolic play, especially sociodramatic play, to be a better predictor of aspects of reading and language achievement in kindergarten children than I.Q. or socioeconomic status. (19)

Play and thought

In defining play as the dominance of assimilation over accommodation, Piaget makes play an integral part of the process of cognitive development. This is illustrated by the correspondence between Piaget's stages of play (sensorimotor, symbolic and games with rules) and the first three stages of intellectual development. For Piaget, play serves two major functions in intellectual development: first, play is a reflector of the child's thought or cognitive abilities, and second, play is a method of exercising newly developed cognitive skills. (20)

Considerable research has been done supporting these two functions of play. (21) Currently, some researchers in the area of children's play suggest that the relationship between play and thought may be more extensive. For example, Rubin (22) and Bruner (23) suggest that beyond merely exercising newly developed cognitive skills, play may serve as an aid in the acquisition of further cognitive abilities. The implication is that children's play may be a facilitator as well as a reflector of cognitive abilities.

One example illustrating the practical facilitating capacity of children's play in terms of cognitive abilities is a study I conducted on the effects of training preschool teachers in techniques for facilitating children's play during their "free play" periods. The subjects of this study were eight preschool teachers and thirty-five preschool children between the ages of three and five years. In eleven sessions, spanning a six-month period, a group of preschool teachers were trained in techniques to: 1) observe learning and development in play, 2) determine and provide the necessary materials for play and 3) appropriately use adult involvement to facilitate children's play.

The variables measured were teacher behavior and the children's verbal expression, divergent thinking ability and play. The study included an experimental and control group and used a pretest, posttest and delayed posttest design. The results of this study suggested that developing play-facilitating techniques in preschool teachers may have an effect on all the variables measured. Increases for the amount of teacher talk and child talk were found in the experimental group with corresponding decreases observed in the control group. The amount of "no verbal interaction" decreased for the experimental group while increasing for the control group. The greatest single contributing factor to these results was the experimental teachers' consistently increasing use of children's ideas in developing dialogue between themselves and their students.

In the area of cognitive abilities, the experimental group significantly increased their verbal expression abilities and was able to demonstrate significant differences in their divergent thinking skills in comparison to the control group. The experimental group showed an increase in the amount of higher level social play and a corresponding decrease in lower level social play, while the control group demonstrated the opposite effects. The sociodramatic play level of the experimental group remained the same, and the control group experienced drops in the higher levels of sociodramatic play and increases in the lower levels.

The resulting data from the pretest, posttest comparison, using an analysis of covariance with the pretest as the covariate, were not only confirmed by an identical analysis of the delayed posttest measurements, but indicated escalated effects. While the results only suggest a relationship between children's play and cognitive abilities, this study clearly demonstrates the interactive and integrated relationship between thinking and play.

Conclusion

Programs for young children, whose goals include advancing intellectual functioning and beginning reading skills, should take into consideration the contributing potential of children's play, especially symbolic play. Such play assists the development of both reading and thought by increasing the child's level of representational skills, thus leading to advances in intellectual growth and to the formation of the symbolic foundations necessary for the complex abilities required to read the printed word. In the final analysis, reading, thought and play all evolve from the child's integrated and interactive search to make sense out of the reality of his/her own world.

REFERENCES

1 Kooij, R. van der, and Groot, R. de, *That's All in the Game: Theory and Research, Practice and Future of Children's Play*, Rheinstetten: Schindele, Verlag, 1977. (Kooij, R. van der and Vrijhof, Heleen J., "Play and development," *Topics in Learning and Learning Disabilities*, D. Kim Reid (Eds.), Vol. 1, No. 1, April 1981, pp. 57-67).

2 Piaget, Jean, *Play, Dreams and Imitation in Childhood,* New York: Norton & Norton, 1951.

3 Bruner, Jerome, "Play is Serious Business," *Psychology Today*, Vol. 8, 1975, pp. 81-83.

4 Vygotsky, L.S., "Play and Its Role in the Mental Development of the Child," in Jerome Bruner et al. (Eds.), *Play-Its Role in Development and Evolution*, New York: Basic Books, 1968.

5 Singer, Jerome, *The Child's World of Make-Believe: Experimental Studies of Imaginative Play*, New York: Academic Press, 1973.

6 Sutton-Smith, Brian, "One Hundred Years of Change in Play Research," *The Association for the Anthropological Study of Play Newsletter*, Vol. 9, No. 2, Winter, 1983, pp. 13-17.

7 Ellis, Michael, *Why People Play*, Englewood Cliffs: Prentice-Hall, Inc., 1973.

8 Chance, Paul, *Learning Through Play*, New York: Gardner Press, 1979, p. 17.

9 Parten, Mildred, "Social Play Among Preschool Children," *Journal of Abnormal & Social Psychology*, Vol. 28, 1933, pp. 136-147.

10 Chance, *Op. cit.*

11 Wolfgang, Charles, *Growing and Learning Through Play*, New York: McGraw Hill, 1981.

12 Smilansky, Sara, *The Effects of Sociodramatic Play on Disadvantaged Preschool Children*, New York: Wiley, 1968.

13 Piaget, Jean and Bärbel Inhelder, *Psychology of the Child*, New York: Basic Books, 1969.

14 Loban, Walter, "The Absolute Bedrock of Reading," *Claremont Reading Conference 45th Yearbook*, Malcolm Douglass (Eds.), 1981, pp. 21-33.

15 Furth, Hans and Wachs, Harry, *Thinking Goes to School*, New York: Oxford Press, 1975.

16 Wolfgang, Charles and Sanders, Tobie, "Defending Young Children's Play as the Ladder to Literacy," *Theory Into Practice*, Vol. 20, No. 2, pp. 116-120.

17 *Ibid.*

18 *Ibid.*

19 Pellegrini, A.D., "The Relationship Between Kindergarteners' Play and Achievement in Prereading, Language, and Writing," *Psychology in the Schools*, Vol. 17, No. 4, October, 1980, pp. 530-535.

20 Piaget, *Op. cit.*

21 Rubin, Ken (Eds.), *Children's Play*, San Francisco: Jossey-Bass, 1980.

22 Rubin, Ken, "Fantasy Play: Its Role in the Development of Social Skills and Social Cognition," *Children's Play*, Ken Rubin (Ed.), San Francisco: Jossey-Bass, 1980, pp. 69-84.

23 Bruner, Jerome, *Under Five in Britain*, Ypsilanti: High Scope Press, 1980.

Natural Learning and Computational Environments

Arleen A. Armantage and *James W. Armantage*

INTRODUCTION

This article summarizes an investigation of a particular claim:

> Computational environments provide a context of
> remarkable power for giving children the ability to
> "control the distance" between their mental structures and
> their experience.

To explain and support this claim, a theory of natural learning is described which clarifies the ideas of mental structures, experience, and "controlling the distance," and the notion of a computational environment is made concrete and practical through reference to microworlds.

The exposition of the theory has three sections:

1. Description of the theory through a minimal set of assertions or propositions,

2. Presentation of a model which simulates the theory and allows for its application,

3. Application of the model to the issue of learning to read print.

Since the theory provides a measure for discussing how natural learning takes place, the model is represented graphically and visually.

The measure — controlling the distance — and its use in a computational environment are explored through a "grammar" microworld. Microworlds can be understood as structures for curriculum development in the local setting, structures that provide materials to work with and operations for building with these materials. Computational environments are defined to be environments that allow student and teacher to choose strategies and techniques for learning, indeed to invent strategies and experiment with them. The appropriate use of these environments, especially those that utilize the computer, is identified in terms of the measure suggested by the theory. It should be noted that computational environments need not utilize computers, and that the appropriate use of computers in these environments is quite different from the currently popular and traditional uses of the computer in education.

The article presents only an outline sketch of the theory, computational environments, and the conclusions drawn. These elements were presented in a detailed and interactive form at the Claremont Reading Conference, January 22, 1983. To the authors the most interesting feature is the measure induced by the theory and its application to identifying and developing appropriate uses for technology in education.

THEORY SUPPORTING NATURAL LEARNING

Assertions About Natural Learning

1. People (of all ages) construct their own knowledge and understanding out of their experience.

2. Every serious thought or idea anyone has *does* make sense to him or her.

3. Ideas people construct themselves are more accessible to them than ones they are fed by others. (1)

4. Intellectual growth involves both thinking and feeling.

Comments

Assertion #1: The self construction of knowledge takes considerable time, is risky and complex, and sometimes involves the changing of ideas.

Assertion #2: Children continually build theories — sometimes incorrect ones — about the world around them. Teachers need to try to understand the sense or perspective of the person they are teaching, often by probing until that person's view makes sense to them. This probing probably also helps the other person understand his view more clearly.

Assertion #4: Feelings provide the motivational force for the intellect. (2)

Model of Natural Learning

Description of model elements

Human Mind: — A live, active entity.
                 — Constantly interacts with situations.

Knowledge: — Something dynamic, which grows and changes.
               — A construction.
               — Involves relationships; new knowledge grows
                 out of previous knowledge.
Student: — A builder.
               — Continuously questing in search of
                 increased understanding.
Teacher: — A provider of the raw materials for
                 building: *experience.* (3)
               — *Also* a learner.
Intelligence: — Continually developing.

Comments on model elements

Note the *active* quality of each element of this model! The net
result of all of this activity is what may be called *mental
structures.* The external or environmental correlate to mental
structures is *experience.* Experience is the interacting of the
mental structures with the situation the individual encounters.
The active character of mind in which mental structures and
experience continually form and re-form each other is graphically
described in the following diagram.

Graphic representation of the model

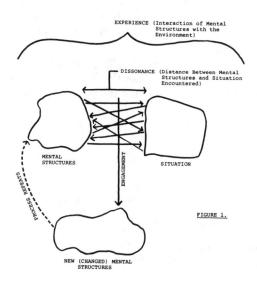

FIGURE 1.

The measure induced by the model

In general, the result of this interaction between the environment and the probing character of the mind is a change in the mental structures; i.e., experience produces learning. However, not every encounter between mental structures and environment leads to an interaction which produces such change. The notion of *dissonance* can help pinpoint more precisely what occurs in this active natural learning process.

DISSONANCE

1.   NO DISSONANCE

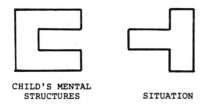

Perfect match.

No need for engagement.

CHILD'S MENTAL
STRUCTURES   SITUATION

2.   MODERATE DISSONANCE

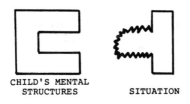

Not a perfect match.

Novel or different enough to invite engagement, yet similar enough to make engagement possible.

CHILD'S MENTAL
STRUCTURES   SITUATION

3.   EXTREME DISSONANCE

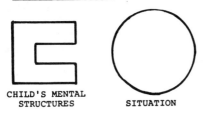

Total mismatch.

No chance of engagement.

CHILD'S MENTAL
STRUCTURES   SITUATION

FIGURE 2.

The degree of match between the learner's mental structures and the situation encountered alternatively represents the *distance* between the learner's mental structures and the situation.

Three-step process of dissonance in natural learning

1. Child encounters it.
2. Child decides to engage or ignore it.
3. If child engages, resolves. (4)

What triggers the change in mental structures is the ability of the child to engage the situation. When there is no dissonance, the child's current mental structures — or his present knowledge

EFFECT OF DISTANCE BETWEEN DISSONANT
SITUATION AND CHILD'S PRESENT
MENTAL STRUCTURES

1.

CHILD'S MENTAL
STRUCTURES

Distance too small.

Situation bores child.

Will not engage.

No change in
mental structures.

2.

SITUATION

CHILD'S MENTAL
STRUCTURES

Distance too great.

Will not engage
(or learns by
rote or
trivializes).

No change in
mental structures.

3.

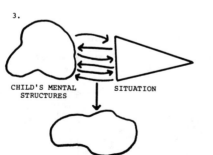

CHILD'S MENTAL   SITUATION
STRUCTURES

NEW MENTAL STRUCTURES

Distance just right
(moderate dissonance).

Engages and
resolves.

Resolution results
in growth and
modification
(further building)
of mental structures.

FIGURE 3.

— mesh perfectly with the situation he encounters. No learning occurs. When the two do not mesh, he experiences dissonance. The crucial element in the learning situation is how much dissonance the learner experiences, or how great the distance is between the situation which the child encounters and his present mental structures.

Natural learning defined in terms of the induced measure

Natural learning occurs in instances involving moderate dissonance, as in Figure 3, in which the distance between the child's current mental structures and the situation encountered is enough to interest and engage him yet not so great as to prevent engagement.

Application of model of natural learning to the language experience approach to learning to read print — a graphic illustration (5)

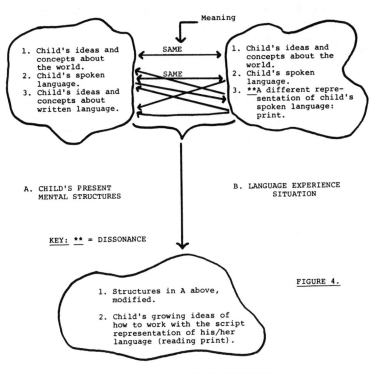

FIGURE 4.

It should be noted that the child moves *straight to meaning* — there are no intermediate steps, such as the teaching of skills — and that dissonance exists in only one area (B.3). The degree of dissonance is moderate, because of the meaning-rich situation which involves *the child's own* ideas about what is important to him, expressed in completely familiar language. This inclusion at the heart of the learning experience of that which the child brings with him (his present mental structures) serves as *the control element;* the learner controls the distance. Since the only novelty or locus of dissonance is the print itself, and since the control element is more powerful than the novelty of print, the distance between the child's present mental structures and the situation is controllable.

In controllable circumstances the motivational involvement is high, and chances are good that the child will engage the situation, work toward resolution, and in time *build new mental structures; i.e., learn to read print.* In so doing, the child experiences the reading of print as a *process*, the understanding of which he has built for himself. (6) In contrast to this natural form of learning how to read print, when learning to read print is taught as a *procedure* to be learned and applied, a *functional literacy* can result which may or may not involve a change in mental structures. If this change in mental structures which accompanies learning how to read print has not occurred, then the person's functional literacy may serve, quite ironically in fact, as a screen or barrier between the person himself and the reading of print except as a kind of decoding activity.

COMPUTATIONAL ENVIRONMENTS AND NATURAL LEARNING — A TECHNOLOGY FOR CONTROLLING THE DISTANCE

The main import of the preceding theoretical exposition is the idea of the distance between the child's current mental structures and the experiences with which the child is presently engaged. If, as the above description suggests, distance is the critical element in learning, then learning environments can be characterized in terms of the amount of dissonance and the appropriateness of the distance. Natural learning would be defined as the collection of those environments where degree of dissonance and amount of distance are appropriate. It is evident to all that not every learning environment is a natural learning environment.

In particular it is unlikely that the school environment can approximate natural learning environments which have been tuned by powerful forces over long time spans for maximum effectiveness. The main problem in the school environment appears to be the difficulty of establishing contexts where dissonance and distance are optimal for each individual. A possible solution to this dilemma is providing an environment where student and teacher can *locally* control the distance rather than having to accommodate to distances fixed by a set of global or external criteria. By substituting the notion of control for that of accommodation, one emulates the active features of the natural learning process. Control permits the learner, be it student, teacher, or both, sharing the experience, to adjust the conditions of the learning environment so that they match more closely those which characterize the natural learning context.

We identify this idea of control with that of the computational environment; i.e., computational environments are precisely those where such control is possible. This identification gives us a measure of *appropriateness* and thus a definitional criterion for the application of technologies to education.

To illustrate the idea of a computational environment during the Claremont Reading Conference we used the idea of a microworld, (7) in particular a *grammar* microworld. Microworlds are structures that provide materials to work with and operations for working with the materials. They are designed so that the user — in this case the child, but it might be the teacher or child and teacher working cooperatively — is always in control, taking as small or large a step at a time as the user feels comfortable with, moving forward or backward, and in general exploring the territory defined by the microworld. The image that one uses to describe working with a microworld is that of discovery, exploration, and invention.

The importance of this imagery is that genuine examples of these activities are always determined by the experience and skill the explorer or inventor brings to the new territory. Microworlds facilitate *local* control of the environment in that they depend for their effectiveness on the interaction between what the discoverer brings to the microworld and what wonders the microworld has to display.

The grammar microworld (8) is a particularly simple and rewarding example of microworlds in general. It is a one-command language which can be implemented in many forms in addition to being implemented on the computer. At the Reading Conference we "taught" our grammar microworld to the audience by using Cuisenaire rods and then "demonstrated" the grammars' characteristics using a computer-implemented grammar microworld. The one command can be interpreted as a replacement rule which says, "Replace the first item in the rule with some combination of elements from the second item in the rule;" e.g., if we use R as the symbol for our rule, we can write

R [Orange] [Pink Green]

which says, "Replace Orange with Pink and Green." By putting a number of these "sentences" together, we can create all kinds of "patterns" ranging from writing sentences; composing music; doing arithmetic; or drawing hills and valleys, trees and bushes, and putting them together in landscapes. An example of a class of grammars that generate sentences of increasing complexity is included in the appendix.

The important element to note is that the child creates his or her *own* grammar; he makes up the rules on the one hand, and he chooses the elements for substitution on the other. The entire process is personal and thus is *controlled*, in the case of our sentence-generating grammars, *by the child*'s own developed sense of the spoken language. The child has freedom to experiment with both syntax and semantics and to develop increasingly sensitive abilities to manipulate language. Note that the child controls the print or script representation of language in terms of his or her sensitivities to the spoken language; idiosyncrasies and standard usage can be mixed, compared, and then appropriate adjustments made — all by the child without appeals to external guidance unless desired. Sophistication with the written language is developed internally at whatever speed the child can handle, with as much repetition and experimentation as the child desires. This microworld and its generic counterpart fulfill the primary function of giving the user control over the environment being investigated and thus the ability to "control the distance" and bring this learning situation into a closer match to the natural learning environment.

Microworlds can be offered to the child or even developed by the child in order to learn or explore a particular new territory. The creation of microworlds is itself a computational environment. It is this fact that allows the teacher to create according to his or her experience a curriculum as closely matched to his or her students' needs as is desired. Thus the design of microworlds is an act of discovery or exploration by the teacher in order to provide local control over the classroom learning environment and to optimize the effectiveness of the instructional process just as the students' use of the microworld optimizes the learning process. "Controlling the distance" appears to be the same measure in both learning and instruction. It is this fact that makes the notion of computational environments so appealing and should, in the very near term, influence how we choose to use technology in the classroom.

REFERENCES

1 The above points are among those which Duckworth stresses when guiding teachers in their attempts at putting into classroom practice the theory of Jean Piaget. Eleanor Duckworth, "Teacher Education," paper presented at the Eleventh Annual Interdisciplinary UAP Conference on Piagetian Theory and Its Implications for the Helping Professions, University of Southern California, Los Angeles, January 31, 1981.

2 Jean Piaget and Bärbel Inhelder, *The Psychology of the Child*, New York: Basic Books, 1969.

3 These and other related elements are developed and discussed in Thomas C. O'Brien, "What's Basic? A Constructivist View," in *Basic Skills, Issues and Choices: Issues in Basic Skills Planning and Instruction*, ed. by Shirley Jackson and Michael B. Kane, Washington, D.C.: National Institute of Education, 1982.

4 Thomas C. O'Brien, "Five Anchors," Teachers' Center Project, Southern Illinois University, Edwardsville, IL 62026. Some 50 publications related to the practical classroom application of the view that learners construct their own knowledge out of experience are available from the center at the cost of printing.

5 Language experience is *one* example of a natural learning approach to beginning reading instruction. Some others would include use of key words, reading to children, and self-selection of books for reading. On language experience see Dorris M. Lee and Roach Van Allen, *Learning to Read through Experience*, Rev. ed., New York: Appleton Century Crafts, 1963. On key words see Sylvia Ashton - Warner, *Teacher*, New York: Bantam Books, 1963; also Jeannette Veatch et al., *Key Words to Reading*, Columbus: Charles E. Merrill, 1973. On self-selection see Jeannette Veatch, *How to Teach Reading with Children's Books*, New York: Citation Press, 1968.

6 This brings to mind the question of "reading readiness." When a child learns to read through a natural learning approach which does not impose externally determined expectations, *the child is always ready, since he controls the distance*. In contrast, reading readiness programs are required when the distance has been predetermined by external criteria. Indeed, the term "reading readiness" may be more appropriately applied to the teacher than to the child; i.e., how well the teacher is fitting the reading task to the child. As Downing noted, "In recent years it has been increasingly recognized that the teacher is the one whose readiness needs evaluating, perhaps even more than the child's." See John Downing and Derek Thackray, *Reading Readiness*, London: University of London Press Ltd., 1971.

7 R.W. Lawler, "Designing Computer-Based Microworlds," *Byte, The Small Systems Journal*, Vol. 7, No. 8, August 1982; Seymour Papert, "Computer-based Microworlds" in *The Computer in the School: Tutor, Tool, Tutee*, ed. by Robert P. Taylor, New York: Teachers College Press, 1980; Seymour Papert, *Mindstorms: Children, Computers, and Powerful Ideas*, New York:

Basic Books, 1980; Daniel Watt, "Logo in the Schools," *Byte, The Small Systems Journal*, Vol. 7, No. 8, August 1982.

8 Neil Rowe, "Grammar as a Programming Language," Logo Memo 39, MIT Logo Group, 1976. MIT Logo memos and "Bibliography of Logo Memos" are available at cost from MIT Logo Group, Building 20C, Room 109, Massachusetts Institute of Technology, Cambridge, MA 02139.

APPENDIX

Sample sentence generating grammars

SENTENCE1

R [SENTENCE1] [NOUN VERB]
R [NOUN] [[DOG CAT BOOK FRIEND]]
R [VERB] [[LIKES HATES BOTHERS]]

SENTENCE2

R [SENTENCE2] [NOUN VERB NOUN]
R [NOUN] [[DOG CAT BOOK FRIEND]]
R [VERB] [[LIKES HATES BOTHERS]]

SENTENCE3 (This sentence illustrates learning through error.)

R [SENTENCE3] [NOUN VERB NOUN]
R [NOUN] [[DOG CAT BOOK FRIEND]]
R [VERB] [[IS ANGRY SMART FAST]]

SENTENCE4

R [SENTENCE4] [ADJECTIVE NOUN VERB ADJECTIVE NOUN]
R [NOUN] [[DOG CAT BOOK FRIEND]]
R [VERB] [[LIKES HATES BOTHERS]]
R [ADJECTIVE] [[FURRY SHAGGY SLOBBERY FRIENDLY GREEN]]

SENTENCE5

R [SENTENCE5] [ADJECTIVE NOUN VERB NOUN ADJECTIVE]
R [NOUN] [[DOG CAT BOOK FRIEND]]
R [VERB] [[LIKES HATES BOTHERS]]
R [ADJECTIVE] [[FURRY SHAGGY SLOBBERY FRIENDLY GREEN]]

SENTENCE6

R [SENTENCE6] [ADJECTIVE NOUN ADJECTIVE VERB
    ADJECTIVE NOUN]
R [NOUN] [[DOG CAT BOOK FRIEND]]
R [VERB] [[LIKES HATES BOTHERS]]
R [ADJECTIVE] [[FURRY SHAGGY SLOBBERY FRIENDLY GREEN]]

SENTENCE7

R [SENTENCE7] [ADJECTIVE NOUN ADVERB VERB ADJECTIVE
    NOUN]
R [NOUN] [[DOG CAT BOOK FRIEND]]
R [VERB] [[LIKES HATES BOTHERS]]
R [ADJECTIVE] [[FURRY SHAGGY SLOBBERY FRIENDLY GREEN]]
R [ADVERB] [[OFTEN PERHAPS PARTICULARLY NEVER ALWAYS]]

SENTENCE8

R [SENTENCE8] [ADJECTIVE NOUN VERB ADVERB ADJECTIVE
    NOUN]

R [NOUN] [[DOG CAT BOOK FRIEND]]
R [VERB] [[LIKES HATES BOTHERS]]
R [ADJECTIVE] [[FURRY SHAGGY SLOBBERY FRIENDLY GREEN]]
R [ADVERB] [[OFTEN PERHAPS PARTICULARLY NEVER ALWAYS]]

SENTENCE9

R [SENTENCE9] [NOUNPHRASE VERBPHRASE NOUNPHRASE]
R [NOUNPHRASE] [ADJECTIVE NOUN]
R [VERBPHRASE] [ADVERB VERB]
R [NOUN] [[DOG CAT BOOK FRIEND]]
R [VERB] [[LIKES HATES BOTHERS]]
R [ADJECTIVE] [[FURRY SHAGGY SLOBBERY FRIENDLY GREEN]]
R [ADVERB] [[OFTEN PERHAPS PARTICULARLY NEVER ALWAYS]]

SENTENCE10

R [SENTENCE10] [NOUNPHRASE VERBPHRASE NOUNPHRASE]
R [NOUNPHRASE] [ADVERB ADJECTIVE NOUN]
R [VERBPHRASE] [ADVERB VERB]
R [NOUN] [[DOG CAT BOOK FRIEND]]
R [VERB] [[LIKES HATES BOTHERS]]
R [ADJECTIVE] [[FURRY SHAGGY SLOBBERY FRIENDLY GREEN]]
R [ADVERB] [[OFTEN PERHAPS PARTICULARLY NEVER ALWAYS]]

SENTENCE11

R [SENTENCE11] [NOUNPHRASE VERBPHRASE NOUNPHRASE]
R [NOUNPHRASE] [DETERMINER ADVERB ADJECTIVE NOUN]
R [VERBPHRASE] [ADVERB VERB]
R [NOUN] [[DOG CAT BOOK FRIEND]]
R [VERB] [[LIKES HATES BOTHERS]]
R [ADJECTIVE] [[FURRY SHAGGY SLOBBERY FRIENDLY GREEN]]
R [ADVERB] [[OFTEN PERHAPS PARTICULARLY NEVER ALWAYS]]
R [DETERMINER] [[ONE THE SOME]]

SENTENCE12

R [SENTENCE12] [NOUNPHRASE VERBPHRASE NOUNPHRASE]
R [NOUNPHRASE] [[[DETERMINER ADVERB ADJECTIVE NOUN]
    NAME]]
R [VERBPHRASE] [ADVERB VERB]
R [NAME] [[MARY FRANK SNOWY SNUGGLES]]
R [NOUN] [[DOG CAT BOOK FRIEND]]
R [VERB] [[LIKES HATES BOTHERS]]
R [ADJECTIVE] [[FURRY SHAGGY SLOBBERY FRIENDLY GREEN]]
R [ADVERB] [[OFTEN PERHAPS PARTICULARLY NEVER ALWAYS]]
R [DETERMINER] [[ONE THE SOME]]

SENTENCE13

R [SENTENCE13] [NOUNPHRASE VERBPHRASE NOUNPHRASE]
R [NOUNPHRASE] [[[DETERMINER ADVERB ADJSTRING NOUN]
    NAME]]
R [VERBPHRASE] [ADVERB VERB]
R [ADJSTRING] [ADJECTIVE [ADJSTRING []]]
R [NAME] [[MARY FRANK SNOWY SNUGGLES]]
R [NOUN] [[DOG CAT BOOK FRIEND]]
R [VERB] [[LIKES HATES BOTHERS]]
R [ADJECTIVE] [[FURRY SHAGGY SLOBBERY FRIENDLY GREEN]]

R [ADVERB] [[OFTEN PERHAPS PARTICULARLY NEVER ALWAYS]]
R [DETERMINER] [[ONE THE SOME]]

SENTENCE14

R [SENTENCE14] [NOUNPHRASE VERBPHRASE]
R [VERBPHRASE] [ADVERB [[VERB NOUNPHRASE]
    [IS ADJECTIVE]]]
R [NOUNPHRASE] [[[DETERMINER ADJSTRING NOUN] NAME]]
R [ADJSTRING] [ADJECTIVE [ADJSTRING []]]
R [NAME] [[MARY FRANK SNOWY SNUGGLES]]
R [NOUN] [[DOG CAT BOOK FRIEND]]
R [VERB] [[LIKES HATES BOTHERS]]
R [ADJECTIVE] [[FURRY SHAGGY SLOBBERY FRIENDLY GREEN]]
R [ADVERB] [[OFTEN PERHAPS PARTICULARLY NEVER ALWAYS]]
R [DETERMINER] [[ONE THE SOME]]

SENTENCE15

R [SENTENCE15] [NOUNPHRASE VERBPHRASE [[] [[AND BUT]
    SENTENCE15]]]
R [VERBPHRASE] [ADVERB [[VERB NOUNPHRASE] [IS ADJECTIVE]]]
R [NOUNPHRASE] [[[DETERMINER ADJSTRING NOUN] NAME]]
R [ADJSTRING] [ADJECTIVE [ADJSTRING []]]
R [NAME] [[MARY FRANK SNOWY SNUGGLES]]
R [NOUN] [[DOG CAT BOOK FRIEND]]
R [VERB] [[LIKES HATES BOTHERS]]
R [ADJECTIVE] [[FURRY SHAGGY SLOBBERY FRIENDLY GREEN]]
R [ADVERB] [[OFTEN PERHAPS PARTICULARLY NEVER ALWAYS]]
R [DETERMINER] [[ONE THE SOME]]

Redefining Learning Disabilities: an Holistic Perspective

Mary Poplin

My intention today is to extend last year's discussion of learning disabilities into the future, the 1990s. I'll seek to accomplish this by elaborating upon the ideas I proposed as the forerunners of holistic thought in special education at last year's Reading Conference.(1) First, I will quickly review two early models of learning disabilities and then spend the bulk of the time we have together defining *two* distinct cognitive models — the cognitive strategy model and the holistic model. I knew so little of these models last year that the entire discussion scarcely covered a page in the yearbook. However, I was like a good democrat — I might not have known what I believed, but I certainly knew what I did not believe. Sometimes our discomfort with the present system is our only signal for change. For years professionals may writhe around with symptoms of paradigm change and yet actually modify very little. Such has been the case with learning disabilities.

One of the learning disability professional's most disturbing preoccupations comes from our past and present emphasis on eligibility criteria. I suspect the discussions of operational criteria for eligibility, while taking up most of our research journals, ultimately provide little more than a series of rationalizations we can all use to defend what we are doing and are going to do anyway. As our colleagues Ysseldyke and Algozzine (1981) have noted, we do not place youngsters in special education because of their test scores, but rather after they have been tested and sometimes despite the test results. For every child in learning disabilities with erratic WISC profiles and low achievement scores, there are two others who have the same scores but are never so placed.

If one is expecting me to criticize that practice, one will be disappointed. If I were to criticize the placement of children in special education and particularly learning disabilities, it would be to criticize it in its entirety — to rant and rave because the

rest of the school is not flexible enough to keep the little Pac
Man addicts in the regular classroom. However, if we are to
continue special education classes, I'd rather see the decisions
made by a group of teachers than by a group of tests. As
inflexible as some educators may be, they certainly are not more
inflexible than the questions on standardized intelligence and
achievement tests.

Of course, this flexibility also allows for discrepancies and
discriminations. As the new economics and right wing
conservatism continue to decrease funds in other special
programs such as bilingual and compensatory education, we will
see more children from these programs finding their way into
learning disabilities classes — not because they are learning
disabled but because our schools are culturally and experientially
emaciated. As our culture becomes more diverse, the discrepancy
widens between what teachers know and have experienced and
what the children know and experience. Special education will
continue to be a holding tank until the time comes, indeed if it
ever comes, when the schools can operate from children's
experiences. We have not yet admitted that the world is not the
same as when we went to school, and in desperation, we cling to
those notions despite new technologies that have revolutionized
learning everywhere but the schoolhouse.

In the 1960s, of course, we were far too busy looking into
the brains of children to see the problems of special education
within any larger context. During this time, professionals viewed
learning disabilities as a product of deficient psychological
processing. It was believed that problems in learning to read,
write, and calculate stemmed from inherent psychological process
problems, such as visual perception (e.g., visual figure-ground,
visual-motor coordination, visual discrimination, and association
and/or memory), auditory perception (e.g., auditory
discrimination, association, memory, and figure-ground), motor
perception (e.g., balance, flexibility, coordination, and strength),
and sensori-motor integration. These problems were presumed to
be the result of dysfunctions that had specific, identifiable
correlations in the brain.

In the 1960s, professionals began to identify students with
learning disabilities by assessing these psychological processes.
Tests were created and administered to measure each of them.
Of course, no one in education has ever assessed any ability that
they subsequently do not intend to teach. Such it was with
learning disabilities; soon materials catalogs and classroom

cabinets were full of books, games, dittos, and exercises designed
to teach all the various psychological process abilities.

Not so surprisingly now, none of these tests of materials
have been shown effective. The tests we used did not differentiate
good learners from poor and, what is worse, most have very poor
reliability and validity in and of themselves. The activities we
undertook to teach psychological processing have not been shown
to increase even those processes they purport to represent. Even
more serious, these programs could not show that children who
received process training became any more ready for academic
school tasks.

Then came the 1970s and the behaviorists became
prominent in special education. Behaviorists proposed that the
way to teach children to read was to take the activity of reading
and break it into its component parts or behaviors. Once reading
was broken into curriculum objectives, it was further reduced by
"task analyzing" all the bits of behavior that went into the
performance of the task. Special educators moved from thinking
almost exclusively about parts of brains to thinking almost
exclusively about parts of curriculum.

Much of our learning disability curricula goals and objectives
are merely modifications of regular class curricula. Learning
disability goals and objectives represent regular classroom
curriculum reduced to its smallest and often most meaningless
components. While we have found that by applying the principles
of reinforcement to these task analyzed skills, we can "train"
students to perform certain behaviors, we have not demonstrated
the relevancy of behaviors to overall school achievement. In fact,
there has been a reluctance to research the long term results of
"learned behaviors." Thus, the questions remain, do students
maintain these discrete academic and social behaviors and do
students generalize these "learned" behaviors to any other
settings or contexts?

Last year I stopped here and started slinging the words
holism and cognition and cognitive strategies around much like
one slurs a word one does not know quite how to pronounce.
However, throughout the last year I have, with the help of my
colleagues and graduate students, better defined things. There's
nothing like a group of hungry graduate students to make one
define one's terms — if not for the sheer joy of intellectual
pursuit — for survival! Of course, the same is true of any
classroom, children or adults. This is why we often remark: "You
never know so much about a topic until you have to teach it."

Now, however, having had their help, I believe I am prepared to try out some new ideas with this ominous group and stand back for questions, corrections, comments, and suggestions.

Perhaps the most disturbing thing in these new reflections is the appearance of an entirely new model that indicates both a move toward holism and a distortion of it. I shall call the new model several things: cognitive strategies, learning strategies, and cognitive behavior modification (CBM, as it is affectionately abbreviated). Now, some of you may laugh, but there are people who believe they can modify cognition or train people to help them modify their own. That's very nice of the CBM researchers, but it reminds me of a paragraph in Tom Wolfe's *Even Cowgirls Get the Blues*, in which a character is musing over what a delightful toy is one's brain, meanwhile enumerating all the things people can do with their brains. The brain, Wolfe goes on to say, is only dangerous when someone else wants to reach over and play with your own. That's a bit of the way I feel about attempts to "modify cognition."

The encouraging part of the cognitive strategies model is that there is recognition, acknowledgement, and emphasis given the role of student action and initiative in one's own learning. There is at least lip service paid to the fact that learning is accomplished best when it comes from within the student, when the student is actively engaged in learning rather than acting as a passive receptor.

The cognitive strategies movement (1980s)

Insofar as there was disillusionment and frustration over the failures of the psychological process and behavioral models to demonstrate maintenance and generalization of skills, the stage was set for the emergence of yet another model to explain, diagnose, and treat learning disabilities. Added to it was a growing body of research suggesting that the *manner* or ways in which one approaches and deals with a learning task is every bit as important as the accuracy of requisite academic behaviors.

Perhaps the best way to describe the perspectives of persons who advocate a cognitive or learning strategy approach is to note how the focus of instruction differs from the behaviorist's focus. Reid and Hresko (1981) state that the difference between the two groups is that cognitive strategists' primary concern is with "how" a person learns while the behaviorists' concern is for "what" a person learns. Rather than teaching pupils correct answers, strategists seek to teach students to create and apply strategies that will help them think through and become actively involved in the solution of problems.

The notion that the most important goal of education is to teach persons ways of going about finding and using facts rather than merely remembering specific facts is not a new one. Knowing *all* the answers is not only impossible, but it obviously presupposes that (1) there always are correct, verifiable answers or simple facts; and (2) the school decision makers are competent to decide which facts would be most beneficial to learn. The position that schools should emphasize the "process" of learning is one that is familiar to readers of Dewey, Spencer, Bruner, Piaget, and others.

The cognitive strategy model that has emerged to identify and train the learning disabled to actively develop and apply learning strategies is based on these premises as well. Meichenbaum (1980), one of the leaders of the cognitive strategies approach, stated the purpose this way:

> The hope was that by "going cognitive," namely by supplementing the behavior management programs by means of self-instruction training or by means of social problem solving training, educators would obtain the generalization and maintenance effect that have previously eluded their grasp (p. 84).

In order to accomplish this purpose, the cognitive strategists developed their ideas from bits and pieces of the theories of Piaget and Inhelder, Kagan, Budoff, Rotter, Kohlberg, and others.

In order to emphasize the processes by which one learns and creates an instructional technology, advocates of the cognitive strategy approach have sought a sort of marriage between certain principles within cognitive psychology (e.g., metacognition, executive functions, attribution theory, computer models of information processing, encoding, and memory) and certain behavioral techniques (e.g., observation, direct measurement, self-instruction, task analysis, time on task, and reinforcement). Whenever such marriages are undertaken there is inevitably a new vocabulary for educators to learn. You can see here why special educators love this model — heaven forbid we should try to help children learn to read rather than to manage their meta-cognitions.

Reassessing the facts and fallacies of both the behavioral and psychological processing models, the theories of Joseph Torgesen (1979) spurred the introduction of the cognitive strategy model into the field of learning disabilities. Torgesen has suggested that what one observes as the problems of the learning disabled may not be the result of either deficit psychological processes (e.g., memory, discrimination, association and/or modality) or deficit skill behaviors (e.g., phonics, sight words, and math behaviors), but rather an inability or ignorance of when and how to call upon these aptitudes and abilities at the appropriate moments. In Torgeson's (1979) words, the learning disabled:

> . . . may not have developed the cognitive and emotional
> characteristics necessary to adapt to the requirements of a task
> and use active and efficient strategies (p. 519).

By 1978, the profound influence this model was to have on the field of learning disabilities had become evident. Three of five major federally funded learning disability research institutes in the United States were heavily influenced by this model. The University of Virginia team of researchers led by Daniel Hallahan sought to target strategies that might enhance selective attention. In 1978, Hallahan defined cognitive strategy techniques as a "blend of modeling, reinforcement, verbal self-instruction, and training in the use of problem solving strategies" (p. 77). A second major research institute relying heavily on the strategies model was begun at the University of Kansas by Donald Deshler. Deshler, Alley, and their colleagues studied the effectiveness of strategies directly applicable in secondary academic school settings, such as defining main ideas, outlining, note taking, and other study skill strategies (generally referred to as learning strategies at the University of Kansas Institute). The researchers at the University of Illinois at Chicago Circle, under the leadership of Tanis Bryan, studied the social strategies used by youngsters, both normal and learning disabled. Of course, in addition to the researchers at these institutions, other professionals have studied and advocated the various cognitive strategies perspectives within the field of learning disabilities, including Wong, Keogh, and Swanson.(2)

The assumptions of this approach regarding the education of the learning disabled are somewhat different than that of the behavioral model, despite the fact that behavioral technology is often applied to train persons to use cognitive strategies. The strategist assumptions are as follows:

1. Efficient learners actively engage in developing and applying specific strategies that allow them to locate, learn, remember, and generalize information to solve problems. Learning disabled students appear passive in their approach to many

learning tasks or problems. They either lack the awareness of such strategies, develop inefficient ones, and/or are slow or fail to develop or apply such strategies.

2. Effective strategies can be defined by observing and interviewing "good learners," and these strategies can then be assessed by observing and interviewing the learning disabled person.

3. Once defined, efficient strategies can be taught by pairing the principles of self-instruction and reinforcement with the appropriate strategy(s).

4. Upon learning these strategies, the learning disabled will generalize to other situations and, thus, become more efficient learners.

Of course, no one undertakes the assessment and instruction of cognitive or learning strategies with so shallow a hope as teaching the individual strategy itself; rather it has been hoped that students will apply the single learning strategies they are taught to many other learning tasks. In this way it has been hoped that cognitive strategy training could circumvent the generalization and maintenance problems of other models, particularly the behavioral model. Knowing techniques to attend to task or to comprehend and remember what one read seemed far more utilitarian than learning bit-by-bit specific pieces of information. However, to date the research on cognitive strategy training with the learning disabled looks as bleak as does the behavioral research. Advocates of this model are also depressed by the lack of generalization and question whether any technique will ever aid the disabled in academic learning.

The reductionist models

At the end of analysis one is tempted to become quite smug about noting the distinctions of each model under which learning disability professionals have operated (e.g., the psychological process, behavioral and cognitive strategy). One is quick to lose that smugness when one realizes that the similarities between each of these models are far more striking than their differences. Taken together, each clearly defines the general philosophic position taken by the learning disability profession since its inception. The positions these models have in common include:

1. An attempt in each case to divide learning into segments (sequential skills, developmental steps, or sequences of strategies).

2. Instruction aimed primarily at meeting school goals rather than life needs.
3. Assessment, evaluation, and special instruction conducted only for the purpose of seeking and remediating deficits and disabilities.
4. Insufficient evidence of generalization and maintenance.

Division of learning

The notion that learning can be broken into parts is not new. It is exemplified by the very structure of the typical school day. Each "subject," including reading, is taught separately from all the others. Even more disturbing, "reading" is seen as equally distinct from written expression, spelling, literature, and grammar, which are also viewed and executed as separate subjects. The distinction is still made today, despite the considerable evidence suggesting that each of these areas of language develop simultaneously and, in fact, complement and embellish the other.

The tendency to categorize and subcategorize learning has led special educators time and again into the same trap. Thus, in the 1960s, professionals in learning disabilities proposed divisions in the psychological processes of the mind (presumably related to distinct areas of the brain). In the 70s, having noted the ineffectiveness of the psychological process model, we began to define the categories, tasks, and subtasks that were observable in reading, math, and even the socialization process. Worried about the failure of students to integrate them into meaningful reading, writing, math, and social behaviors across time, setting, and tasks, special educators once again sought to divide the learning process into "strategies."

In an effort to define our observations and translate them into a learning environment, we have bastardized the wholeness, the spontaneity, and the excitement of learning. Learning, when broken down into processes, objectives, and strategies becomes meaningless, for in doing so, we divorce it from the child's previous experiences, information, interests, and talents. Shuy (1981) comments that for many years adult curriculum developers have held the same fallacious assumption that the smaller one can break down a learning task, the simpler it will become. That simply is not what the child development literature or children tell us.

School goals

Because "special education" is the creation of the public
school system, it is not surprising that emphasis has been given
to those goals, associated with schooling for normal children, i.e.,
reading, math, and writing. Although most school goals
emphasize the importance of developing the potential of each
individual student, most go about doing so in ways which
emphasize this important goal indirectly, at best. For example,
that student who *cannot* learn to read the print of the English
language is not prevented from becoming familiar with the texts
of good literature. There is little provision for a non-reader of
normal or above intelligence to become acquainted with the ideas
of Sylvia Plath, Shakespeare, Gabriel Garcia Marquez, Doris
Lessing, or Virginia Wolfe. Nor do we allow students who
cannot *write* to deliver orally their own ideas or their answers to
questions. In other words, the higher cognitive functions of the
sciences, humanities, and arts can be accessed in school only
through print. Before the technological explosion which has
brought us such things as television, taped books, films, etc., our
insistence on achieving knowledge through print may have been a
more valid requirement.

Because special education is part and parcel of the school
system and more importantly, because learning disabled students
today are so often "mainstreamed" in regular classrooms, our
attention is even more intensely directed to the goals and
objectives of the regular classroom. Learning disability specialists
have little time to examine critically the curriculum being
selected and have even less opportunity to choose substantially
different goals and objectives. I am, of course, suggesting here
that the goals and objectives we have uncritically adopted need
closer inspection.

Deficit-driven assessment and instruction

Thirdly, all of the previous models under which the field of
learning disabilities have operated are deficit-driven. Diagnosis,
assessment, and instruction all focus upon pinpointing problems
and disabilities. Naturally, as in any field (e.g., medicine,
psychology, and education), whatever factors are assessed are
also treated. If our intent was *not* to dwell on the problems of
individuals, we would not spend so much effort and so many
resources to locate them. If a student who has a reading problem
is diagnosed and classified for "special" services, then it is
almost guaranteed that he/she will be subjected to even more

hours of reading instruction. Then, need we ask ourselves why students with learning disabilities do not like school, become disinterested, depressed, or truant? Of course, the only deficits that are selected for assessment or remediation are those that help meet school ends; a student who is not talented in music or art is rarely a candidate for special education.

Failure to generalize

Lastly, and most revealing, there has been virtually no evidence to suggest that our remedial efforts have long term positive effects. While the behavioral models can demonstrate at least the short-term retention of specific subskills of reading, math, and writing, there is still little to suggest that these subskills are maintained for any length of time, generalized across settings and tasks, or ever become integrated or assimilated into the student's own life interests and goals. There is even less convincing evidence that psychological processes, as we define and teach them, are learned or integrated into the lives of students. Cognitive strategy research is plagued by the same problems as its behavioral predecessors. Perhaps if we utilized better the worlds of children and adolescents as a base for our instruction, students would see relevance for practicing and applying the objectives we select as targets for instruction.

The holistic model

Diametrically opposed to the reductionist view of education is the holistic view. Rather than being derived from an empiricist perspective, like the reductionists, the holistic perspective is grounded in structuralist philosophy. Structuralism emphasizes the role of the individual in structuring or building meanings from their own experiences. In educational philosophy, structuralism, or holism (also called constructivism), is somewhat akin to the broader and more dynamic concepts of Deweyian, Brunerian, and Piagetian ideas of education and learning.

The holistic explanation for learning is a dynamic one where the most critical variable in learning is the collective experiences of the learner. In addition to past and present experiences, other variables recognized as having effects on learning include physical variables (e.g., genetics and the integrity of the nervous system), personality characteristics of the learner and teacher, natural interests, physical characteristics of the setting, abilities, talents, and aptitudes.

The search for meaning, the building of one's own meanings and structures for incoming information, and the integrity of the mind in solving problems are all emphasized in the holistic view of education. Because the role of the learner in constructing meaning is viewed as the single most critical and relevant variable, the holistic model (more than any other) stresses that learning best occurs where there is active involvement in the learning task.

Ideally, of course, special education would not exist where a truly holistic view of education prevailed; therefore, the task of defining holism in learning disabilities is made even more difficult. And, in fact, the assumptions of a special education classroom will not be different from those assumptions of the holistic regular public school classroom, a college science classroom, or in a teacher training program. In this discussion of holism in special education I have tried to follow the same outline as that used earlier in discussing the psychological process, behavioral, and cognitive strategy models. Because these assumptions are relatively new to most of us who think of ourselves as "special educators," I encourage you to play with these different ideas regarding the diagnosis, assessment, and instruction of students. Holistic assumptions regarding the education of students with learning disabilities might include the following:

1. Learning disabilities are the result of some inopportune interaction between the child's neurology, previous experiences (in school and other environments), interests, personalities, aptitudes and abilities and the experiences, goals, physical characteristics, personalities, interests and abilities in the learning environment. (Note that if we were being true to the holistic philosophy we would omit the words "disabilities" and "some inopportune" and leave the holist view of learning.)

2. Informal assessments and inventories are made of the child's previous experiences, interests, personalities and current abilities.

3. Instruction is designed from knowledge of these interests, abilities and experiences (including the selection of classroom placement, teacher, and materials). Goals of instruction and criteria for performance emphasize successful completion of goals necessary in adult life.

4. The desired result of holistic instruction is a more happy, well-adjusted growth and learning-oriented human being.

The differences between special education under the holistic model and current special education methods and procedures are drastic. First of all, there are no attempts to break subjects into curriculum objectives or task analyses; more importantly, there are no attempts to break education or learning into subjects (e.g., reading is not separated from writing or social studies). The object or goal of special education will not be directed toward being re-placed in the regular classroom or passing competency or other achievement tests. Curriculum is not viewed as a set series of objectives to be met by using a limited array of materials. Instead, curriculum structure is more an inherent knowledge of child and adolescent development and the experiences, talents, and interests of the individual students. The teacher is responsible for bringing new, relevant, and interesting experiences to the student that encourages the gaining of competence in a wide variety of possible abilities.

The most dramatic of all changes to be effected by adopting a holistic view of learning disabilities is the change in attitude from the deficit-driven assessment and instruction to an ability-driven model of instruction. Rather than special educators identifying and explicating problems, weaknesses, and disabilities, the holistic model emphasizes the assessment of student strengths and interests and the matching of these *ability* characteristics with educational programming.

The holistic model can be successful only to the degree that we can dramatically depart from the past. It asks us to shed artificial notions regarding divisions in learning. Perhaps the most difficult and revealing task will be the extent to which we can shed deeply rooted assumptions that the purpose of special education is to cure specific disabilities. We must look on special education not as preparation for schooling but as life itself, leading to the gradual improvement of the quality of that life.

NOTES

1   See *40th Yearbook of the Claremont Reading Conference*, 1982, pp. 41-52.
2   See special volumes of *Topics in Learning and Learning Disabilities*, 1982, Volume 2, Numbers 1 and 2.

REFERENCES

Hallahan, D. University of Virginia learning disabilities institute. *Learning Disability Quarterly*, 1978, 1, 1, 77-78.

Meichenbaum, D. Teaching thinking; A cognitive-behavioral approach. Austin, Texas: Monograph #2, *Society for Learning Disabilities and Remedial Education.* 1980.

Reid, D.K. & Hresko, W. *A cognitive approach to learning disabilities.* New York: McGraw-Hill, 1981.

Torgesen, J. What shall we do with psychological processes? *Journal of Learning Disabilities*, 1979, 12, 8, 514-521.

Ysseldyke, J. & Algozzine, R. *Critical issues in special education and remedial education.* Boston: Houghton-Mifflin, 1982.

Reading Instruction As Seen from a Special Education Perspective

Donald D. Hammill

This paper discusses current instructional practices in reading as seen from a special educational point of view. In addition, some correlative evidence is offered in support of one approach to instruction.

Approaches to Instruction

Generally speaking, all instructional practices seem to be on one of two basic types: indirect or direct.

Indirect instruction

In indirect instruction, X activities are engaged in to produce Y results. For example, one might teach children to recall strings of digits, to walk a balance beam, or to crawl and creep properly, because such activities are thought to be in some way a part of, related to, or prerequisites for, reading. A characteristic of this kind of training is that the prescribed activities don't look at all like reading and can only be related to reading in terms of highly abstract constructs.

To illustrate, the goal here is to train hypothetical processes, basic abilities, or faculties in the brain (mind) that are supposedly related theoretically to reading, e.g., visual/auditory preception, memory, closure, sensory integration, sequencing, attention, movements, etc. The argument is made that in order for a child to read, he or she must attend, perceive, recall, and so forth, requisites that are seemingly true in some abstract sense. Such instruction is often referred to as "process training."

Direct instruction

In direct instruction, X activities are engaged in to produce X results. For example, one might teach a child to name letters of the alphabet, to recognize when a book is upside down, to see the main themes of paragraphs, and to comprehend the thematic as well as the phonic nature of written language, because such activities are thought to constitute various important aspects of reading. The relevance that an individual places on any one or on any set of activities depends, of course, on how he or she conceptualizes reading. Regardless, everyone would agree that the activities just mentioned are all closely associated with reading.

Advocates of direct (on-task) teaching are frequently heard to say, "If one wants to teach Johnny to read, expose him to reading," or "One learns to read as a consequence of reading." Professionals who espouse direct instruction can be separated readily into two different (and often contending) camps — the atomistic and the holistic orientation.

Atomistic. To atomistically inclined individuals, the whole (reading) is the sum of its parts (skills). For example, the word *cat* is believed to be comprised of three separate graphemes, c - a - t. Teaching children the sounds that go with the letters and having them say them fast is considered the heart and soul of atomistic education. Some atomistically inclined professionals do teach reading comprehension, but even here they tend to think of comprehension in terms of sequenced skills and conceive of it as being merely one of the many reading subskills. Sometimes this type of instruction is called "skill-centered" or "bottom-up."

Rather than relying on the child's natural language and interests, scope and sequence charts comprised of phonemically regular words and arbitrarily sequenced skills are used as guides for selecting material to be taught. Since contrived vocabularies are essential to instruction, the interest level of the reading material is usually low. Because of this, one often finds that behavior modification and management programs are used in conjunction with atomistic instruction. Invariably, atomistic instruction is curriculum or program centered even when individuals are being taught. Oral reading is emphasized.

Holistic. To holistically inclined individuals, the whole (reading) is never the sum of its parts (skills). These people would not break a word into its phonemic or graphemic parts for fear of destroying its meaning. In point of fact, the more dogmatic holistic educators would probably not even teach words in isolation, only in context. In choosing strategies, activities, and content for instruction, these teachers rely heavily on their knowledge of the student's home environment, desires, and natural language. The approach is decidedly child-centered. Silent reading for comprehension and retelling are mainstays in instruction. This type of instruction is frequently called "meaning centered" or "top-down."

Of course, in practice, most professionals find themselves positioned somewhere between polar opposites, i.e., no one is completely atomistic or holistic, nor are they completely direct or indirect in their instructional efforts. This has led some individuals, e.g., S. Jay Samuels, to postulate a third approach to instruction, the interactional. In this approach, professionals incorporate both atomistic and holistic principles into their instructional and diagnostic attempts.

Still, individuals do tend to gravitate toward one foci or another, an observation that is certainly obvious when professionals talk about *why* they teach in this or that way or discuss their educational philosophies.

A Special Education Perspective

Both the direct and indirect orientations just briefly described have at one time or another been pervasive in American special education. The indirect education emphasis was paramount from around 1930 to 1975. This was the heyday of "process training." The movement began with the perceptual hypotheses of Strauss and Werner, among others, and was operationalized in the programs of Frostig and Horne, William Cruickshank, Ray Barsch, Gerald Getman, and Newell Kephart. This trend continued with renewed vigor when Samuel Kirk incorporated these concepts into his ideas about "psycholinguistic" training (a la 1957 Osgood). These concepts of indirect instruction never received the degree of acceptance in the fields of speech or reading that they did in special education, where for years they were dominant. Since the early 1970's, however, this approach has come under increasing attack from special education researchers (see the work of Stephen Larsen, J. Lee Wiederholt, Joe Jenkins, Frank Velluntino, Lester Mann, Michael Epstein, Ken Kavale, James Ysseldyke, Douglas Carnine, and myself). Today few articles are published in peer-reviewed journals supporting the benefits of indirect instruction.

Since 1975, the mainstream of special education has turned to the use of direct instruction methodologies. Doubtless to say, the proponents of atomistic instruction are pervasive today. The theories and programs of Siegfred Englemann, Douglas Carnine, Thomas Stephens, James Kauffman, Tom Lovitt, Joe Jenkins, Anna Gillingham, among many others, have a practical, heady appeal. Only recently, at the start of the 1980's, are the holistic

ideas of Jean Piaget, Frank Smith, Jerome Bruner, and Ken and
Yetta Goodman beginning to seep into the special education
current to join there with those advocated by the neo-Fernaldites.
Hopefully before long, these ideas will stimulate the development
of programs, strategies, and research. Holistic education is now
the frontier of special education. Though philosophically pleasing
(to me), it remains to be seen whether this approach, either alone
or as a part of interactional efforts, will be preferable to or equal
with purely atomistic approaches.

In Support of Direct Instruction

In addition to the results of a considerable and growing body
of efficacy research which indicates clearly that with regard to
reading, process training and indirect methods don't work or
aren't worth the effort, there are other kinds of research that
support the use of direct instruction methods. Dr. Gaye McNutt
and I surveyed the findings of 322 research reports that correlated
reading with a wide variety of variables. We felt that much could
be learned about the nature of reading by determining just what
reading was and was not related to. If reading were correlated
with perceptual variables, for example, it would indicate that
there might be something to the perceptual hypotheses concerning
reading. If it were not correlated with perception, then this, too,
would indicate that perceptual factors were relatively unimportant
in reading.

After conducting a meta-analysis on 8,239 coefficients
reported in the studies, we concluded that the best predictors of
reading were variables that made use of writing in some way,
e.g., spelling, math skills, capitalization and punctuation use,
sound-letter relations, grammatic writing, and letter discrimination.
Affective, motoric, and perceptual abilities were found to be
completely unrelated to reading at any age. Most spoken
language, phonemic, and reasoning (intellectual) abilities were
significant but surprisingly were not particularly powerful
predictors of reading (see Hammill and McNutt, *The Correlates
of Reading: The Consensus of Thirty Years of Correlation
Research.* Austin: PRO-ED, 1981). Since reading was related
mostly to abilities that involved the use of written symbols, we
felt that direct instruction methods would be most beneficial. It
was unlikely that training abilities known to be unrelated to
reading would result in increased reading proficiency.

Helping Children with Learning Problems — The American Approach

Gilbert R. Gredler

The current interest in learning problems continues unabated in the United States. The reasons for this phenomenon are numerous and varied. The intent of this paper is to review the present status of the field and to offer an assessment of important

The first severe reading disability cases were mentioned in the British medical literature by Hinshelwood and W. Pringle Morgan in 1895.(12, 16) In 1897 James Kerr, another British physician, wrote of examining children who had many features of learning disabilities such as those mentioned by Morgan. In 1917 Hinshelwood published a monograph on severe reading disability which was, at that time, called "congenital word blindness." Hinshelwood also stated that severe reading disability tended to run in families, and he emphasized that not all cases of such disability were the result of neurological conditions. In 1932 Ronne emphasized that severe reading disability was a "unitary condition and not a haphazard coincidence [due to] circumstances as neglect of school, change of school, lack of diligence, an unfortunate home, and poor intellectual endowments — " (12, p. 19) and these difficulties continue on into adult life. Thus by the 40s, a condition is definitely recognized where a child of normal intelligence may have extraordinary difficulty in learning to read. Hermann, a Danish neurologist, said that a severe reading disability case is a condition that shows "a defective capacity for acquiring at the normal time, a proficiency in reading and writing corresponding to average performance —." (p. 12, 18)

What is acknowledged today is the existence of a small core of reading disabled children who show extreme difficulties in learning to read. The latest research confirming the existence of this core is Clark's (5) study of 1,544 Scottish children. One hundred twenty children were found to be having difficulty in reading after three years of school. Reading retardation was defined as having a reading age two or more years below the child's chronological age. This group comprised eight percent of the total group of children in that school system. At age ten, after five years of schooling, one-half of this group was still two to three years retarded in reading, an incidence rate of 3.8 percent.

At first, diagnosis of severe reading disability was based almost solely on exclusion. However, specialists soon began to suggest certain signs as being important: "various errors occur frequently — such as reversal and rotations of certain letters." (12) Gradually a list of characteristic symptoms took shape. This list has expanded and changed over the last 50 years.

There have been a number of theories enunciated in the past 40 years to help explain severe reading problems. Rabinovitch, (18) an American psychiatrist, helped conceptualize an approach to severe reading disabilities by postulating a three-fold classification of reading disorder. Primary reading retardation, he said, is a condition where learning to read is impaired, but without the existence of definite evidence as to brain damage. Rabinovitch explains that such a child would show "a disturbed pattern of neurologic organization." In secondary reading retardation there is no question as to the child's capacity to learn, but this capacity is negatively affected by factors exogenous to the child's neurologic organization. Such factors would be an emotional condition such as anxiety, depression, or hostility; or the child's reading could be affected by limited school opportunities. A third type of reading retardation is retardation associated with brain damage. While Rabinovitch later revised his points somewhat, these essentials remain.

Currently one of the most popular theoretical positions among educators as to causative factors of severe reading problems is the maturational lag school. This term refers to the lack of normal maturation of selected functions of the cerebral cortex.(23) However, the danger in this approach is that when the term "maturational lag" is used, many consider that the child is automatically immature developmentally in all behavioral areas. The term "immature child" is very popular in American educational circles, and the automatic solution for a child so labeled in kindergarten or first grade is to retain him in order to "overcome" his immaturity. While it is common sense to state that the maturational level is a function of chronological age, it is definitely incorrect to conclude that if children who are at risk at age five or six just repeat their grade, then all will be well. Supposedly all their maturational functions will have matured by then, and no further efforts will be needed to help them in learning. While DeHirsch is an advocate of the maturational point of view, she states in her study of children who showed reading failure that "chronological age alone is not only inadequate but misleading as a predictor.(10)

Herman (12) strongly opposed the idea of a maturational lag as an explanation for the existence of severe reading disability. He mentions that young children can easily pick up two to three languages, whereas this type of linguistic learning declines rapidly after age ten; therefore, a period of lesser maturity seems to be favorable for linguistic development. He argues that it would seem foolish to argue that reading development is so different. He states that the maturation of nerve fibers is promoted by repeated use; therefore, one is "fully justified in arguing that immaturity is a prerequisite for the establishment of learning, and furthermore, maturational processes are facilitated by practice of what has been learned." (p. 31)

It must be remembered that in the controversy over the term, "minimal brain dysfunction," the use of the label arose from physicians' concern with a group of children who showed extraordinary difficulty in learning to read. The term MBD was used to help account for learning problems at a time when many educators and psychologists only looked at emotional factors as causative of poor reading. It is conceded that the syndrome consisted of an overinclusive list of behavioral signs, family factors, and various examination findings. (9) Kinsbourne (13) considers that children who have unexpected difficulty in mastering material in the first grade are having temporary lags in mental development. He also makes the important point that perhaps the differences we find in individual children may not really be that important but for the fact of the rigid demands of society which, when imposed on the child in school, become of heightened importance.

As stated previously, a number of investigators linked the child's various ability deficits to "soft signs" indicating brain dysfunction. Later these same deficits would be considered "correlates" of severe reading disability,(14) thereby bypassing the issue of possible brain dysfunction in the child. Very popular in the 1940s to the 1960s, the use of the term "minimal brain dysfunction" has now gone out of favor.

The delay model then became popular and for the past 10

years has been the theory most in favor among American psychologists attempting to explain severe reading problems. This model considers the child's neurological development as its key element. However, instead of emphasizing possible structural damage, it focuses on developmental changes and the child's slower pace of development. Some consider that such delays may be genetic in origin or possibly due to molecular changes within the body not observable through present diagnostic methods. (13)

Another approach to the severe reading problem not often discussed, but important, is the difference model. This approach considers that the child's behavior patterns are not abnormal per se but that the development of the various cognitive abilities shows sufficient variation that the child has difficulty meeting the demands that the regular school invokes. (13) This school of thought is not popular since it obviously places a major responsibility for the child's lack of success on those in authority, i.e., school personnel. It raises the issue of an inadequate curriculum and too rigid educational goals.

Almost any term used to explain severe reading difficulty has its opponents, but it is important to mention that none of these theories can be "proven." There is no hard evidence that we can obtain which would firmly indicate that there is actual brain damage, nor are there medical tests which firmly indicate that the child is developmentally delayed.

Valtin (22) feels that the issue of dyslexia is more of a deficit in research strategy than in the reading state of the child. She states that a number of studies of severely retarded readers are suspect. Valtin discusses the hazard of drawing conclusions about poor readers when using a matched control design. The matched pairs would tend to include the better readers among the dyslexic group and the poorer readers from the normal reading group. Therefore, she states, conclusions on differences found between the two groups must be tempered by this fact. Also she mentions that research results are affected by the differential use of Full Scale, Performance or Verbal IQ as the matching variable.

However, it is now well accepted that there are various subgroups of poor readers, and as long as that is acknowledged, then legitimate conclusions about characteristics about reading disability can certainly be arrived at. Investigators have correctly assumed that Performance IQ can be used as a legitimate matching variable. Doehring (11) states: (The Performance IQ seems to provide) "an adequate means of differentiating children with specific reading disabilities from children whose reading disability was associated with more generalized intellectual subnormality." (p. 129) Doehring (11) also points out it would be difficult to obtain a large enough group of poor readers if normal Verbal IQ was chosen as the criterion. Also, if both Verbal and Performance IQs had to be equal, then probably no group of reading retardates could have been assembled for his study. Doehring found in his sample of 39 reading retarded children that not one child with a Performance IQ of 90 had a Verbal IQ equal to or higher than the Performance Quotient.

In an attempt to meet objections to research on reading, Mattis et al., (15) compared brain damaged dyslexics and developmental dyslexics with a group of children who were brain damaged and reading successfully. They concluded that (1) there are several independent clusters of deficiencies in higher cortical functions which serve to limit the development of reading skills, and (2) these deficiencies may occur in the areas of language, blending fluency, and/or visuo-spatial perception. Their theoretical approach encompasses both the idea that the reading disturbance may include not only an actual deficit in one of these process areas but also discrepancies in the development of subprocesses within a specific skill area, all of which combine to then limit the necessary integration of skills so that progress in reading will occur. This study more than any recent investigation points out the value of use of carefully selected psychological tests to measure functions underlying the reading process.

Rutter (21) feels that the psychologist can make a distinct contribution by determining more precisely a child's neuropsychological difficulties and defining the type and kind of improved function that the child makes under certain kinds of learning conditions. This type of contribution can be best seen in Bale's (3, 4) research. Bales found that no single factor explained all the child's reading retardation but that a combination of visual-perceptual, auditory perception, language difficulties, and motor impairment were involved. He said that there was sufficient evidence from his studies to come to "a deductive hypothesis which links dyslexia and a causal relationship with developmental, behavioral and birth stresses." (p. 9)

Recent research in the pattern of intellectual ability found in children with severe reading disability is reported by Richman and Lindgren. (20) Using the Weschler and Hiskey-Nebraska Scales, they found three main subgroups of children: those with good abstract reasoning; a group with good sequencing ability; and a group poor in both areas. There was an extraordinary difference in the reading levels of these three groups. While only

eight percent of the abstract reasoning group scored more than
one standard deviation below the mean on a reading test, 21
percent of the sequential memory group did so, and 89 percent of
the children with poor performance in both abstract reasoning
and sequential memory ability did so. It should be noted that in
this group, whose Verbal IQs ranged from 81-89, more than one-
half (51%) were adequate readers as measured by their
performance on a standardized reading test. This is important to
remember in view of the present thrust by some to emphasize
poor reading of children as mainly due to low IQs. (1)

A number of objections have been made to the use of tests in
the diagnosis of severe reading problems. They have ranged from
lack of adequate validity and reliability criteria; bias against
specific subcultural groups; to lack of sufficient information from
the test to mount a treatment program. In a slashing attack on the
use of an LD test battery, Coles (6) considers that the use of
these tests is illogical and that low scores on such tests do not
demonstrate the child has a valid learning disability.

Coles correctly points out that there is no such thing as a
standard LD battery, and this has been a problem in the field of
psychology for years. While at first glance it would appear that
Coles has fashioned a horrible indictment of the use of tests in
attempting to diagnose LD, unfortunately he has overstated his
case. He does make legitimate points as to the influence of social
class factors on test results. Coles admits he has concentrated on
the use of individual tests in determining learning disability and
not on the use of a composite profile "in large part because
literature on these tests has assumed that each part of the battery
has the strength to stand on its own, independent of the whole
battery." (p. 328) However, most leaders in the area of learning
disability do not agree with this assumption. (3, 8, 9, 11, 15)
And this is the major error of Coles' article. Sophisticated
investigations of LD for the past 15 years have emphasized the
need and value of a composite analysis of suitable measures of
perceptual, conceptual, and language functioning.

What Coles' criticisms point out is the sad state of diagnostic
judgment as practiced by many professionals in the United States
today.

Arter and Jenkins (2) vehemently argue against the continued
use of the modality approach until a "more adequate research
base" is established. They call for a moratorium on advocacy of
diagnostic-prescriptive teaching and on the classification and
placement of children utilizing differential processing ability tests.

However, it would appear that this more adequate research base has been partially provided by the recent investigations of Naylor and Pumphrey. (17) Their work raises significant questions as to whether such a wholesale indictment should be accepted.

Naylor and Pumphrey (17) worked with 60 poor readers aged seven and eight years. A deficit in psychoeducational functioning as measured by the ITPA was found in auditory closure and visual sequential memory. Three intervention programs were utilized, with one group receiving a language program based on ITPA type activities; another group utilized materials from the Peabody language development program. A third group, the control, worked with a number program to help offset the Hawthorne effect.

The results showed that both language subgroups improved in psycholinguistic development as measured by the ITPA. But, more important, the two language groups made significant gains in word comprehension and word recognition as compared to the controls, both at the end of the treatment program and 10 months later. This research is important for several reasons. It demonstrates the value of the use of a language program in improving psycholinguistic functioning and achievement in reading.

Naylor and Pumphrey (17) further postulate that the effectiveness of their remediation is also due to the use of reading and writing activities in the treatment approach, and they suggest that the Kirk treatment approach reflects more of a general language orientation where a number of subskills are worked on during the course of treatment. In this carefully organized research, Naylor and Pumphrey have shown the efficacy of a modality approach to the remediation of reading problems in one group of seven- and eight-year-olds.

There continues to be a core of children who continue to show difficulty in attaining proficiency in academic skills and yet are of normal intelligence. This small group of children, variously estimated at from two to four percent of the school population, possesses a constellation of symptoms which have been described in quite similar terms through the last 90 years, though the technical vocabulary has changed. What the passage of years has brought has been a gain in refinement of measuring the variety of processing difficulties a child might have.

What has definitely changed over the last 90 years is our thinking as to the causes of severe reading disability. This area is still beset with a great deal of conflict, much of it quite emotional. Originally, 'hard core' cases were conceived as "congenital" and probably hereditary in origin. (12) Negative reaction to this opinion has come from psychologists and educators. (2) However, it has been pointed out that use of this terminology by the medical profession has been partly due to the fact that psychology and education have been too prone to dismiss all severe reading problems as reflecting emotional problems within the child and his family. (13)

Fortunately, the charge of vagueness, arbitrariness in diagnostic signs, is not accurate. There has been definite progress in conceptualizing and classifying reading disorders, which in turn have helped to resolve some of the conflicts which have plagued the field in the past.

While the debate continues on as to the etiology of the condition of severe reading disability, at present there can really be no resolution of the problem. Given present means of investigation of severe reading disability, conclusive evidence for any position cannot be garnered. However, as has been shown, a number of researchers have helped in arriving at a more adequate conceptualization of the severely reading disabled.

One of the most important studies was carried out recently by Darby. (8) Utilizing multivariate statistical techniques, he was able to discern four distinct subtypes of reading disabilities. They included: (1) a group with mainly verbal fluency problems; (2) a subgroup with deficient visual perceptual problems; (3) a subgroup with deficiency in both areas; and (4) a group with no deficiencies in performance in either area. The existence of this last group demonstrates that, even today, we will find children who show severe reading problems for whom we have difficulty in finding a suitable psychological explanation.

Is the strength of the learning disability movement mainly a reflection of the bureaucratic inefficiency and inflexibility of the American school system, with continued emphasis on the lockstep of grades? Yet another approach to learning problems within the school is that of mastery learning. The degree of learning is a product of time allowed for learning, motivation, aptitude, quality of instruction, and ability to understand instruction. According to mastery theory, even if children are normally distributed in regard to aptitudes, if every learner receives the optimal quality of instruction and the learning time required, then a majority of children could be expected to attain mastery of the material. To the extent that a school attempts to involve the children in a mastery learning approach, perhaps there would be fewer LD classes in that school.

The learning disability movement has given hope to a number of parents whose children have constantly had trouble with learning problems. So much has been said about parents being at fault for their children's learning problems that the message of the learning disability movement, "we absolve you of blame," has fallen on ready ears. However, it is important to remember there is a definite core of children with severe reading problems whose needs in the past have not been met within the school system. The learning disability movement has helped the school to pay more attention to such children. It is to be hoped that the 1980s will see new stress given to more innovative intervention approaches to helping the learning disabled child within the public schools.

REFERENCES

1 Ames, L.B. Learning disabilities: Time to check our roadmaps? *Journal of Learning Disabilities, 1977, 10,* 328-330.

2 Arter, J.A., & Jenkins, J.R. Differential diagnosis - prescriptive teaching: A critical appraisal. *Review of Educational Research,* 1979, *49,* 517-555.

3 Bale, P. Perceptual, motor and language deficits in dyslexic children. *Dyslexia Review,* 1980, *3,* 6-9.

4 Bale, P. Prenatal factors and backwardness in reading. *Educational Research,* 1981, *23,* 134-143.

5 Clark, M.M. *Reading difficulties in schools.* London: Heinemann Educational Books, 1979.

6 Coles, G.S. The learning disabilities test battery: Empirical social issues. *Harvard Educational Review,* 1978, *48,* 313-340.

7 Critchley, M. *The dyslexic child.* London: Heinemann Medical Books, 1970.

8 Darby, R.O. Learning disabilities: A multivariate search for subtypes. Unpublished doctoral dissertation, University of Florida, 1978.

9 Denckla, M.B. Minimal brain dysfunction and dyslexia: Beyond diagnosis by exclusion. In Blaw, M.E., Ragin, I., & Kinsbourne, M. (Eds.), *Topics in child neurology.* New York: Spectrum Books, 1977.

10 DeHirsch, K., Jansky, J.J., & Langford, W.S. *Predicting reading failure.* New York: Harper & Row, 1966.

11 Doehring, D.G. *Patterns of impairment in specific reading disability.* Bloomington, Indiana: Indiana University Press, 1968.

12 Hermann, K. *Reading disability.* Copenhagen: Munksgaard, 1959.

13 Kinsbourne, M., & Caplan, P.J. *Children's learning and attention problems.* Boston, Massachusetts: Little, Brown & Company, 1979.

14 Kirk, S. Educating exceptional children. Boston, Massachusetts: Houghton Mifflin, 1972.

15 Mattis, S., French, J.H., & Rapin, I. Dyslexia in children and young adults: 3 Independent neuropsychological syndromes. *Developmental Medicine and Child Neurology,* 1975, *17,* 150-163.

16 Naidoo, S. *Specific dyslexia.* London: Pitman Publishing, 1972.

17 Naylor, J.G., & Pumphrey, P.D. The alleviation of psycholinguistic deficits and some effects on the reading attainments of poor readers: A sequel. *Journal of Research in Reading.* In press.

18 Rabinovitch, R.D. et al. A research approach to reading retardation. In McIntosh, R., & Hare, C.C. (Eds.), *Neurology and psychiatry in childhood.* Baltimore: Williams & Wilkins, 1956.

19 Richman, L.C. Language mediation hypothesis: Implications of verbal/ performance discrepancy and reading ability. *Perceptual & Motor Skills,* 1978, *47,* 391-398.

20 Richman, L.C., & Lindgren, S.D. Patterns of intellectual ability in children with verbal deficits. *Journal of Abnormal Child Psychology,* 1980, *8,* 65-81.

21 Rutter, M. et al. *A neuropsychiatric study in childhood.* London: Heinemann Medical Books, 1970.

22 Singleton, C.H. The myths of specific developmental dyslexia I. *Remedial Education,* 1975, *10,* 109-113.

23 Valtin, R. Dyslexia: Deficit in reading or deficit in research? *Reading Research Quarterly,* 1978-1979, *14,* 200-225.

24 Vernon, M.D. Varieties of deficiency in the reading process. *Harvard Educational Review,* 1977, *47,* 396-410.

A New Approach to Reading*

McCay Vernon

If you ask the question, "What major improvements have been made in reading instruction over the last 50 years?" answers would vary tremendously. The ultra traditionalists who currently advocate a return to the McGuffy Readers would argue that there has been no progress. In fact, they would claim that we have regressed over the 200 plus years since the American Revolution. In moments of despair, many of us have almost agreed with this view.

Professionals in the field of reading might cite as major steps forward in the last half century factors such as the application of psycholinguistics. Implementing knowledge from psycholinguistics to reading has led to a re-focus on comprehension and meaningful text material rather than isolated skill work. The use of effective layout, e.g., headings and sub-headings to make material more readable, is a part of this general approach.

A second advance reading authorities might point to is an emphasis on early childhood pre-school preparations. SESAME STREET and HEADSTART are important dimensions of this thrust. Research results on the value of pre-school are conflicting.

A third major development in reading has been the more sophisticated diagnosis and remediation of reading disorders as functions of sensory modalities. The nature of specific learning disabilities has developed from this line of thinking. Special focus remediations, for example, the introduction of the Fernald Method and related procedures, Wepman's work, and the development of tests such as the ITPA, illustrate progress toward defining reading problems more specifically. The corollary to this diagnostic approach is that once an accurate diagnosis is made, remediation can ideally be more problem specific.

A fourth milestone in the field of reading over the last 50 years was (not, has been) the influx of federal government

---

*The Peter Lincoln Spencer lecture, named for the founder of The Claremont Reading Conference, and its director from 1932 until 1958.

monies resulting in the "Right to Read" movement of the 60s and 70s. The aforementioned SESAME STREET, HEADSTART, and other grant-type programs were a part of this. The full impact of these federal programs is hard to assess accurately but to some degree they have had an omnipresent if diffuse influence. As you are all aware, such federal expenditures are at present a matter of history.

Depending on your own perspective, you may or may not see the work on reading for gifted children as the fifth major development in reading over the last half century. Certainly, work in this field of exceptionality has, as work with exceptional children in general, proven a highly fertile ground for new concepts and techniques in teaching reading.

The point of this historical perspective is that when we look at major progress in reading over the last 50 years, one conclusion is so obvious as to be a truism. It is that reading is an extremely complex process which does not lend itself to simple corrections of its pathology. Thus, the developments that have been made chip away at aspects of the problem rather than represent major breakthroughs or cures to reading disability. In other words, research in reading is analogous to cancer research, in that progress has been made toward reducing aspects of the problem, but a full understanding of the nature of the basic processes of either still eludes us.

TOTAL COMMUNICATION APPROACH

The new approach to reading to be presented here is called Total Communication. It involves the use of fingerspelling and sign language of deaf people, along with natural gestures, to help normally hearing children learn. By way of explanation, fingerspelling (see photos 1, 2, 3, 4, and 5) is simply a system of separate hand positions for each letter. Sign language, by contrast, is comprised of hand positions that stand for entire words or phrases (see photos 6, 7, 8, and 9).

The most readily apparent technique to use as a remedial reading tool is fingerspelling. Fingerspelled letters correspond directly to printed letters. Moreover, many of the hand positions of manually formed letters are shaped like the printed letter. Even for those letters whose manual formation and printed formation are not identical, there are generally noticeable similarities. Stated somewhat differently, the manually formed letters are icons of their printed counterparts (Jacobs, 1859). This maximizes the value of the manual letters as an aid to learning printed ones. In actual practice, fingerspelling is generally used in teaching phonics-related skills. Signs are more helpful in sight-word reinforcement.

Most current reading instruction involves combining visual and auditory components. Teachers are therefore already experienced at including these elements in their instruction. This prepares them for using Total Communication.

In presenting the method to you, first the theory, clinical data, natural observations, and research underlying its use will be examined. Finally, some practical values and applications of the technique will be illustrated.

Theory, Clinical Data, Research, and Natural Observations Contributing to the Rationale for Total Communication

Characteristics of remedial reading techniques

The first line of theoretical support for the use of total communication comes from an analysis of existing techniques that are successful with disabled readers. These techniques usually have at least one of three basic characteristics. Many are multisensory (Abrams, 1968; Charuk, 1974; Fernald, 1943; and Segel, 1974). For example, they involve tracing words, feeling sandpaper letters, or handling letters that are three dimensional (Myers, 1978). Others include physical movements by the students. The work of Asher Kusudo (1974), Creedon (1973), and Offir (1976) illustrate this approach. The third characteristic of successful techniques with disabled readers is that they motivate students.

Idiographic vs. alphabet languages

Ideographic languages, for example, some forms of Japanese and Chinese, which do not involve alphabet letters and phonetic rules, are easier to read (Hamanaka and Ohashi, 1974; Markowicz, 1973; and Zhon, 1980). Among children who use these "picture" languages, there are far fewer reading problems (Hamanaka and Ohashi, 1974; and Zhon, 1980).

The American Sign Language and the manual alphabet used by deaf people combine all of these desirable characteristics of remedial reading techniques. As indicated, the manual alphabet consists of separate hand positions for each of the 26 letters of the alphabet. Signs, in contrast, are individual hand movements that stand for an entire word or phrase. Many signs are ideographic, which makes them especially vivid and appealing.

They motivate children and are easy to remember and associate with the reading of printed words.

Thus sign language and fingerspelling have fundamental characteristics that theoretically offer significant potential for use with children who have trouble learning to read, or mastering language, and for all youngsters beginning to learn to read.

By fingerspelling a word, a child gets strong kinesthetic feedback and reinforcement along with added visual input. Of course, the whole idea of associating reading with a pleasurable motoric activity has great appeal for young children who almost universally relish the chance for physical activity in school (Asher and Price, 1967). Moreover, manual communication does not have the negative association which a paper-pencil task conjures up for many youngsters. In fact, this lack of writing, while strong kinesthetic input is retained, may make fingerspelling a technique preferable to many other approaches.

Children of deaf parents

Clinical observations on children of non-speaking deaf parents gave the first clue to the potential of Total Communication (Vernon and Coley, 1978; Vernon, Coley, and Ottinger, 1979). Because these deaf parents use fingerspelling (and sign language) at home, their children are exposed to it even though they are not deaf. Thus, a sort of "experiment of nature" is created whereby the effects of signing and fingerspelling can be assessed.

The end result of the "experiment of nature" is that all normally hearing children of average or above IQ, who have non-speaking deaf parents, read prior to entering school (Vernon and Coley, 1978). They read fingerspelling which is cognitively identical to reading printed words (Klima and Bellugi, 1979). In fact, many read regular printed words, because they make the connection between the manual letter and the printed one (Hofsteater, 1959; Klima and Bellugi, 1979; and Vernon and Coley, 1978). Not only do these children read but they also write; i.e., they use fingerspelling expressively.

The implications of this unique "experiment of nature" have tremendous generality for the teaching of reading to all children. It means that given Total Communication as a part of a reading readiness program, the early development of reading and writing skills would be greatly facilitated. Gifted children would be reading by age three years, because this is what happens now with the gifted offspring of congenitally deaf parents. Children of average or above intelligence using Total Communication could be reading at four to five years of age, if this were the goal.

Additional evidence of the potential value of fingerspelling in teaching reading to hearing children comes from studies of children who not only have deaf parents but who are themselves deaf (Bellugi and Klima, 1975; Kannapell, 1974; Vernon and Koh, 1970, 1971). Many of them are fluent fingerspellers well before they even enter school. This means that, like hearing children of deaf parents, they can read and write (manually) before having been taught to do so formally. These children of deaf parents learn this from a combination of fingerspelled words and signs manually communicated to them by their parents in the form of sentences; that is, they are not taught the alphabet as such in many instances. Even more surprising, they can "write" similar sentences to their parents; i.e., they can fingerspell and sign sentences. Once these deaf children enter school, they rapidly and easily learn to read conventional print symbols. In fact, many deaf children of deaf parents come to school able to read, because their parents have already taught them to associate the manual and print alphabet symbols (Hofsteater, 1959).

In stark contrast to the studies of deaf children of deaf parents are the studies of deaf children who do not have early exposure to fingerspelling or sign language. The reading level of these deaf children is generally inferior (Meadow, 1968; Vernon and Koh, 1970, 1971).

Essentially, what these findings on both hearing and deaf children of deaf parents indicate is that, if given only manual communication (fingerspelling and sign language), they read at a very early age. If speech were added in a classical conditioning framework such as involved in Total Communication, learning would be even more effective.

Sign language and primates

The simplest, most direct explanation for why Total Communication works may be that sign language is easier to learn than conventional language. Clinical evidence for this comes from work with primates. If primates cannot only learn it, but teach it to their own offspring, this certainly suggests that it is readily learned (Cantfort and Rimpau, 1982; Gardner and Gardner, 1975; Mayberry, 1976; Premak, 1971).

Hemispheric dominance

It may be that the brain hemisphere opposite that used for conventional auditory language learning is involved in the motor-linguistic functioning of manual communication (Abbott, 1975; Chen, 1971; Glass, Gazinaga, and Premak, 1973; Goodglass and Kaplan, 1965; Kimura, 1973; and Reed, 1971). Thus, individuals with left hemispheric damage, which often causes the loss of conventional speech, language, and reading, may be able to develop manual communication skills, because motor function in most people is in the right hemisphere. With regular children, the use of Total Communication brings both brain hemispheres to bear on the task of reading.

Findings from deaf and hearing aphasics

Once again, some of the initial evidence on Total Communication comes from the field of deafness. It has long been recognized by teachers and others who work with deaf children that a significant number of these youth are aphasic (and/or dyslexic) in that they are totally unable to master printed or oral/aurally presented language (Mindel and Vernon, 1972). Yet, they are usually fluent in sign language (Vernon, 1969). There are no childhood sign language aphasics (apraxics). This rather remarkable fact was seized upon by a number of speech pathologists and rehabilitation specialists who have generalized it by teaching sign language to non-deaf aphasics, including stroke victims (Balick, Spiegel, and Greene, 1976; and Chen, 1971). Once aphasics master signs or fingerspelling, these communication skills are used to facilitate reading and speech. Results have been positive (Balick, Spiegel, and Greene, 1976; Chen, 1971; Chester and Egolf, 1974; Duffy and Pearson, 1975; and Skelly, Schinsky, Smith, Donaldson, and Griffin, 1975). In brief, the normally hearing individuals they studied who were aphasic and, therefore unable to communicate via conventional means, learned basic sign language. This enabled them to make their wants known, and it played a major part in the overall linguistic rehabilitation.

Classical conditioning and total communication

Perhaps the most powerful rationale for the value of Total Communication comes from psychological learning theory, namely the principles of classical conditioning. Appropriately used, Total Communication presents the reading stimuli to the child in visual, auditory, and kinesthetic modes simultaneously, all very closely together in time. Thus, the stimuli are learned or associated by classical conditioning, i.e., the presentation of a conditioned and an unconditioned stimuli in temperal proximity. This process is fundamental to much or all of human learning. To be successful, an approach to reading must involve conditioning. Sometimes the paradigm used is paired associate learning.

Other rationales

Sign language and fingerspelling do not require auditory memory and auditory processing. This may be another factor accounting for the method's effectiveness (Fristoe and Lloyd, 1977). Finger-ground differentiation may also be enhanced by use of the visual mode, as contrasted to the audition and the context in which speech stimuli are often used (Fristoe and Lloyd, 1977).

Finally, with speech sounds it is not possible to meaningfully sustain the phonemes indefinitely. By contrast, with manual communication an alphabet letter or a sign can be presented at a rate appropriate to the learner. Fristoe and Lloyd (1975) provide an excellent discussion of some of the ways in which visual language may be easier to learn than auditory or written language.

In sum, when we look to widely diverse fields such as remedial reading, cross-cultural studies involving Japanese and Chinese languages, human exceptionality (deafness and aphasia), primate research, the neurology of laterality and language, basic learning theory, perception, and cognition, there is a tremendous amount of data to support the use of Total Communication to teach regular, normally hearing kindergarten and primary age children to read. Ironically, however, the first applications of the method have not been with regular children but with exceptional children. As you know, this has been the history of many new developments in reading.

Practical Aspects, Applications and Use

We will now look at the technique of Total Communication in practical terms, i.e., its value and its use. In a written paper such as this, the actual hands-on experience needed to go over lesson plans and to teach the specific steps in how to use the method is not feasible. However, information immediately following this narrative explains how to get free materials about the method. There is also information on how to obtain a book which includes over 50 easy-to-use lesson plans, instructional games, learning stations, and reproducible student sheets for classroom use. The book shows how to adapt the method to any elementary level, K-6, or pre-school programs.

Teacher concerns

The major concern of teachers is that they will have to learn a whole new language. This is not the case. If it were, the method would not be practical. For many of the applications, all that is required of the teacher is that she take about 20 minutes to learn the manual alphabet. This can be done with the students during class time. Speed and facility in fingerspelling are not required. For example, in certain lesson plans only the final consonant sound is spelled, if this is the letter or sound being taught.

Similarly with signs — they can be used to help introduce new vocabulary in a basal reader. Before the story is to be introduced, the teacher can take 5 minutes or less to learn the signs for a half dozen or fewer words that may be difficult for the class. When these words are used, the teacher signs and says them and has the class do the same thing. Using this approach, students learn the words quickly when they are introduced in print form.

Thus, not only does the method require very little teacher time, but the only cost is for the basic book with the lesson plans and explanations. The lesson plans in the book are in ready-to-use form. Most of them require only that the teacher take five minutes or so before class to read them.

Because signs can give every student a chance to respond without using paper and pencil, some Total Communication activities can be substituted for traditional written assignments, thereby lessening some of the teacher's paper correcting chores.

Individualization

Many of the activities suggested in the book involve an every-pupil response to meet individual needs. For instance, one lesson involves all children in a group fingerspelling letters to indicate which vowel is heard in given words. In a matter of seconds, every child is being "heard" by the teacher. All children are actively and simultaneously participating in an orderly manner.

Additionally, no one child is put in the embarrassing situation of being singled out when they make a mistake.

The teacher in this lesson can see everyone's response and make mental or written diagnostic notes relative to children who seem unsure or confused, so that further help may be provided. All the children can be immediately reinforced by a statement such as, "If you have the same answer showing as Pat, you have the idea. Let's try another and see if more of you understand."

Children who are having difficulty with a skill will probably copy the responses of others rather than not participate. This modeling is advantageous in several ways. It provides immediate feedback by instantly giving the student the unknown response, much as programmed learning or self-checking centers do. The child's hesitation is immediately obvious to the teacher who may then plan further reinforcement. A manual type of response, however, allows children to escape the embarrassment of publicly admitting they do not have the answer.

Motivation

Children are used to saying, seeing, and hearing words, but feeling words adds a new dimension. Almost without exception, students are enthusiastic about signs and fingerspelling. They take naturally to the play acting and secret codes of Total Communication. They are thrilled to "act out" this new "secret code" in their school work especially if they have grown blase about filling in the blanks, doing workbook pages, and playing sight word games.

One teacher reported that she was reading a book about sign language. The book, which had the manual alphabet on the inside front cover, was lying on the reading table when three children came for instruction. One of them started leafing through the book and became fascinated with the manual alphabet. The questions came from every direction. "What's this?" "How does it work?" "How do you make my name?" "How do you make your name?" and then the big one, "Could we use this to do our words?" The children's excitement indicates the potential of the Total Communication approach in teaching reading.

The teacher who decides to use the Total Communication approach for teaching language arts has the advantage of using an approach that is totally new and motivating to children. Once exposed to it, they are eager to learn more and use it in new ways.

Success

Children who have trouble with language arts because they "can't sit still," or because it is so difficult for them, tend to especially benefit from this technique. The Total Communication approach encourages them to be physically active, yet not chaotic. They do not have to spend inordinate amounts of time passively listening. They can actively, physically participate in the lesson. It can make language come alive for children who have previously not experienced success in reading and other language skills.

Independence

Using the Total Communication approach fosters independence even when children are unsure of their footing, because they are having difficulty or are tackling something new. This technique can wean a child away from dependence on the teacher and encourage him or her to take steps toward becoming an independent reader. For example, in prompting children who stumble over a word in oral reading, the teacher can begin to fingerspell the word. In many cases, before the spelling is done, the student will have the word out. Thus, the child does not have to be told the word but just urged on a bit until she or he succeeds in recognizing it.

Teachers report that children who have been exposed to this type of manual prompting learn to self-prompt. One child was observed during an initial attempt at independent reading. She came to a word which she did not recognize. She used her hand to fingerspell the word. Although the teacher was watching from a distance and could hear the child whisper the sounds, she gave no help. The child immediately recognized the word after fingerspelling and went on reading.

Teachers who have watched children using fingerspelling to self-prompt observe that once the difficult words are learned, the children no longer have a need to use fingerspelling with those words, and they stop (Greenberg, Vernon, Dubois, and McKnight, 1982).

Illustrating concepts

The Total Communication approach is a valuable technique for many skills, and perhaps, one of the best for some. For example, fingerspelling and signs are naturals for helping children understand the concept of rhyming words, opposites, and expressive oral reading.

Partner learning

Partner learning, assigning two children to help each other practice a skill, is an effective technique that can be further enhanced by the Total Communication approach. For example, two students in need of initial consonant identification practices, can be given a set of picture cards. The children can take turns flashing cards that have the initial consonant on the back. The partner can make and say the sound for the manual alphabet letter to indicate the initial consonant. Not only will activities such as this motivate students but also facilitate learning by introducing kinesthetic input.

Large groups

Teachers can use the Total Communication approach in whole class instruction. It is particularly effective for practicing basic skills that must be learned by rote, e.g., homophones. The approach can also provide instant class tests. When a new skill, such as distinction between fact and opinion, has been introduced, children can be informally tested at the end of the lesson. For instance, the teacher can read some statements and direct students to show the manual alphabet "O," if the statement is an opinion, "F," if it is a fact.

Small groups

In small groups, the Total Communication approach can be used to spark interest in a new concept. For example, letting children use signs to mime the action in verbs is an exciting way to introduce the concept of action words.

When a teacher wants to review briefly a concept taught earlier, the Total Communication approach can be useful. Having the children respond manually to a quick oral review gives the teacher a chance to reinforce without the fuss and time required for a paper and pencil activity.

The Total Communication approach is a natural for small group situations in which the teacher wishes to change pace by using an instructive game. Learning games which are already familiar, such as Scrabble or Bingo, become even more motivating when fingerspelling and sign language are used.

Summary

A method for use in teaching reading to preschool, elementary, and exceptional children has been presented. It incorporates the major characteristics of current remedial techniques and other major advances in reading. For example, it is multisensory, it involves the child physically in the reading process, it is highly motivating, and it is ideographic.

The method incorporates current psychoneurological knowledge about laterality. It is soundly based in research and clinical data. It uses classical conditioning principles of human learning, and it applies recent theory on perception and cognition. From the teacher's viewpoint, it can add excitement and effective teaching to education, yet the time investment required of the teacher is minimal, and there are no costs other than the textbook.

The method is not a panacea for reading problems. No such magic exists. However, it is a practical method usable with all children at preschool and K-6 levels, with exceptional children, and with students in adult basic education.

Materials on Teaching Reading Using
Total Communication

I. Free materials describing in general terms the method and its rationale:

   A. *The Sign Language of the Deaf and Reading-Language Development,* McCay Vernon, Joan Coley, THE *READING TEACHER, Vol. 32, #3.*

   B. *Programs, Materials, and Techniques,* McCay Vernon, Joan Coley, and Jan Hafer DuBois, JOURNAL OF *LEARNING DISABILITIES, Vol. 13, # 4, April 1980.*

   C. *The Use of Sign Language in the Reading-Language Development Process,* McCay Vernon, Joan Coley, and Paula Ottinger, SIGN LANGUAGE STUDIES (1979), *89-94, Vol. 22, Linstok Press, Inc.*

   All of the above are available free from McCay Vernon, Psychology Department, Western Maryland College, Westminster, Maryland 21157.

II. The basic text on the Total Communication Method which includes over 50 clearly described complete lesson plans, reproducible student sheets for classroom use, and instructions on how to adapt the method to any elemental level, K-6, or preschool program is now available (see address below).

   The research and theory involved in the method are covered along with its use with learning disabled children and all exceptionalities.

   The Language Arts Handbook: A Total Communication Approach. Greenberg, J.C., Vernon, M., DuBois, J.H., and McKnight, J.C. Published 1982 by University Park Press, 300 N. Charles Street, Baltimore, Maryland. Price $19.95.

REFERENCES

Abbott, C. "Encodedness and Sign Language." *Sign Language Studies*, Vol. 7 (1975), pp. 109-20.

Abrams, J.C. Neurological and Psychological Influence on Reading. In H.K. Smith (Ed.) Perception and Reading. Proceedings of the International Reading Association. 12.4, 1968, 63-67.

Asher, J.J., J.A. Kusudo, and R. de la Torre, "Learning a Second Language Through Commands: The Second Field Test." *Modern Language Journal*, Vol. 58 (1974), pp. 24-32.

Asher, J.J. and B.S. Price. "The Learning Strategy of the Total Physical Response: Some Age Differences." *Child Development,* Vol. 38 (1967), pp. 1219-27.

Balik, S., Spiegel, D., Greene, G., "Mime in Language Therapy and Clinical Training." *Archives of Physical Medicine and Rehabilitation.* 1976, 57, 35-38.

Cantforth, T.E. and Rimpan, J.B. "Sign Language Studies with Children and Chimpanzees." *Sign Language Studies,* 1982, *34,* 17-72.

Charuk, J.M., The Effects of Visual-haptic Training on Reading Achievement. Dissertation Abstracts International, 1974, *34,* 9, 5707A.

Chen, L.C., "Manual Communication by Combined Alphabet and Gestures." *Archives of Physical Medicine and Rehabilitation,* 1971, *52,* 381-384.

Chester, S.L., Egolf, B.D., "Nonverbal Communication in Aphasia Therapy." *Rehabilitation Literature,* 1974, *35,* 231-233.

Creedon, M.F., Language Development in Nonverbal Autistic Children Using a Simultaneous Communication System. Paper presented at the Society for Research in Child Development (Philadelphia, Pa., March 31, 1973). ERIC Document Reproduction Service No. ED 078624.

Duffy, R.J., Duffy, J.R., Pearson, K.L., "Pantomime Recognition in Aphasics." *Journal of Speech and Hearing Research,* 1975, *18,* 115-132.

Fernald, G., *Remedial Techniques in Basic School Subjects.* New York: McGraw-Hill, 1943.

Fristoe, M. and Lloyd, L.L. The Use of Manual Communication with the Retarded. Paper presented at the Gatlinburg Conference on Research in Mental Retardation. Gatlinburg, Tenn., 1977.

Gardner, B.T., and Gardner, R.A. "Evidence for Sentence Constituents in the Early Utterances of Child and Chimpanzee." *Journal of Experimental Psychology General,* 1975, *104,* 244-267.

Glass, A.M., Gazzaniga and D. Premak. "Artificial Language Training in Global Aphasics." *Neuropsychologia,* Vol. 11 (1973), pp. 95-103.

Goodglass, H. and E. Kaplan. "Disturbances of Gesture and Pantomime in Aphasia." *Brain,* Vol. 86 (1965), pp. 702-20.

Greenberg, J.C., Vernon, M., Dubois, J.H., and McKnight, J.C. *The Language Arts Handbook: A Total Communication Approach.* Baltimore, Md: University Park Press, 1982, p. 147.

Hamanaka, T., Ohashi, H., "Aphasia in Pantomimic Sign Language," *Studia Phonologica,* 1974, *8,* 23-35.

Hofsteater, H.T. *An Experiment in Preschool Education.* Bulletin #3, Vol. 8. Washington, D.C.: Gallaudet College, 1959.

Jacobs, J.A. "The Relation of Written Words to Signs, the Same as Their Relation to Spoken Words." *American Annals of the Deaf and Dumb,* Vol. 11, No. 2 (1859), pp. 65-78.

Kannapell, B. "Bilingualism: A New Direction in the Education of the Deaf." *The Deaf American,* Vol. 26, No. 10 (1974), pp. 9-15.

Kimura, D. "The Assymmetry of the Human Brain." *Scientific American,* Vol. 228 (1973), pp. 70-78.

Lane, H. *The Wild Boy of Aveyron.* Cambridge, Mass.

Klima, E. and Bellugi, U. *The Signs of Language.* Cambridge, Mass: Harvard University Press, 1979.

Markowicz, H., Aphasia and Deafness. *Sign Language Studies,* 1973, *3,* 61-72.

Mayberry, R. "If a Chimp Can Learn Sign Language, Surely My Non-Verbal Client Can Too." *ASHA,* 1976, *18,* 223-28.

Meadow, K.P., "Early Manual Communication in Relation to the Deaf Child's Intellectual, Social and Communicative Function," *American Annals of the Deaf,* Vol. 113 (1968), pp. 29-41.

Mindel, E.G., Vernon, M., *The Grow in Silence.* Silver Spring, Md.: National Association of the Deaf, 1972, 225.

Myers, C.A., "Reviewing the Literature on Fernald's Techniques of Remedial Reading," *Reading Teachers,* 1978, *31,* 6, 614.

Offir, C.W., "Their Fingers Do the Talking," *Psychology Today,* Vol. 10 (1976), pp. 73-78.

Premak, D., "Language in Chimpanzee," *Science,* 1971, *172,* 808-822.

Reed, J., "Aphasia and Language Function in the Deaf," *American Annals of the Deaf,* Vol. 116 (1971), pp. 420-26.

Segel, E.C., "Improving Perception through the Haptic Process," *Academic Therapy,* 1974, *9,* 419-431.

Skelly, M., Shinsky, L., Smith, W.S., Donaldson, R.C., Griffin, J.M., *Archives of Physical Medicine and Rehabilitation,* 1975, *56,* 156-160.

Vernon, M., *Multiple Handicapped Deaf Children: Medical and Educational and Psychological Considerations.* Reston, Va. Council of Exceptional Children, 1969, 121.

Vernon, M. and Coley, J.D. "The Sign Language of the Deaf and Reading-Language Development." *The Reading Teacher.* 1978, *32,* 297.

Vernon, M., Coley, J.D., and DuBois, J. "Use of Sign Language with Hearing Students Having Severe Reading Problems." *Journal of Learning Disabilities,* 1980, *13,* 4, 46-51.

Vernon, M., Coley, J., and Ottinger, P. "The Use of Sign Language in the Reading Language Development Process." *Sign Language Studies,* 1979, *22,* 89-94.

Vernon, M., and Koh, S.D. "Early Manual Communication and Deaf Children's Achievement," *American Annals of the Deaf,* Vol. 115 (1970), pp. 527-36.

Vernon, M., and Koh, S.D. "Effects of Oral Preschool Compared to Early Manual Communication on Education and Communication in Deaf Children," *American Annals of the Deaf,* Vol. 116 (1971), pp. 569-74.

Zhon, Y. "The Chinese Finger-Alphabet and the Chinese Finger-Syllabary," *Sign Language Studies,* 1980, *28,* 209-216.

Spelling, Language Experience and the Learning Disabled

Michael James

This critique will summarize the development of children's orthography by posing four questions. First, what attempts have been made to understand the problems associated with spelling competence? Second, what are the spelling strategies typically observed in young children, and can these strategies be applied to the learning disabled speller? Third, in the field of learning disabilities, what has been discovered regarding the development of orthographic competence, and finally, is there a place for this research in the classroom?

Until recently, linguists viewed English orthography as a distorted mirror image of speech. Teaching and learning were, as a consequence, seen as engaging the rote skills in an effort to counteract the seeming randomness in the construction of words. As Richard Hodges has put it, spelling has been considered "an erratic artifact of its historical development."(1) As a result, we have come to think of our writing system as an imperfect conglomeration of symbols which have confused and irritated even the most articulate and eminent of scholars, George Bernard Shaw among them. With letters representing more than one sound and sounds being represented by more than one letter, a student could only expect frustration. It was thought that learning to spell depended not only on accuracy of pronunciation, but upon heavy doses of memorization and perception training. A word mispronounced would undoubtedly be misspelled, and a word not memorized, in all likelihood, would be soon forgotten.(2)

Throughout the present century, emphasis in spelling research has been upon determining the most efficient means of achieving competence through memorization and drill. James Mendenhall provides us with a rich example of what we now see as an inordinate concern for the relatively unimportant surface patterns of English orthography. In *An Analysis of Spelling Errors*,(3) Mendenhall asserted that problems in spelling could be solved if certain bothersome questions could be answered. For example, he asked, is there a particular "hard spot" in a word and, if so, where is it located? What letters are most frequently associated with error, and how does one cope with the significance of pronunciation in spelling?

It was not until the advent of the computer that spelling research began to undergo significant change. In 1966, a Stanford University research team headed by Paul Hanna began a most ambitious task. Entitled Project 1991,(4) the Hanna group undertook an analysis of the letter-sound relationships within some 17,000 different words with the objective of determining "once and for all" the alphabetic nature of the English language. Directing the computer to apply over 300 graphemic-phonemic rules generated from that massive list, the Stanford group devised a computer program to "spell" the 17,000 word bank.

The result of the first application of rules produced 8,000 correctly spelled words, or nearly half the total. This seemingly remarkable result has, as one might expect, been hailed by spelling reformers as proof that the English writing system needs to be retooled; after all, there were some 9,000 misspelled words left over. Interestingly, nearly 37 percent of those 9,000 remaining words contained only one error. Nearly all of the "errors" were the result of an *insufficient computer program*, not because English is essentially a chaotic system of writing. Any evaluation of the Stanford Project must consequently be based on the final result of the computer's effort; nearly 15,000 of the 17,000 words would have been spelled correctly had the program contained provisions for higher order phonological analysis as well as those accounting for scribal idiosyncracies.

Within the last decade, Noam Chomsky's conceptions of transformational grammar have provided a theoretical background for some ideas on how children acquire the psycholinguistic abilities needed to spell. To define how we use language, the Chomskian hypothesis stresses not the relationship found in the surface patterns of English but something called the lexical representation.(5) This abstract level can be thought of as a linguistic data bank. The generative-transformational theory, overly simply stated perhaps, postulates that each of us has the facility to generate language guided by generalizations drawn quite intuitively from this lexical data bank. Instead of being comprised of single words stacked one upon the other as language theories held for so long, transformational grammarians believe we store only what is needed, sets of linguistic data.

Then, when called upon, there is derived from these sets what we observe as the surface patterns of language: words presented as meaningful units. Each of us, therefore, can be seen to possess a storehouse full of language rules through which we make our linguistic selves known. This data bank allows us, as language users, to generate linguistic decisions governing the production of "correct" language, such as stress and vowel alternation, at very nearly automatic rates.(6) If Chomsky's conception of a lexical data bank is valid, then acquiring the skills of written language might best be facilitated through processes which emphasize learning to generalize, as evidence increasingly suggests we do in learning to speak, rather than through methods that stress learning through memorization.

Chomsky's theories of how children acquire and use language have led researchers to formulate a new model of the spelling process. Instead of children being *taught how to spell,* recent studies in linguistics and Piagetian developmental psychology offer us evidence that *children will develop, quite intuitively,* efficient spelling strategies as a consequence of attempting to spell as they undergo various experiences in writing their first language. As these experiences grow, so do spelling skills. In light of these findings, spelling has come to be understood as a highly complex, *evoked* intellectual process,(7) quite a different view from the popular perception of it as a relatively low level activity in which skill is believed to result primarily through memorization and imitation.

One of the first studies initiated to validate this developmental model of spelling was conducted by Charles Read during a series of pre-school observations near Boston. (8) Among the data collected by Read was information suggesting that young children's spelling is both abstract yet systematic in character. Read observed that young writers first rely on a letter-name strategy in which they substitute the closest sounding letter name for a medial short vowel, i.e., MAT is spelled for met and top is spelled as TIP. What may seem confusing and haphazard to adults is, to a child, quite clear; the first sound heard in articulating the long *i* is nearest the sound heard for *o* in hot or *u* in cup.(9) Read's observations were not isolated examples. Carol Chomsky found youngsters writing stories only they could read. From her observations, Chomsky believes that children should begin their journey with print through writing.(10)

Along similar lines, a small group of researchers, among them Edmund Henderson from Virginia and James Beers from

William and Mary College, have studied older children as well as the dialectically different child,(11) to determine how they acquire spelling skills. They believe, as do Charles Read and Carol Chomsky, that young children invent words based on a strict "child" interpretation of phonology; indeed, Henderson calls these young writers "super phoneticans."(12) They have found that children invent similar letter patterns for similar sound patterns; in other words, how 6-year-old Bobby "invents" a word as he attempts its spelling will often be similar to how 6-year-old Sara spells the same word in her writing.

Henderson and Beers, extending Read's original research, followed first and second graders through experiences with "creative writing."(13) They observed that children gradually refine their invented spellings, moving toward increasing competence in understanding and using conventional orthography, only falling back to earlier spelling strategies when new vocabulary is encountered.

From their studies, Henderson and Beers concluded that learning to spell is a developmental phenomenon which passes through at least four stages of refinement. The initial phase of learning to spell is born out of every child's natural interest in "writing" about his environment. This pre-phonetic/pre-literate stage encompasses the 3rd and 4th year, when children, not having any permanence with written language, "spell" with scribbles, ABC blocks, letters and numbers.(14)

The second phase in orthographic development, beginning usually in the 4th year, emerges as youngsters begin to acquire some knowledge of the letter-sound system. Often during this time, children will use single letters to represent words. Writing samples may, for example, show the letter D being used to represent the word *dog*, or the letter K being used to "spell" the word *car*. Sometime during late kindergarten or early first grade, and depending on the amount of exposure to printed language, the child passes into a vowel transition stage. During this stage, children exhibit a remarkable ability to manipulate the language to meet their ever-growing spelling needs. Sight vocabulary is usually written correctly, but word inventions demonstrate extremely complex representations. First grade writing samples show what appears to be a disregard for the nasal sounds, m and n. A five- or six-year-old writer may spell KADE for candy or write GOWIG for going.(15) It is the articulation position of the consonant, however, that follows the nasal sounds that accurately predict for the child when m and n will be omitted. Youngsters do not ignore the nasals; they simply do not "hear" them.

For the young writer, spelling accuracy increases as his experience with written language increases. The next level is a transitional one, and it is closest yet to the conventional orthography of adults. A seven- or eight-year-old might spell table as TABL or house as HOUS. As with oral language, experimentation with higher order phonological rules leads to over-generalizations in which bike is written as BIEK, or "kind of" is spelled as CINEDOVE. The concluding phases, less distinct and taking place over the next few years, leads to a considerable command of conventional orthography.

Studies of children's orthographic development demonstrate that spelling competence is largely the by-product of increasing linguistic maturation, not the primary consequence of low-order, psycho-motor skill development. Read, Henderson, and Beers underscore one particular concept in this regard: a child's interpretation of phonological information is abstract and extremely complex; to enlarge and extend his growing awareness of written language does not depend or result from providing lists of words to memorize. Spelling success, drill, and habits are not necessarily synonymous.(16)

The learning disabled speller

The research cited so far has dealt exclusively with a "typical" population of learners; some of Read's subjects were extremely bright, highly gifted youngsters.(17) What, then, can be applied to the learning disabled speller?

Until last year, research with the learning disabled speller centered around identification and remediation: when, where, and how do I intervene for optimal success? Remediation treatments for years have been built on neurological assumptions derived from a medical model of learning disabilities. Elena Boder's Diagnostic Screening Procedure is one such attempt, based on results from spelling tests, to classify dyslexics into deficit groups.(18) However, if we understand recent linguistic inquiries as suggestive of the developmental nature of word knowledge, then Boder's definition of dyslexia based on an equation derived from a spelling test misses the mark.

Recently, two studies have been reported which depart from the familiar position taken so far by spelling researchers in special education. In a longitudinal study using secondary sources, Louisa Cook analyzed the spelling abilities of 15 learning disabled students.(19) From her data, Cook believes learning disabled children lack what she calls the "cognitive-linguistic" maturity of their younger, normally achieving school peers. In her analysis of the Wide Range Achievement Test (spelling sub-test) over a period of four years, Cook found most students displayed an emerging awareness of conventional orthography. She infers from these data that developing strategy shifts can be utilized to measure the effectiveness of language instruction.

In a series of studies and interviews focusing on the linguistic development of learning disabled children, M. Gerber of U.C. Santa Barbara and his colleague, R.J. Hall, report learning disabled spellers, in many cases, are deficient in "cognitive flexibility" as they struggle to encode the language. What is of particular interest here are their findings regarding the learning disabled child's *perceptions* of the spelling process:(20)

1. When questions arose regarding personal goals and limitations, as well as what was considered conducive to a successful spelling environment, most of the children believed books in the home and encouragement to study greatly affected spelling ability.

2. Although learning disabled children perceived the importance of books and encouragement, they seemed to view spelling ability from a single perspective, whereas their normally achieving peers interpreted spelling ability from many perspectives.

3. When questioned about personal preferences regarding self-selection versus teacher-selection of spelling words, every learning disabled child, except one, felt they would do better if they could select their own spelling words. Words would be easier to learn and easier to remember.

It has been my own experience that preferences for self-selection arise from a child's mode of instruction. Teachers have insisted their preference for teaching in the study of language is best for the student. Seldom have students been given the opportunity to make curricular decisions.

Conclusion

Teachers ask, as they should, from all this research what can be used in the classroom? Let me offer the following ideas.

First, classrooms should be places in which children are encouraged to explore the utility of their language. An instructional system that dictates to children that they parrot adult language is disrespectful of a child's natural curiosity and developmental characteristics.

Second, teachers need to become aware of the developmental spelling strategies employed by their students. The ability accurately to analyze a student's writing and then make the necessary pedagogical decisions is of critical importance.

Third, teachers should refrain from asking children to "sound it out." This may sound heretical, yet the research indicates that children should not be confused by asking them to sound out a word when they have already done so. Suggestions should be offered as alternatives.(21)

Fourth, alternatives might include student designed lists of words taken from their stories and then categorized according to any number of themes, sounds, structures, or subjects. Language experience classrooms should have little visible wall space; they should be covered with words, stories, and pictures. It has been my experience that, as children create language, their ability to use language will increase tremendously.

Fifth, it is important to remember that all individuals are idiosyncratic learners. We are in different places at different times. Thus, learning must be individualized, and the bulk of our teaching should start with what our students produce with their writing. Simply stated, teachers need to teach from what students write, dictate, or draw.

Finally, all of these opinions offered as suggestions are only possible when it is understood that every language has a richness deserving of respect. Only by being surrounded with the literary successes of many civilizations can we ever hope to achieve literacy with our children.

REFERENCES

1 Hodges, R., "Research Update: On the Development of Spelling Ability," *Language Arts*, Vol. 59, No. 3, March, 1982, p. 285.

2 Furness, E., "Mispronunciations, Mistakes, and Method in Spelling," *Elementary English*, Vol. 33, No. 4, October, 1956, pp. 508-511.

3 Mendenhall, J., *An Analysis of Spelling Errors* (Teachers College, Columbia, N.Y., 1930).

4 Hanna, P., Hanna, J., Hodges, R., and Rudorf, E., "Phoneme-Grapheme Correspondence as Cues to Spelling Improvement," *U.S. Government Printing Office* (U.S. Office of Education, Washington, D.C., 1966). The title "Project 1991" came from the number assigned by the U.S.O.E.

5 Chomsky, N., "Phonology and Reading" in *Basic Studies on Reading*, Levin, H., and Williams, J., ed. (Basic Books, N.Y., 1970).

6 Chomsky, C., "Reading, Writing, and Phonology," *Harvard Educational Review*, Vol. 40, No. 2, May, 1970, pp. 197-219.

7 Hodges, R., *Learning to Spell* (ERIC Clearinghouse on Reading and Communication Skills and the National Council of Teachers of English, Urbana, Illinois, 1981).

8 Read, C., "Pre-School Children's Knowledge of English Phonology," *Harvard Educational Review*, Vol. 41, No. 1, February, 1971, pp. 1-34.

9 Beers, J., Henderson, E., "First Grade Children's Developing Orthographic Concepts," *Research in the Teaching of English*, Vol. 2, No. 2, Fall, 1977, p. 133.

10 Chomsky, C., "Invented Spelling in the Open Classroom," *Word*, Vol. 27, No. 3, Fall, 1975, pp. 499-517.

11 Stever, E., "Dialect and Spelling," in Henderson, E., Beers, J., ed., *Developmental and Cognitive Aspects of Learning to Spelling: A Reflection of Word Knowledge* (International Reading Association, Delaware, 1982), pp. 46-51.

12 Henderson, E., "Word Knowledge and Reading Disability," in Henderson, E., Beers, J., ed., *Developmental and Cognitive Aspects of Learning to Spell*, p. 140.

13 Beers, J., Henderson, E., "First Grade Children's Developing Orthographic Concepts," p. 141.

14 Read, C., "Pre-School Children's Knowledge of English Phonology," p. 3.

15 Beers, J., Henderson, E., "First Grade Children's Developing Orthographic Concepts," p. 139. Goodman, Y., "The Roots of Literacy" in Douglass, M., ed., *The Claremont Reading Conference Yearbook, 1980* (Claremont Colleges, Claremont, California, 1980) pp. 21-23.

16 *Op. Cit.,* p. 33.

17 *Ibid.,* p. 31.

18 Boder, E., "Developmental Dyslexia: A Diagnostic Screening Procedure Based on Three Characteristic Patterns of Reading and Spelling," in Douglass, M., ed., *The Claremont Reading Conference Yearbook, 1968* (Claremont Colleges, Claremont, California, 1968) pp. 173-187.

19 Cook, L., "Misspelling Analysis in Dyslexia: Observations of Developmental Strategy Shifts," *Bulletin of the Orton Society*, Vol. 31, 1981.

20 Gerber, M., Hall, R.J., *Development of Spelling in Learning Disabled and Normally Achieving Students* (Society for Learning Disabilities and Remedial Education, Austin, Texas, in press).

21 See the following articles for additional suggestions: Gentry, J., Henderson, E., "Three Steps to Teaching Beginning Readers to Spell," *The Reading Teacher*, March, 1981, pp. 632-637; Gentry, J., "Learning to Spell Developmentally," *The Reading Teacher*, January, 1981, pp. 378-381; Templeton, S., "Spelling First, Sound Later: The Relationship Between Orthographic and High Order Phonological Knowledge in Older Students," *Research in the Teaching of English*, Vol. 13, No. 3, October, 1979, pp. 255-264; and Zutell, J., "Some Psycholinguistic Perspectives on Children's Spelling," *Language Arts*, Vol. 55, No. 7, October, 1978.

Oral and Written Language Differences and Becoming Literate

Herbert D. Simons and *Sandra Murphy*

The beginning stages of learning to read in school have been and continue to be the subject of intense interest and controversy. Part of this controversy has to do with the relationship between the language skills children already possess when they come to school and the language skills they have to acquire. The focus of attention in teaching reading has shifted back and forth over the years from emphasizing new language skills (while more or less ignoring old skills) to emphasizing old skills and deemphasizing new ones. The decoding-meaning debate can be looked at in these terms, because decoding proponents emphasize the acquisition of new skills, while meaning proponents focus on the language skills children have already acquired.

Participants in the debate have tended to assume that learning to decode is the major task facing children who are learning to read, that oral and written language differ only in mode, and that translating print to speech is the major task facing beginning readers. However, recent work in linguistics has focused on a number of ways that oral and written language differ other than in mode. This suggests that there are other new skills to be learned beyond decoding in order to master printed language. The acquisition of these new language skills requires a shift from oral language based strategies to written language strategies. In the remainder of this paper we would like to discuss two of the major differences between oral and written language, the new demands they make on beginning readers, and the problems these demands create.

Oral and written language differences

Oral and written language typically differ along a number of dimensions (Rubin, 1978; Schallert, Klieman, and Rubin, 1977). They differ in function, vocabulary, syntax, cohesion, dependence upon the situation, use of multiple channels, amount of feedback, and amount of shared background information. These differences are matters of degree, and their prominence depends upon the language activity under consideration. The language activities that show the greatest contrasts are face-to-face conversations between people who know each other well and written academic prose. Other oral and written language activities fall somewhere between these two extremes with respect to the features mentioned above.

These differences can be traced in large part to differences in the situations in which they are produced. In typical oral language activities participants share the same temporal and spatial situation. This state of affairs has several important consequences. First, reference can be made directly to the temporal and spatial context. Second, in oral language the communication is sent over several channels. Prosodic and nonverbal channels are used in addition to the lexical channel. Thus, tone of voice and gestures, etc. can be used to convey the speaker's message. Third, oral conversation is characterized by turn taking and feedback. This results in shorter stretches of discourse, shifting topics, and more assumed information which must be filled in by the listener.

In contrast, in the typical written language situation the reader and writer do not share the same temporal and spatial situation and usually do not even know one another. The audience is generalized, and the communication is typically not anchored to a specific time and place. As a result, there is less motivation for the characteristics of spoken language mentioned above. Reference is rarely made to the situation. Instead, it is generally confined to the text through the use of coreferential relationships. The communication is limited to the lexical channel. Nonverbal or gestural information cannot be used, and prosodic information is minimal apart from that supplied by punctuation. There are no turns or immediate feedback, shared background knowledge cannot be assumed, and feedback on omitted information cannot be provided. This results in longer stretches of discourse with less frequent topic shifts. More information is explicitly provided in words and less is carried by the situation and shared knowledge.

Because of this difference in dependence upon the situation, oral language can be thought of as situation dependent and written language can be thought of as text dependent (Smith, 1982). This terminology will be adopted here. In this paper we

will focus on two related aspects of the differences between
written and spoken language discussed above, the use of
situation-dependent language and the assumption of shared
knowledge. We will provide some examples and evidence of the
effects that these aspects of language use have on learning to
read. The data come from an ethnographic study of a first grade
classroom (Gumperz and Simons, 1981) and from an
experimental study of second grade students (Murphy, 1983).

The shift from situation-dependent to text-dependent language

One consequence of the situational differences between
written and spoken language is that in oral communication words
may be used to refer to participants and objects in the situation.
This type of reference is called exophoric reference (Halliday and
Hasan, 1976). Exophoric reference signals the listener or reader
that the information is to be retrieved from the situational
context. For example, if in a conversation the speaker says:
"Will you please put the cheese over there," the interpretation of
"you" and "there" depends upon knowing or being present in the
situation in which the utterance occurs. "You" and "there" are
being used exophorically. On the other hand, in the sentence,
"Johnny walked over to the table, and he put the cheese on it,"
the words "it" and "he" are used endophorically in that "he" is
coreferential with "Johnny" and "it" is coreferential with the
table. Endophoric reference signals the reader that the
information is to be retrieved from the text itself. Exophoric
reference is more characteristic of spoken language while
endophoric reference is more characteristic of written language.

Many exophoric words are also deictic in that they must be
interpreted in relation to a particular time, location, or speaker
(Fillmore, 1975). In the first example above, "you" and "there"
are deictic, because they must be interpreted from the point of
view of the speaker. Deictic terms must be anchored in the text
in written language, because the receiver of the message is
separated in time and space from the sender. Fillmore's (1975)
well known example in which a note is found in a bottle floating
in a river shows what happens when deictic terms are not
properly anchored. The note reads, "Meet me here tomorrow
with a stick about this big." "Me," "here," "tomorrow," and
"this" must be interpreted from the point of view of the speaker
and the situation in which the message was encoded in order for
it to be understood, but this is impossible because the producer
and receiver of the message are separated in time and space.

Deictic terms are used differently in written language than in
spoken language. Information about the situation must be
provided in the text, and, they must be interpreted from the
perspective of the writer or the speaker indicated by the text. The
deictic categories include pronominal (May *I* ride *your* bike?);
temporal (Give it to me *now*.); and spatial aspects of meaning
(Put it *there*., Give me *that*.). Certain motion verbs (e.g. come,
go) contain all three components (e.g. person, place, and time).

   One problem for children learning to read is learning how to
interpret such terms when they are used endophorically and
without the situational cues which are present in oral language
situations. Children, whose language background is essentially
oral and who have come to depend upon situational cues for
interpreting oral communication, must give up this dependence
and create an imaginary context to interpret exophoric as well as
endophoric forms. For example, in the sentence, "She said, 'He
liked it here'," the child must learn to interpret "here" as
referring to the location of "She" rather than to the location of
"he" or the writer of the sentence.

   This problem arises in the texts children encounter when
they begin to learn to read. The following examples from primary
grade texts include deictic terms which must be interpreted
without the support of a real world situational context. They must
be interpreted from the perspective of the character identified in
the text.

> But wait! Someone was *there*! 'That's just the old baby,'
> thought Nicky. But no! it was just the baby. Butch was
> *there*, too. (Anastasio, Smith and Wardhaugh, 1975)

The proximal-distal contrast which underlies the distinction
between "here" and "there," must be interpreted in relation to
Nicky, the main character of the story. "There" refers not only
to the location of the baby and Butch, but to a place other than
where Nicky is at that moment in the narrative.

> Sally said to Jill, '*Come* to *my* house *tomorrow*.' (Rubin,
> 1978)

When reading this passage, the child must realize that "my"
refers to Sally, that "tomorrow" refers to the day after the
utterance is produced, that "come" indicates that Sally will be at
home the next day, and that Jill will come from some location
other than Sally's house. The deictic words "come," "my," and
"tomorrow" must be interpreted in relation to Sally and to the

hypothetical "moment" she utters the invitation in the context of the narrative.

In the examples above, the reader must interpret the deictic terms from the perspective of a character introduced into the text rather than from his own physical perspective. He must create an imaginary context and interpret the text in terms of that context. The precise mechanisms by which such words create problems for beginning readers is not totally clear. In some cases they may misinterpret deictic terms and actually misunderstand the text (Murphy, 1983). In addition, the process of creating contexts to anchor these terms may add extra processing time and effort to the reading process and thus slow reading progress for some readers. One would expect individual differences in children's ability to adapt their oral language strategies with respect to deictic processing to written language, and that these individual differences would translate into differences in reading achievement. Thus children's ability to suspend their dependence on the physical context in oral language use should act as a predictor of their ability to do this in reading written language which, in turn, should predict their reading achievement.

One way to test this line of reasoning is to give children a task in which the production of situation-dependent language is inappropriate and to see if individual differences in ability to suppress situation-dependent language are related to reading skill. The task chosen was a modified referential communication task (Krauss and Glucksberg, 1969). In this task, children were asked to describe nine abstract geometric figures so that a classmate who was not present could at some later time pick out each of the figures from listening to a tape recording of their descriptions. In this task, referring to the physical situation with unanchored deictic terms such as "this," "that," "here," and "there" would be inappropriate, because the listener doesn't share the situational context with the speaker. Despite the inappropriateness of exophoric reference to the physical context, subjects produced descriptions like the following:

1. *This* one just looks like a uh something right *here*, like *this* part right *here,* looks like a key.
2. It . . . it's round and it curves right to *here*, goes down and like *that* . . . and it comes back like *that*, sort of straight.
3. *That* look like part of a . . . right *here*. *These* look like two fingers. *That* look like a vase, like you put water in *there*.

In these examples, the use of the deictic words "here," "there," "this," and "that" is inappropriate, because the listener in this task does not share the speaker's physical context. There were large individual differences in the production of these terms. We correlated the number of such terms produced, adjusted for the number of clauses produced, and found a significant negative correlation with reading achievement as measured by a standardized reading comprehension test ($r = -.39$, $p > .01 < .05$). Higher proportions of deictic references were associated with poorer reading skill. The children who were most dependent upon the use of the situation to anchor their descriptions were the poorer readers. This supports the notion that the shift from situation-dependent oral language to text-dependent written language causes problems for some children and affects their reading skill.

The inability of some children to adjust their oral language strategies to produce language that is independent of the language strategies to produce language that is independent of the situation indicates that they may have trouble with deictic terms when learning to read written text where there is no situational context to anchor such terms. However, the communication task evidence is indirect in nature, and there may be other explanations for the correlation other than the hypothesized one. What direct evidence is there that children have trouble creating a context for the interpretation of deictic terms when they appear in written text? They are, after all, exposed to endophoric uses of these terms in oral language when they listen to narration, and they may not present a problem when they are encountered in written text.

More direct evidence for the problem is provided by a study conducted by one of the authors of this paper (Murphy, 1983). She studied second grade children's comprehension of deictic terms in oral and written tasks. Children were given deictic terms embedded in oral and written discourse and asked to interpret them. In the oral discourse the deictic terms were anchored in the physical context, while in the written discourse they were not. She studied pronouns, verbs of motion, and demonstratives. A sample written text from the last category follows:

> Tina, Suzie, and Patty sit down at a table.
> Everyone has a bag.
> A penny is in one of the bags.
> 'Suzie,' says Patty.
> 'Get the penny in the bag *here*.'

Children were asked who had the penny. In order to answer the question correctly, a student must interpret the deictic word "here" correctly. In the written text, the deictic word must be interpreted in terms of the situation described in the text. The interpretation of the word is thus text dependent. This same task was given to the children orally. The same physical situation was set up, the participants spoke the same words, and the same question was asked. In the oral task, the terms were used exophorically, and they were anchored in the physical context. The interpretation of the word "here" depended upon the physical arrangement of the participants. In the oral task, the children could use the situation to interpret the discourse. In the written task, they had to shift from situation-dependent to text-dependent strategies. Murphy found that the written task was significantly harder than the oral task and that performance on both tasks correlated with reading achievement. The absolute level of performance showed that interpreting these terms was a problem for many second grade children. This finding provides more direct evidence of the problems children encounter when shifting from oral situation-dependent language to written text-dependent language and supports the findings of the communication task study.

The shift away from situation-dependent language is part of the more general problem of how much knowledge the sender of the message assumes that the receiver of the message has. Assumed knowledge doesn't have to be explicitly stated, while new knowledge must be included in the message. Thus the sender has to judge how much to say and how much can be left unsaid. As mentioned above, oral and written messages differ in this respect. In most oral situations, the fact that the participants may know each other, share the same physical context, and provide feedback which allows the message to be adjusted, means that in oral language more information can be assumed. In written language where these conditions do not pertain, the audience is often unknown and generalized. Thus the writer cannot assume as much information and must be more explicit while avoiding redundancy. This creates problems in the beginning stages of learning to write and requires a shift in language use strategies. This can be seen in the modified referential communication task described above in which the use of exophoric reference reveals the mistaken assumption that the physical situation is somehow shared. The amount of assumed knowledge has been misjudged. This sort of misjudgment also appears in another task administered to the subjects of our study. This task, the pear narrative (Chafe, 1980), requires the subjects

to recount the contents of a short film involving the stealing of
some pears to a listener who has not seen the film. Thus the
content of the film is not shared by speaker and listener, and it is
inappropriate to make the assumption that it is. However, some
children appear to assume it is, and treat parts of the film as
given information, using the definite article and other forms of
definite reference to signal that the information is shared, as can
be seen in the following examples:

> *the* lamb
> and *the* lamb has . . . ate one apple
> So then . . . um . . . this boy came
> and . . . stopped by *the* tree
> and the man wasn't looking
> *the* whole basket
> and he took *the* whole basket

Although the pragmatic schemas associated with picking
apples allow a listener to infer that "the tree" must be the one in
which the man is picking "apples," and that "the basket"
probably contains "apples," it requires extra inferencing to do so.
The lamb, however, has no part in schemas associated with
apples or picking them, and the use of the definite article is in
effect a discourse miscue. Since the listener had not seen the
film, it misdirects the listener to either look to the previous text
for information about the referent or to expect elaboration to
establish identification.

Besides using the definite article, the children also use other
forms for definite reference, which occasionally results in
sequences which are uninterpretable for persons who have not
seen the film and which are difficult to understand for persons
who have. For example:

> and these other three boys
> they was waiting for *him*
> they was makin *him* do *it*
> just cause
> with *that* thing

The numerous instances of repair strategies in the children's
protocols, in which they backtrack to fill in necessary information
they have omitted, suggest that some of them may be having
difficulty coordinating the sequencing of events to be recalled
with the demands of signalling information in a text-dependent
task, i.e., a task that is not supported by a shared experience
between speaker and listener. Not all instances of omitted

information are repaired, however, and their use of definite reference suggests that at times they may be relying on direct reference to knowledge of a shared experience as a strategy.

The problem of assuming too much shared information, and consequently not providing anchoring in the text, shows up in children's performance with written language as well. Unanchored expressions, exophoric reference, and the treatment of new information as given can be found in first grade children's writing, as can be seen in the following examples of the children's short diary entries:

    1) We had a good time today.
    2) I like the monkey, and the rabbit and the skeleton.

In the first example the reader isn't provided with any information to identify the "we" or the day referred to as "today." In addition, the nature of the activity which provided the good time is left unspecified. A more successful entry is provided by another student. "I played on the swing with David." In the second example above, the use of the definite article indicates that the writer has assumed that the reader shares knowledge of the monkey, the rabbit, and the skeleton.

The problem of deciding how much knowledge to assume on the part of the receiver of the message with respect to shared information and reference to the context shows up in various production and reception tasks. The problems arise because the language strategies used to accomplish these ends differ between written and spoken language. There are still other aspects of the shift in strategies that have to do with giving up a dependence upon prosodic cues to chunk the discourse and signal given and new information and the necessity of producing a coherent sustained discourse. The problem of giving up a dependence upon prosody shows up in children's oral reading where intonation and stress anomalies and failure to observe punctuation conventions occur. The problems with producing sustained coherent discourse show up in oral and written productions and recall after reading. These other problems have been discussed elsewhere (Simons and Murphy, in press).

Learning written language use strategies

The question now arises as to how children learn to make the transition to text-dependent language. Conclusive statements about activities which may facilitate this transition must of course await more research on the manner and pace of this transition, the nature of individual differences, etc. However, we do have some evidence and some speculations about the nature of such activities. In general, reading and writing instruction do not explicitly focus on the issues discussed here, although some of it obviously affects the transition. For example, factual comprehension questions and exact recall activities that focus on information explicitly stated in the text may help children focus on the need for explicitness in text-dependent language. Another activity that has been studied to some degree (Michaels and Cook-Gumperz, 1981) may play a role in this transition. It is the activity known as sharing time or show and tell, where children are required to describe an object or give a narrative account of some past event. Michaels and Cook-Gumperz argue that this activity is implicitly designed to bridge that gap between situation-dependent language and text-dependent language. The teacher's questioning strategies in the classroom studied suggest a text-dependent model; i.e., the teacher appears to be trying to get the children to produce text-dependent written features in their oral discourse as can be seen in the following examples:

1. C: Yesterday, when I came home my mother took me to a store and I bought these.
   T: What are they?
   C: Bells.
   T: Little Jingle Bells.

2. C: Saturday I got a Tom and Jerry game.
   T: How do you play it?
   C: (starts to open game)
   T: Pretend I can't see it.

3. C1: I went to the beach and I found this little thing in the water.
   T: For goodness sake, what is it?
   C2: A block.
   Cs: A block, a block.
   T: A block. When did you go to the beach?

In these examples, the children are using the physical context to anchor the discourse which is perfectly appropriate in an oral situation where all the participants can see the objects being discussed. However, the teacher with her implicit, literate model attempts to have the children anchor their discourse lexically by naming objects and the time and place of the events being described. Sharing may be one activity which helps children to make the transition from oral to written language by shaping their language so that it exhibits written features. However, neither the teacher nor the children are aware of this implicit function of the activity. Moreover, written language features are not always appropriate in an oral language situation. It seems that more explicit recognition of the differences between oral and written language would be helpful so that the school's role in facilitating the transition to literacy could be more systematic and based upon the ease or difficulty with which children are making the transition. It may be helpful to develop reading, writing, and language activities that explicitly focus on several aspects of the transition and systematically train for it. For example, oral language activities which are intermediate between oral and written discourse, such as the referential communication task or talking on the telephone, may be helpful in fostering the transition. The development and sequencing of these activities will require more detailed analyses of classroom literacy and language activities to identify those that focus on the transition. Such activities could then be more explicitly directed to this purpose. In addition, we will need to study activities that prepare children to make the transition. Some of these activities could then be incorporated into the classroom in preschool and the primary grades and used as a basis for advice to parents on preparing their children for success in school. In general, we need to identify activities that explicitly help children make this transition and use them as part of literacy instruction.

BIBLIOGRAPHY

Anastasio, D. Smith, C.B. and Wardhaugh, R. *Colors*. Macmillan, 1975.

Chafe, W. The deployment of consciousness. In *The pear stories, vol. III advances in discourse process*, Freedle, R.O. (Ed.). Ablex Publishing Corp., Norwood, N.J., 1980.

Fillmore, C.J. *Santa Cruz lectures on deixis*, 1971, University of California, Berkeley. Reproduced by the Indiana University Linguistics Club, November, 1975.

Gumperz, J. and Simons, H. *Language at school and home: A comparative ethnography of children's communication strategies*. Final Report. National Institute of Education, 1981.

Halliday, M.A.K. and Hasan, R. *Cohesion in English*. London: Longman, 1976.

Krauss, R. and Glucksberg, S. The development of communication: competence as a function of age. *Child Development*, 1969, *40*, 255-261.

Michaels, S. and Cook-Gumperz, J. A study of sharing time with first grade students, discourse narratives in the classroom. In Gumperz, J. and Simons, H. (Eds.) *Language at school and home: A comparative ethnography of children's communication strategies.* Final Report. National Institute of Education, 1981.

Murphy, S. Comprehension of Deictic Categories in Oral and Written Language. Unpublished doctoral dissertation, University of California, Berkeley, 1983.

Rubin, A. *A theoretical taxonomy of the differences between oral and written language.* Center for the Study of Reading. Technical Report #3731. University of Illinois at Champaign-Urbana, 1978.

Schallert, D., Kleiman, G. and Rubin, A. *Analyses of differences between written and oral language.* Center for the Study of Reading. Technical Report #29. University of Illinois at Champaign-Urbana, 1977.

Simons, H. and Murphy, S. Spoken language strategies and reading acquisition. In Cook-Gumperz, J. (Ed.) *Language, Literacy and Schooling.* Heinemann Educational Books. (In press.)

Smith, F. *Understanding reading.* New York: Holt, Rinehart and Winston, 1982.

Phonics First, Second, or Not at All

Harry Singer

> All the world's a stage,
> And all the men and women merely players.
> They have their exits and their entrances
> And one man in his time plays many parts . . .
> Shakespeare, *As You Like It*

These Shakespearian lines are an appropriate
introduction, because I am going to tell you about a short play
in two acts that could have occurred on this stage. The first
act, entitled "Phonics First," takes place in a school's
conference room. You have the role of a teacher. Then we
have a long intermission that provides background knowledge,
consisting of a personal anecdote, information on writing systems,
and some research on reading acquisition. You draw on this
information for a long speech delivered with great conviction in
the second and final act, entitled "Phonics First, Second, or Not
at All."

Act I: Phonics First

Your principal has called a meeting to satisfy a federal
requirement for educationally handicapped children. An
individual educational program (IEP) has to be written for one of
your students. The student's parents will be there too. You were
glad you had taken the inservice training course in writing IEP's.
The meeting seems to be going well until it gets to plans for
reading instruction. Then the parents hand you a statement,
which reads, in part:

> We insist that sequential phonics ("phonics first") should
> be used in teaching our child to read and write . . .

While you are still surprised at this demand, the parents explain
that they had read Rudolph Flesch's (1981) book on *Why
Johnny Still Can't Read.* (1, 2) On pp. 147-148, they said
Flesch advised all parents of learning disabled students to copy
the statement he had written and present it at the IEP meeting
which the federal government, under PL 94-142, now requires all

schools to conduct for planning the education of handicapped children.

Intermission

You are not sure how you should reply to the parents, but fortunately you have an intermission to reflect on what has occurred and to think about your reply. You know that the debate over "phonics" versus "whole-word" instruction has been going on for over the past 150 years and has not been resolved. You realize that Flesch recently heated up the debate by conceding that schools teach phonics, but most of them do not start with it. If you read his book, you know that in it Flesch presented no valid evidence that "phonics first" enables all children to read successfully or that "phonics first" results in superior reading achievement for any students. In fact, Flesch did not conduct any research on what effect "phonics first" would have on children's reading development. Nor what effect it would have on reading instruction for educationally handicapped children.

I don't know what reply you'll give to the parents. But I'll tell you what I told the Reading Reform Foundation, one of Flesch's staunch supporters, when I was invited to speak to its annual convention. Perhaps you can use what I said in your reply. The foundation's annual convention was held in Houston on August 14-16, 1981. The motto of this group, which is on the front of its publication, *The Reading Informer*, states: "Our sole aim: To restore intensive phonics to the teaching of reading throughout the nation."

Anecdote on teaching reading

I started my talk with an anecdote on teaching my son to read. It illustrates the main point of my talk. When my son was two years old, I started to read to him at bedtime using the exposure method. I sat next to him so that he could see the book in the proper left-to-right position, learn to turn the pages correctly, look at the pictures as I read, and get exposed to the print. I became familiar with a host of children's authors and their characters, including Berenstain's Bears, Rey's Curious George, and Dr. Seuss's (Geisel's) Aunt Annie's Alligator. As my son's language and curiosity improved, he switched over to the conversational method of learning to read, occasionally asking questions about the story, or the print, and finishing sentences whenever I hesitated. But, remembering the admonishments I had given to parents about letting teachers teach reading and practicing what I preached, I, as a parent, didn't try to teach him to read. When he was about five years old and about to enter kindergarten, I knew he was on the verge of knowing how to read. He could identify many words, but I still desisted from giving him any instruction. Then one evening, his ten-year-old sister who was playing school with her friends, took him into her room to be her student. She taught him how the printed letters could be sounded out. Her instruction was all he needed. He then demonstrated to me that he could now read his books himself. Although I had read to him for three years, to this day his sister takes credit for teaching him to read. She taught him what Philip Gough (1976) refers to as deciphering text, the key for breaking the code. As any cryptographer knows, once you have the key for breaking the code, you can readily apply it throughout the coded message. The key to the code was the alphabetic principle. But to understand how the key can break the code and some limitations in using the key, you have to remember how the alphabetic system developed, changes that have occurred in it over the past 500 years, and the relationship between the English writing and sound system.

Development of the alphabetic writing system

The development of a writing system started with Egyptian hieroglyphics (sacred carvings) in which symbols represented objects. Then a rebus was created in which symbols stood for syllabic sounds. Next, Hebrews modified the writing system by using symbols for consonants, which they wrote from right to left. They later indicated vowels by a system of dots and dashes *under* the consonants. Today the vowels are only used in teaching children to read; they are often not present in adult writing. For example, the Torah, the five books of Moses, does not contain any vowel markings. This omission of vowels saves about 20 percent of writing space, as compared with writing in English. Any ambiguities in reading the words tend to be resolved by the context.

The Greeks adopted the Hebrew consonantal system, invented letters for the vowels, and placed them *next* to the consonants. Their linear consonant and vowel system, which is the ancestor of all alphabetic scripts in use today, was at first written from left to right on one line and right to left on the next line. Eventually, their scribes developed the convention of writing only from left to right.

Thus the English writing system gradually evolved from interactions among the Egyptians, Hebrews, and Greeks. It was further modified and transmitted to us through the Romans who spread it throughout their Empire (Gaeng, 1971).

Non-alphabetic writing systems

The Chinese writing system also started with picture writing but did not progress beyond logographic writing, the use of characters to represent morphemes, which are syllabic-sized units of meaning such as we have in some of our Arabic numerals and chemical symbols. (3) Although their characters have phonetic elements in them, they are used only as analogies to help with pronunciation. Chinese logographs have an advantage over the alphabetic writing system. The Chinese system is more closely related to meaning. Nevertheless, the Chinese first use pin-yin, literally spell-sound, which is a syllabary with Mandarin pronunciation, for initial phonics reading instruction, then pin-yin above or next to ideographs to help in their pronunciation, and gradually a shift is made to ideographs alone as students learn to identify them (Sheridan, 1980). (4)

The Japanese also have two writing systems: Kana, a syllable system that linearly represents sounds in the language, is used for initial reading instruction. Kanji consists of some 1850 characters borrowed from the Chinese some 500 years ago. These lexical units are substituted gradually over grades 1 to 9 for Kana to help speed up writing and reading. However, the Japanese continue to use Kana to represent grammatical units. Thus, the Japanese, like the Chinese, also shift from relying solely on a syllabary (Kana) to use of whole words (Kanji). Both the Chinese and the Japanese also utilize sentence constraints for word identification and construction of meaning.

Complex correspondence between
English writing and sound systems

Although our alphabetic writing system is more closely related to its sound system, we have multiple methods of teaching beginning reading. One reason is that the alphabetic writing system does not have a simple correspondence to its sound system. Over the last 500 years, the English writing and sound systems, which at the beginning of this time period were in closer correspondence, have diverged considerably (Nelson, 1970). Essentially, English orthography (spelling) became frozen while its phonology (sound system) continued to change. Many letters now stand silent but serve as signals or markers; some sounds are represented by two letters (*kick* and *country*), some letters have different sounds (*of* and *from*), some words are spelled alike but are pronounced differently, depending on whether they are nouns or verbs (*produce* vs *produce*), or present and past tense verbs (*read* vs *read*). Some words retain the same spelling even though their vowel has shifted its sound (*nation* vs *nationality*), and so forth. English has borrowed words along with their spellings, or a reasonable adaptation of their spellings, from Latin, Greek, French, and other sources, so that more than half of the words of written English are now non-Germanic in origin and therefore do not have a simple spelling-to-sound correspondence. Although the relationship between the English writing and its sound system is complex, it is still regular or rule-governed (Venezky, 1970); otherwise, we would not be able to communicate through writing (Reed, 1970).

Although all writing systems may be optimal for representing their respective languages (Chomsky, 1970; Wang, 1981), and although all language systems have semantic, syntactic, and sound subsystems, it is possible to start reading instruction in any language with an emphasis on one or a combination of these subsystems. In American reading instruction, methods of instruction have changed in a surprisingly systematic way from an alphabet to a story method; historical events in the country have influenced the changes in the methods and goals of instruction (Smith, 1965; Singer, 1981).

Historical changes in methods of American reading instruction

Prior to the American Revolution, when teachers and parents both had the responsibility for teaching reading, the *New England Primer* used an alphabet and syllabary method for teaching reading. After the American Revolution, Noah Webster's Blue Backed Speller, with an emphasis on spelling and pronunciation, was popular until the *McGuffey Eclectic Readers* took over in the 1840s. The McGuffey readers used all the previous methods but did feature a whole-word approach. Horace Mann, the father of public school education, championed the whole-word method, because he had been to Germany where he had seen the Pestallozian whole-word method in use. He argued that the whole-word method would teach students to read faster with better comprehension than they could with the spelling method. McGuffey readers were used until about 1880, when

Pollard's Synthetic Phonics Method became popular, and
remained in use until about 1900, when a sentence-story method
replaced it. Next came an emphasis on silent reading in about
1915. Then in the 1920s with the advent of the experience chart
method, children's stories became the basis for teaching reading.
In the 1930s a split occurred between those who favored a
project method of learning to read vs. those who favored a
systematic, basal reader method. The basal reader, with its
introductory emphasis on whole words, was the dominant
instructional approach when Rudolph Flesch (1955) wrote a
best-seller on *Why Johnny Can't Read and What To Do About
It* (substitute phonics for whole-word instruction). Subsequently
Jeanne Chall, now a Professor of Education at Harvard, began a
study for the Carnegie Foundation, which was later (1967)
published as *Learning To Read: The Great Debate*. She had
reviewed all the research over the preceding 50 years and
proclaimed that there was a continuum of reading instruction with
a code-emphasis on one end and a meaning-emphasis on the
other. However, the research on methods of teaching reading was
not done well enough for her to come to a clear-cut conclusion
on which method is best for beginning reading. She and others
called for a study of the various methods of beginning reading.
This study, which occurred some 15 years ago, was reported by
Bond and Dykstra (1967); it is known as "The First Grade
Study." I shall briefly review this study because it is germane to
our purpose.

The First Grade Study

The First Grade Study investigated five different types of
reading programs.

1. An Initial Teaching Alphabet method which has a 44-
    character alphabet and purports to have one sound for
    each symbol.
2. A linguistic emphasis in which children are taught through
    sequencing of word patterns; these patterns enable them to
    discover symbol-sound correspondences by a method of
    minimal contrastive pairs of words. For example, "pen"
    and "pin" differ in one phoneme.
3. A purely synthetic phonics program which starts with one
    symbol-sound correspondence, then teaches another, and
    combines the two to make a whole word. Gradually, this
    approach leads to the reading of sentences and finally
    stories.

4. A language experience approach in which students dictate stories about their experiences to the teacher who writes them on the board so that students can read their own stories. Subsequently, students write and read their own and each other's stories. (Individual conferences between student and teacher for learning relationships between spoken and written language and for guidance are also an important feature of this method.)

5. A basal reader supplemented with phonics materials.

About 30 teachers taught each program. What the researchers wanted to know was whether any one method would lead to superior comprehension at the end of grade one on the Metropolitan Reading Achievement Test. Bond and Dykstra (1967) found greater variations in achievement within a method than between methods. In short, nobody could claim that any one method led to superior comprehension. However, Bond and Dykstra did report that those methods, such as Lippincott's and Sullivan's programmed instruction, which Flesch (1981) lists among his "Phonics Five," had an edge in the first grade over basal readers such as Macmillan's, which Flesch lists in his "Dismal Dozen." But Ruddell (1968) reported that by grade three, the basal reader was superior. He had compared Sullivan's programmed instruction with the Harper-Row Basal Reader. He supplemented both of them with instruction in syntax and morphemics (meaning units). Sullivan's programmed instruction supplemented with syntax and morphemics was superior at the end of grade one, but Harper-Row won out by grade three, perhaps because after students had learned to identify the words, meaning became the crucial component and it was developed better by the basal reader.

None of the researchers in the First Grade Studies had investigated the effect of the different methods on development of the subsystems underlying reading achievement. However, Buswell (1922) had shown that different methods of teaching reading in first grade produced differences in eye-movement patterns in reading. More recently, Barr (1973-74) observed that instructional practices tend to determine whether first graders will first try to decode words, then learn to use their semantic and syntactic systems, and still later integrate the two, or whether they will follow a different sequence of learning to read. But, she did not systematically vary instruction and assess the development of the underlying systems. These subsystems are graphophonemic, morphemic, semantic, and syntactic.

Subsystems underlying beginning reading achievement

However, Katz and Singer (1976) did test an hypothesis from the substrata-factor theory which focussed on the systems underlying reading achievement. This hypothesis states that different methods will differentially develop the subsystems underlying reading achievement. Individuals can then mobilize these subsystems to obtain reading comprehension. In short, the hypothesis assumes that there is more than one pattern of subsystems for obtaining reading comprehension. In their initial attempt to test this hypothesis, Katz and Singer secured the original First Grade Studies data and reanalyzed them. But they found the data were inadequate for trying to answer what they considered to be a key question: Do the various methods of teaching beginning reading lead to systematic differences in the subsystems underlying reading achievement?

Katz then decided that for her doctoral dissertation, done under my direction, she would do an experimental and statistical study to test the hypothesis that methods of instruction are functionally related to the acquisition of subsystems for learning to read. She secured permission from two elementary schools to do her study on their students. However, she could not interfere with the students' regular instruction, which consisted of *Open Court* for some students and *Ginn 720* for others. What she could do was to provide supplementary instruction. She randomly assigned the students to four different methods of supplementary instruction. Essentially, Katz tested her hypothesis by conducting a study in two phases. In the first, she had four teachers, not currently employed by any school system, provide supplemental instruction to first graders who had been randomly assigned within two schools to supplementary instruction in each of four subsystems: graphophonemic, morphemic, semantic, and syntactic. After ten weeks of supplementary instruction, an analysis of variance design revealed significant systematic differences among the criterion-referenced tests given to all the groups. Each group was significantly superior to the others on the supplementary method it had been taught. As in the First Grade Study, she also found that differences among the groups in comprehension on the *Metropolitan Reading Instructional Tests* were not significant.

Next, for each group, Katz computed a multiple regression equation for determining the predictors of comprehension. Her data, derived from her criterion-referenced tests and the *Metropolitan Reading Instruction Tests,* revealed that each group's multiple regression equation for predicting reading comprehension contained the same predictors, but each group's lowest predictor was in the very subsystem in which the group had received supplementary instruction.

Katz found that methods of instruction interact with students' (13) capabilities to differentially develop subsystems underlying reading achievement. More specifically, she noted that beginning readers' pattern of acquisition of graphophonemics, morphemics, semantics, and syntactics is functionally related to differences in methods of instruction. In short, in contrast to the First Grade Studies, methods of instruction in beginning reading *do make a difference*. Katz's finding, which is in agreement with Buswell's (1922) early study and Barr's (1973-74) more recent investigation, has important implications for instruction, diagnosis, and improvement of reading.

In general, what Katz's study shows is that beginning readers tend to learn what you teach them. If you provide a syntactic emphasis, they will develop more in that subsystem than in the others. If you stress phonics, they will progress at a faster rate in acquisition of that subsystem. If you give them supplemental instruction in morphemics or in semantics, those subsystems will become better developed. Even though each group was best in the subsystem emphasized in its supplementary instruction, each group nevertheless mobilized all four subsystems for attaining reading comprehension. The implication for general reading instruction is clear: Students must acquire and integrate all the subsystems to become independent readers. For diagnosis and improvement of reading, it is also clear: If a beginning reader is strong in one subsystem and weak in another, then help this student overcome whichever subsystem is weak. Indeed, Burt and Lewis (1946) in England found that *a change in method per se* helped remedial readers improve the most, perhaps because in switching to a new method they got help in a subsystem in which they had been weakest and had not been stressed or had not been a part of their previous method of learning to read.

Katz (1980) also found that at the end of first grade, the *Metropolitan Reading Achievement Comprehension* subtest correlated only .27 with a word recognition factor, but .73 with a reasoning-in-reading factor that was heavily saturated with semantics and syntax. These results suggest that towards the end of grade one, when students have begun to master the graphophonemic aspect of reading, individual differences in comprehension are more attributable to semantic and syntactic factors; that is, at this point in their reading development, differences in comprehension are due more to general language abilities and to reasoning factors than to word recognition. Hence, general instruction should reflect the differences in the importance of these two factors at the end of grade one. Of course, those students who are still in need of emphasis in word recognition at the end of grade one should receive it.

A sound program for beginning reading

From these data, you realize that there are three major components in learning to read: (1) acquiring correct responses to printed words, such as sounds for letters, syllables, whole words, and blending sounds together; (2) learning to use language abilities of semantics, syntax, phonology, and general information for anticipating words, constructing meanings, and drawing inferences; and (3) learning to integrate responses to print along with language abilities. Of course, readers must apply this instruction to *r*ecreational, *e*nrichment, *a*pplied, and *d*evelopmental reading in order to have a comprehensive instructional program. This program is known by its acronym: R-E-A-D.

Now we shall return to my anecdote about my son. In using the exposure and conversational methods in teaching reading to my son, I was only stressing one of the components, use of language background. My daughter added to his repertoire the second component, responses to printed words. Then my son integrated both of these components to become an independent reader. My conclusion from the research evidence and from my personal experience in teaching reading is that a program which includes both responses to printed words and use of language abilities, teaches students to integrate them, shifts in emphasis from word recognition to reasoning-in-reading as students progress in learning to read, and has students practice with a variety of reading materials is a sound program for teaching reading.

Act II: Phonics First, Second, Or Not at All

Prepped with the knowledge gleaned during the intermission and from other information already in your repertoire, you return to the IEP Conference. When it is your turn to speak, you give a long speech in which you wisely select and state the appropriate information for your reply to the parents. You tell them, "We know that students need to learn to identify printed words. Phonics is one way to do so. It works well for words like 'cat,' and 'sat' but not at all for words like 'right.' We have to teach these kinds of words as whole words, or as a combination of an initial consonant 'r' plus a phonogram 'ight,' or through the use of context, 'The teacher told the boy who answered correctly, that's _____ .' We have to teach some words, such as 'shepherd' by first dividing the word into its two meaningful parts (morphemes) of 'shep' and 'herd;' then the student can sound out each part. We have to use a variety of techniques, because the English language does not fit just one of them."

Some teachers may start with phonics, but they soon have to add other techniques. Even Lippincott, a strict phonics approach, teaches 'the' as a whole word. It also uses context in the form of pictures to help teach word identification.

Other teachers start to teach reading by having children tell stories, then the teacher writes the story on the board, and teaches children to read their own story. She is having them capitalize on their language background while learning techniques for word identification. This teacher is emphasizing 'language first.'

When a child, such as yours, does not make normal progress, then we listen to the child read, perhaps administer some tests, and diagnose the child's difficulty. On the basis of observation and test information, we formulate an instructional plan to overcome the child's difficulties. That is what we have done for your child. We are meeting to present our findings and discuss our plan with you. If your child needs phonics first, we will teach it first."

NOTES

1   The answer: the schools are not teaching "phonics first." This priority for phonics is an implicit concession by Flesch that the schools are teaching phonics now. Twenty-five years ago, he accused the schools of not teaching phonics at all (Flesch, 1955).

2   A satirical reply entitled, "Why Rudolph Can't Read" was written by Sam Sebesta (1981). He had Rudolph follow a strict "phonics first" regime before and after he started school. As a result, Rudolph ended up as an educationally handicapped child.

3   One explanation for lack of further progression is that Chinese logographs are an optimal way of representing the Chinese language (Wang, 1981), just as English orthography is an optimal way of representing the English language (Chomsky, 1970).

4   But it does have its limitations. For example, the Chinese writing system does not lend itself to use in typewriters and computers. To remedy the limitations of Chinese orthography, Chairman Mao tried to install an alphabetic system in China, but failed.

   The Japanese are more fortunate than the Chinese because they can more readily adapt their dual writing system to technological tools.

REFERENCES

Barr, R. The effect of instruction on pupil reading strategies. *Reading Research Quarterly,* 1974-75, *10,* no. 4, 555-582.

Bond, G.L. and Dykstra, R. The cooperative research program in first grade reading instruction. *Reading Research Quarterly,* 1967, *2,* 5-142.

Burt, C. and Lewis, R.B. Teaching backward readers. *British Journal of Educational Psychology,* 1946, *16,* 116-132.

Buswell, G.T. *Fundamental Reading Habits: A Study of Their Development.* (Supplementary Educational Monographs No. 21). Chicago, Ill.: University of Chicago Press, 1922.

Chall, J. *Learning to Read: The Great Debate.* New York: McGraw-Hill, 1967.

Chomsky, N. Phonology and reading. In H. Levin and J. Williams (Eds.), *Basic Studies on Reading.* New York: Basic Books, 1970.

Flesch, R. *Why Johnny Can't Read and What to Do About It.* New York: Harper, 1955.

Flesch, R. *Why Johnny Still Can't Read.* New York: Harper and Row, 1981.

Gaeng, P.A. *Introduction to the Principles of Language.* New York: Harper and Row, 1971.

Gough, P. One second of reading. In H. Singer & R. Ruddell (Eds.), *Theoretical Models and Processes of Reading.* Second Ed. Newark, Delaware: International Reading Association, 1976.

Katz, I. The effects of instructional methods on reading acquisition systems. Unpublished doctoral dissertation, University of California, Riverside, 1980.

Katz, I. and Singer, H. Effects of instructional methods on reading acquisition systems: A reanalysis of First Grade Studies data. Paper presented at the International Reading Association's Annual Convention, Anaheim, California, 1976.

Nelson, F.W. Linguistics and reading: A commentary on chapters 1 and 3. In H. Levin & J. Williams (Ed.), *Basic Studies on Reading.* New York: Basic Books, 1970.

Reed, D. A theory of language, speech, and writing. In H. Singer and R.B. Ruddell (Eds.), *Theoretical Models and Processes of Reading.* First Edition. Newark, Delaware: International Reading Association, 1970.

Ruddell, R.B. A longitudinal study of four programs of reading instruction varying in emphasis on regularity of grapheme-phoneme correspondences and language structure on reading achievement in grades two and three. Project No. 3099 and No. 78085, University of California, Berkeley, 1968.

Sebesta, S. Why Rudolph Can't Read. *Language Arts,* 1981, *58,* No. 5 545-548.

Sheridan, E.M. Literacy and language reform in the People's Republic of China. ERIC: ED 185 541, 1980.

Singer, H. Teaching the acquisition phase of reading development: An historical perspective. In O.J.L. Tzeng and H. Singer (Eds.), *Perception of Print: Reading Research in Experimental Psychology*. Hillsdale, N.J.: Erlbaum, 1981.

Smith, N.B. *History of American Reading Instruction*. Newark, Delaware: International Reading Association, 1965.

Venezky, R. Regularity in reading and spelling. In H. Levin & J. Williams (Ed.), *Basic Studies on Reading*. New York: Basic Books, 1970.

Wang, W.S.-Y. Language structure and optimal orthography. In O.J.L. Tzeng and H. Singer (Eds.), *Perception of Print: Reading Research in Experimental Psychology*. Hillsdale, N.J.: Erlbaum, 1981.

Critical Reading
That Makes a Difference

Fehl L. Shirley

The development of individuals who read critically is an important goal of reading instruction and of education in general. A statement of the Educational Policies Commission asserts that the primary purpose of education is to produce "a rational thinking individual, who has developed both critical and creative thinking, and who uses those intellectual abilities in becoming a useful and productive member of society."(1) Also, concerned with the critical awareness of sophisticated media by elementary, secondary, and college students, the National Council of Teachers of English resolved to encourage teacher education programs that promote the understandings and insights students need to evaluate critically "the persuasive techniques found in political statements, advertising, entertainment, and news."(2)

Since students today are assaulted by propaganda unequaled even by the Nazi Germany propaganda machines, instruction in critical reading/thinking is essential in helping them analyze the language of the commercial and political persuaders. By the time children enter school at the age of five or six, they have viewed thousands of commercials; by the age of sixteen, they have watched over 640,000 commercials.(3) In order to become intelligent and articulate citizens, training is required in the new media literacy.

The Federal Trade Commission Staff Report containing the petition for the regulation of television advertising of candy and other sugared products to children discusses the imbalance between the mechanisms of the persuaders and the resources of the persuadees.(4) On the one hand, the commercial advertisers, representing a multibillion dollar industry, have sophisticated personnel with well-financed scriptwriters, actors, technicians, psychological analysts, and motivational researchers. On the other hand, there is the uninformed citizen or naive, gullible child. According to Feinbloom: "An advertisement to a child has the quality of an order, not a suggestion."(5) For some preschool children, those characters inside the television set are real, speaking to them. It is difficult for young children to separate reality from fantasy. Even teenagers tend to accept the claims of advertisers except when personal experiences influence them otherwise, according to a study by Linn and associates at the University of California, Berkeley's Lawrence Hall of Science.(6) Commenting on the effect of advertisements on teenagers, Linn said: "Advertisers, it appears, succeed in defeating critical analysis of their potentially misleading messages."(7) The adolescents of the study were aware of the persuasive appeal and intent of the advertisers, but they apparently did not know how to deal with it. Therefore, as well as training the future persuaders through marketing and psychological curricula, instructors need to train the future persuadees of our country in the critical analysis of propaganda techniques and language manipulation by writer or speaker.

In order to facilitate the critical awareness of persuasive techniques by students, teachers require a functional concept of critical reading. The literature abounds with varied definitions of critical reading, which, for the most part, are listings of skills or component abilities (8, 9, 10, 11, 12, 13). In their review of the major conceptions of critical reading, Lunstrum and Taylor (14) included the view of critical reading as critical thinking expressed by Ennis as the accurate assessment of statements based on the knowledge of methods of inquiry and logical reasoning.(15) Hash (16) adapted elements of Ennis' (17) comprehensive critical reading model to guides presenting dialogues in narrative form on critical issues. This view of critical reading as critical thinking, also emphasized by Russell (18), is the position maintained in this paper.

In consideration of the varied and numerous listings in the literature of skills involved in critical reading and until more factorial and empirical studies are made, the writer submits a tentative working model of the critical reading process for the use of elementary and secondary teachers. The model encompasses the following five phases:

1. Awareness of the denotations and connotations of words.
2. Suspension of judgment
3. Interpretation
4. Problem solving
5. Insight

The phases of the critical reading process are interdependent since the reader uses a cluster of abilities in interpreting a communication; in problem solving, all the phases of the critical reading process are utilized. As well as the cognitive and affective abilities inherent in the process, the context of the situation is taken into consideration in analyzing persuasive language.

The five phases of the functional critical reading model are described below as well as suggested instructional procedures for elementary and secondary teachers.

Phase 1. Awareness of the denotations and connotations of words

It is essential for students to distinguish between denotations (explicit meanings) and connotations (suggested meanings) in order for them to understand what the author or speaker means and what he or she wants to suggest. The surface meaning may be quite different from the deeper, implied meaning. Sensitivity to the connotative power of words makes students aware of the effect of words on their imaginations, feelings, and thoughts. Words have the power to exalt spirits, strengthen feelings of honor, courage, nobility, pride or sympathy. But words may also evoke feelings of intolerance, vanity, fear, jealousy, and suspicion of the new or different.

Teachers can help elementary and secondary students become aware of the emotion producing power of words and analyze words for their connotative overtones through the following activities:

1. Students are presented a concrete object, such as a shoe or a glove, and asked to define the object. The teacher then appeals to the senses by asking for words that suggest how the object feels, smells, looks, sounds, and tastes. These associative words are incorporated into language experience stories. Students compare the literal and associate meanings. Positive and negative attributes are suggested by students for the object, and comparisons are made of the effect of the words on the individual.

2. Poetry, which employs symbolism, imagery, and analogy, is used to show the skillful use of connotation. Students compare the literal meaning of tiger with the suggestiveness in Blake's, "The Tiger." Students give, also, the literal interpretation of lines of poetry, such as the first line of Frost's poem, "The Fog," and become aware of the poet's selection of words to connote certain effects:

The fog comes	The condensed water
on little cat feet.	vapor comes on little
	lower extremities of
	the *Felis catus.*

3. Students tell which words they would rather use to describe themselves:

   cautious/cowardly
   touchy/sensitive
   coy/modest
   hypocritical/tactful
   teenager/adolescent/youth/juvenile/kid
   accelerated student/gifted student/"honor" student

4. Students analyze the connotative qualities of current brand names, book titles, song titles, names of restaurants, and names of characters in books.

5. Students identify the emotionally-laden words in newspaper articles and analyze the motives of the writers in using the words. Students rewrite the articles from other points of view.

6. Students identify and analyze words they believe were used by the writers of advertisements as suggested by Altick.(19)

   Example: YOU ARE WHAT YOU (EAT, WHEAT, CONSUME, SWALLOW).

   > Add the (excellence, value, goodness, price) of Kretschmer Wheat Germ to any food you (eat, wheat, consume, swallow). It's the heart of the wheat, (of course, naturally, necessarily, consequently) packed with (power, force, energy, strength) and protein, iron, zinc, vitamin E and most B vitamins. (Join, Add, Attach, Tag) it to your diet. (Affix, Add, Unite, Annex) it to your life.

   Students discuss the reasons for their selections and whether they felt the rejected words might be more effective.

Phase 2. Suspension of judgment

Realizing the emotion producing power of words, the student at the second phase of the critical reading process reflects in a rational manner rather than reacting impulsively. This "caveat emptor" phase is concerned with the suspension of judgment until the evidence is considered. The reader has a questioning attitude, resisting efforts that are being made to influence his or her thinking and behavior.(20) This phase implies that the reader may change his or her beliefs "but not by accepting totally an author's viewpoint."(21) The reader is able to live with uncertainty, reinforcing or revising ideas as new information is acquired.

Although a difficult task to accomplish, teachers can attempt to encourage elementary and secondary students to suspend judgment regarding persuasive language by the following techniques:

1. Students consider the context of the situation in which the communication takes place. Students consider who is saying what to whom, under what circumstances, for what purpose, and with what result. Students realize that language manipulation may be good or bad depending upon the motives of the speaker and the context of the situation. Students compare the euphemisms used during the Vietnam War, such as "accidental delivery of ordnance equipment" for shelling your own troops, or "an aerodynamic personnel accelerator" for a parachute, with such euphemisms as are expressed to show sympathy or to avoid embarrassing or hurting another person's feelings.(22)

2. Students are alerted to subliminal or indirect advertising in the mass media. Teachers present examples of subliminal embeds as suggested by Lombard (23), who stressed that advertising analysis be a part of the elementary curriculum so that students can become sensitized to nonverbal influences on their attitudes and behavior.

3. Fables are used to show situations encountered by animals that are analogous to the dilemmas of people in television commercials.(24) In Aesop's fable, "The Fox and the Crow," the crafty fox, as the seducer, flatters the naive and gullible crow into opening his beak to sing, thereby dropping the cheese to the ground for the greedy fox. Viewers of television commercials can be misled, as was the crow, by the artful phrases of advertisers that flatter and goad consumers to buy their products. Other examples from children's literature are used to help students understand propaganda techniques. propaganda techniques.

4. Students role play sales situations where high pressure tactics are used and situations that are "low key" in sales technique. In playing the different roles, students identify with the customer, the salesperson, and the employer. Cartoons are drawn summarizing the situations depicted.

5. Tours of television studios are arranged. In this way, students become aware of the ways television commercials are designed, produced, and financed.

6. Since students are exposed to immediate or simplistic
   solutions to problems through television, magazine, and
   newspaper advertisements, opportunities are presented for
   students to study problems in a scientific way with sustained
   attention, effort, and patience. Linn observed that, in the
   interest of expediency, adolescents tend to forsake
   thoroughness and thoughtfulness and, in the realm of
   advertising, "appear to make decisions based on limited
   information when given the opportunity to gather evidence for
   a decision."(25) McCracken (26) described a year-long study
   of semantics in which secondary students examined the
   language pollution in their environment, including lectures,
   college applications, the language of Watergate, book reviews,
   local newspaper editorials, advertisements, and televised
   political speeches. The instructor believed that this sustained
   year-long study was more effective than short, hurry-up units on
   semantics.

Phase 3. Interpretation

   After the phase of suspending judgment, the reader needs
further clarification of the meaning of the ideas evoked by the
words. The individual reads between and beyond the lines,
making hypotheses, drawing inferences and generalizations.

   The teacher's ability to ask questions that elicit interpretive
responses is of value at this phase. Also, students are encouraged
to generate their own questions that guide their thinking before,
during, and after reading. Studies by Cohen (27) and Andre and
Anderson (28) have shown that a question-producing set in
students can lead to improved comprehension.

   A pattern for questioning used to analyze communication,
persuasion, and propaganda is Rank's (29) intensify and downplay schema. This pattern emphasizes the intensification of
language through repetition, association, and composition and the
down-playing of language through omission, diversion, and
confusion. Rank substituted the new schema for the older
Institute of Propaganda list of seven techniques which he did not
believe was appropriate for contemporary propaganda; the new
pattern is applied to verbal and nonverbal communication,
spoken and written, and other symbolic language. Questions
related to the different aspects of the Rank schema are given
below:

INTENSIFY

Repetition

What words, slogans, symbols, names, colors, and tunes are repeated?
What patterns of repetition do you observe?
What reasons can you suggest for these repetitions?

Association

With what subject matter is the appeal associated?
—tribal pride
—ideals
—heroes
—experts
—folk sayings
—most people
—progress
—sensual pleasures
What nonverbal associative techniques are used?
—visual settings
—musical accompaniment
To what audience is the appeal directed?

Composition

What nonverbal patterning is employed?
—visual (color, size, shape)
—aural (music)
—mathematical (quantities, relationships)
—temporal (pacing)
—spatial (spacing, distancing)
—patterns of pitch, stress, and juncture
—facial expressions
—body movements
What verbal patterning is used?
—choice of words that intensify

DOWNPLAY

Omission

What facts are omitted?
Why were these facts omitted in your opinion?
What euphemisms are used to downplay the unpleasant?
Why do you think these euphemisms were used?

Diversion

What tactics are used to draw attention away from the significant issues?
—emphasizing the nonrelated
—employing emotional attacks or appeals
—using humor or entertainment
—using tactics that drain the energy of others

Confusion

What tactics are used to confuse thinking?
—using faulty logic
—shifting definitions
—using equivocations
—employing circumlocution
—manifesting contradictions and inconsistencies
—using unintelligible jargon

—connotations and
denotations
—use of punctuation
to intensify
—use of unusual
patterns to intensify

The Rank schema is also appropriate for editorials and other persuasive discourse to help students analyze emotional appeals, associative techniques, tactics of omission, and other ways of manipulating verbal and nonverbal communication.

Phase 4. Problem solving

Problem solving is the search for truth; it involves critical reading/thinking or the accurate assessment of statements based on two criteria: (1) the scientific method and (2) standards of logic.(30)

The components of the scientific method of identifying a problem, making hypotheses, gathering data, analyzing and interpreting data, generalizing, verifying generalizations, and reporting the results require critical reading of a more complex order. The application of the scientific method to commercial propaganda is demonstrated by two studies, one at the elementary and the other at the secondary level.

Wright and Laminack (31) describe a first grade program in which the children listened to commercials, tested products, recorded claims and test results, and also made their own brand of liquid detergent, which they named Everysoap. Their advertisement for this product read:

New Everysoap
New Everysoap is different colors. Everysoap will make
your hands softer and prettier. It will get your dishes
cleaner. New Everysoap makes long lasting bubbles. It's
new! Try some today! (32)

All the first graders had the experience of washing their hands with the new Everysoap. In this way, they tested the claims of the commercial. Some children considered the claims as valid; others said they did not experience any difference between the new Everysoap and the soap they were accustomed to using. The teacher observed that the children were better able to distinguish whether the advertiser's claims were facts or opinions as a result of product testing.

Reeves (33) described projects undertaken by his high school students who subjected testable advertised claims to experimental verification by testing the claim, making observations, drawing conclusions, reporting the results of the experiments to the class, and writing letters to manufacturers and the ad agencies stating the results of their tests and asking for responses. A few examples of the claims tested included the claim of Ivory Liquid that it is so rich and thick, "it even whips," the claim that "there are 106 chunks of beef in every can" of Dennison's Chili, the claim that zip-coded mail arrives faster than regular mail, and the ketchup claim, "comes out slowest." About 80 percent of the advertisements tested were found to be as advertised, 15 percent were "somewhat misleading," and about 5 percent turned out to be "not as advertised." As a result of the experiments, Reeves stated that the attitudes of the students toward business and advertising tended to be more favorable.

As well as using empirical methods, advertisements are analyzed logically for the validity and soundness of their reasoning. The tool of logic is the syllogism or sequence of assumptions and conclusions. In analyzing selected ads, students formulate syllogisms:

> Bothered with gasid indigestion? Make this simple test and prove to yourself that Alkaheist is the best antacid you can buy. Drop a single handy Alkaheist tablet in a glass of water. See how quickly it dissolves? It gets to work fast, fast, fast in your stomach — faster than any other tablet! Get Alkaheist today!
>
> Major premise: The tablet that dissolves faster relieves
>   acidity better.
> Minor premise: Alkaheist dissolves faster.
> Conclusion: Therefore, Alkaheist relieves acidity better.

(34)

Since the major premise cannot be accepted as true, the derived conclusion is considered unsound, and the rationality of the advertisement is questionable.

The sweeping deductions of characters in crime dramas on television and in detective and adventure stories are examined by students for the soundness of their statements. For example, the lack of qualifiers is evidenced frequently in Sherlock Holmes' confident deductions.

Students are encouraged also to identify and study in a scientific and logical way the vital problems of current interest related to environmental damage, the international arms race, the growing population, traffic and urban congestion, crime, health, unemployment, and other issues of concern. In this way, tentative hypotheses and alternative solutions are considered. The critical reader, through problem solving, exercises reflective and evaluative thinking, weighing carefully the evidence for making critical decisions.

Phase 5. Insight

Insight is defined in two ways: (1) as "reasonable understanding and evaluation of one's own mental process, reactions, abilities;"(35) and (2) as "the capacity to discern the true nature of a situation."(36) Combining these two views of insight is the task of the critical reader at this last phase. The individual has achieved insight in perceiving himself or herself as a discerning reader who criticizes systematically and independently his or her reasoning processes, attitudes, and behavior in response to patterns of persuasive language, abiding by standards of objectivity and impartiality. The reader who has achieved insight has a critical attitude or a critical spirit (37) reflected in the predisposition to ask questions, to search for sound reasons, and to make independent judgments. This last phase is the culmination of the critical reading program reflected in the ongoing process by the insightful reader of acquiring internal monitoring criteria for making discriminating responses.(38)

An attempt has been made to describe a functional concept of critical reading which can be used, modified, or expanded by elementary and secondary teachers to inculcate in the young the survival skills of a critical attitude, the ability to analyze persuasive techniques, and the capacity to evaluate the motives and the language of author and speaker.

REFERENCES

1 Educational Policies Commission. *The Central Purpose of American Education.* Washington, D.C.: National Education Association, 1962, 12.

2 Dieterich, Daniel (Editor). *Teaching about Doublespeak.* Urbana, Illinois: National Council of Teachers of English, 1976, ix-x.

3 Rank, Hugh. "Teaching about Public Persuasion: Rationale and a Schema." In *Teaching about Doublespeak*, editor Daniel Dieterich. Urbana, Illinois: National Council of Teachers of English, 1976, 5.

4 *FTC Staff Report on Television Advertising to Children.* Washington, D.C.: Superintendent of Documents, U.S. Government Printing Office, February 1978.

5 Quoted by Dr. Richard Feinbloom, Harvard Medical School, in *Hearings on Broadcast Advertising and Children* before House Committee on Interstate and Foreign Commerce, 94th Congress, 1st Session, July 1975.

6 Mehren, Elizabeth. "Teen-agers Taken in by Ads." In *For Teachers Only,* Educational Service of the "Los Angeles Times," November 2, 1982, 1-2.

7 *Ibid.,* 1.

8. Tyler, R.W. "Measuring the Ability to Infer," *Educational Research Bulletin,* 1930, 475-480.

9 Anderson, H.C., Marcham, F.G., and Dunn, S.B. "An Experiment in Teaching Certain Skills of Critical Thinking," *Journal of Educational Research,* 1944, *38,* 241-251.

10 DeBoer, J.J. "Teaching Critical Reading," *Elementary English Review,* 1945, *23,* 251-254.

11 Spache, G.D. *Toward Better Reading.* Champaign, Illinois: Garrard Publishing Company, 1963.

12 Eller, W. and Wolf, J.G. "Developing Critical Reading Abilities," *Journal of Reading,* 1966, *10,* 192-198.

13 Dawson, M.A., Compiler. *Developing Comprehension — Including Critical Reading.* Newark, Delaware: International Reading Association, 1968.

14 Lunstrum, John P. and Taylor, Bob L. *Teaching Reading in the Social Studies.* Urbana, Illinois: ERIC/RCS, 1978, 62.

15 Ennis, R.H. "A Definition of Critical Thinking," *Reading Teacher,* 1964, 10, 599-612.

16 Hash, Ronald J. *The Sighting of Sasquatch: A Critical Reading Guide.* Muncie, Indiana: Ball State University, 1974.

17 Ennis, R.H., *op. cit.*

18 Russell, David. *Children Learn to Read.* Boston: Ginn and Company, 1961.

19 Altick, Richard D. *Preface to Critical Reading.* New York: Holt, Rhinehart and Winston, 1965.

20 Russell, D., *op. cit.*

21 Spache, George and Berge, Paul. *The Art of Efficient Reading.* New York: Macmillan, 1966, 145.

22 Rank, Hugh. "The Teacher-Heal-Thyself Myth." In *Language and Public Policy,* editor Hugh Rank. Urbana, Illinois: National Council of Teachers of English, 1974.

23 Lombard, Jim. "Advertising," *Elements: Translating Theory into Practice,* 1979, *7,* 4-6.

24 Cacha, Frances B. "Propaganda Techniques via Children's Literature." In *Teaching about Doublespeak,* editor Daniel Dieterich. Urbana, Illinois: National Council of Teachers of English, 1976, 89-91.

25 Mehren, *op. cit.,* 2.

26 McCracken, Nancy. "A Student-Centered, Process-Oriented, Interdisciplinary Non-Unit on Doublespeak." In *Teaching About Doublespeak,* editor Daniel Dieterich. Urbana, Illinois: National Council of Teachers of English, 1976, 135-142.

27 Cohen, Ruth. "Learning to Ask Questions." *Resources in Education,* July 1977.

28 Andre, M.E.D.A. and Anderson, T.H. "The Development and Evaluation of a Self-Questioning Study Technique," *Reading Research Quarterly,* 1978-1979, *14,* 605-623.

29 Rank, Hugh. "Teaching about Public Persuasion: Rationale and a Schema." In *Teaching about Doublespeak,* editor Daniel Dieterich. Urbana, Illinois: National Council of Teachers of English, 1976, 3-20.

30 Ennis, R.H., *op. cit.*

31 Wright, J.P. and Laminack, L. "First Graders Can Be Critical Listeners and Readers," *Language Arts,* 1982, *59,* 133-136.

32 *Ibid.,* 135-136.

33 Reeves, Bruce. "Ad-Man, Business-Man, Teacher-Man." In *Language and Public Policy,* editor Hugh Rank. Urbana, Illinois: National Council of Teachers of English, 1976, 65-71.

34 Kehl, D.B. "The Electric Carrot: The Rhetoric of Advertisement and the Art of Persuasion." In *Language and Public Policy,* editor Hugh Rank. Urbana, Illinois: National Council of Teachers of English, 1976, 56.

35 English, H.B. and English, A.C. *A Comprehensive Dictionary of Psychological and Psychoanalytical Terms.* New York: David McKay Company, Inc., 1966, 264.

36 Morris, W., Editor. *The American Heritage Dictionary of the English Language.* Boston, Mass.: Houghton Mifflin Company, 1976.

37 Siegel, Harvey. "Critical Thinking as an Educational Ideal," *The Educational Forum,* 1980, *45,* 7-23.

38 Baldwin, R.S. and Readence, J.E. "Critical Reading and Perceived Authority," *Journal of Reading,* 1979, *32,* 620.

Reading Comprehension Instruction: What Has Been and What Might Be

Diane Lapp and James Flood

What has been

Emphasis upon reading comprehension is a relatively recent phenomenon in the history of reading instruction; comprehension was not considered an important goal of instruction until the nineteenth century. Speculation concerning the reasons for this apparent oversight are diverse. However, one common explanation seems favored by most educational historians. They explain that readers needed help in getting started, they required instruction in decoding strategies; but, once these strategies were acquired, they needed no further help in reading. This simple view of the process of reading and reading instruction perhaps worked well enough in former societies, because most readers were well educated by the standards of their day. Their education and breeding provided sufficient background knowledge to enable them to read with understanding what was required of them. It must be noted that most citizens of the day were not required to do a great deal of reading.

If one were to trace the teaching of reading comprehension to previous societies, it would quickly be noted that little or no attention was given to teaching students to read with comprehension. Mathews, in *Teaching to Read: Historically Considered* (1966), concluded that the Greeks and Romans did not consider the teaching of reading to be a difficult or troublesome task. In all accounts of early reading instruction in the Greek and Roman Empires, only decoding/word analysis aspects of learning to read are discussed. The account of Dionysius of Halicarnasses (20 B.C.) and Quintillian account (1st century A.D.) demonstrate this point accurately. The history of the teaching of reading is extremely sketchy until the Norman Conquest in England. Davies (1973) claimed that all we know about the teaching of reading was that it was assigned to secular priests by order of the Pope (Davies, 1973); he points out that instruction in reading in the thirteenth and fourteenth century, conducted in "petty" schools, included teaching the alphabet, syllables, and the prayerbook. During the Reformation (1517), reading instruction was conducted by teachers in grammar schools, the feeder schools to the universities. It consisted of instruction in letter naming, the catechism, and the primer.

The first mention of comprehension as a component of reading instruction seems to have been made by Friedrich Gedike in 1797, when he criticized the "shockingly slow, inflectionless, uncomprehending manner" in which students read. However, his concerns were not appreciated by educators of the time, and his suggestions for having children immersed in the literature of their own culture were ignored.

The earliest reading instruction recorded in the United States was provided by Puritans who first employed *The Hornbook*, followed by *The New England Primer*. Both emphasized knowledge of the alphabet, vowels, consonants, and syllables (Huey, 1908). The principal modes of instruction were memorization and recitation, and success in reading was assessed by the ability to pronounce words correctly (and, presumably, recognize their meaning). The first movement toward including comprehension materials in a reader came with Noah Webster's American Spelling Book (1783) in which he included 10½ pages out of 158 of literature. N.B. Smith (1965) in her historical account of the teaching of reading, called this a first step toward meaningful reading instruction. Smith points out that:

> until the nineteenth century, it seems safe to conclude that for the most part instruction in reading did not focus on whether the reader understood what he read. The task was still one of fluent and accurate pronunciation. Comprehension, it must have been felt, was a by-product.

Smith reports that the first use of the term, "comprehension," was used by Webb (1856) in his *Normal Readers,* when he suggested "a full comprehension of the matter to be read" as an instructional goal of the third reader. Although the major objective of the McGuffey readers, also popular at this time, was elocution, there was some minor emphasis on comprehension with the instruction of questions asking for retellings, interpretation, and judgment.

During the twentieth century, reading comprehension instruction was indirectly enhanced by the birth of the scientific movement. In 1924, W.S. Gray coined the term "intelligent silent reading," calling for a new emphasis on comprehension.

By the second decade of the twentieth century, a great deal of attention and emphasis was being placed upon discovering the construct necessary for measuring reading comprehension. Investigations of the 20s, 30s, and 40s attempted to isolate skills related to comprehension; this resulted in what Farr (1971) described as a period of subskill proliferation. In time, this emphasis on assessment gave way to a definition of comprehension that Roser suggests we are perhaps "stuck with" today, and that definition is totally pragmatic: "that which the reading comprehension test tests."

All reading programs today include materials that are intended to develop and enhance comprehension abilities. Diverse literature is included in all of these programs, and provision is made through teachers' manuals for instruction in comprehension. Although abundant and effective materials are currently available through reading programs, libraries, book clubs, etc. for teaching reading comprehension, an effective instructional model for teaching comprehension is needed.

It is our intent in the remainder of this paper to describe a framework for instruction that we believe will be useful in designing a reading comprehension curriculum.

A definition of reading comprehension

Before presenting our framework, it is necessary to define what we mean by the term "reading comprehension." Most simply stated, reading comprehension is the acquisition of information from printed material. It is more than decoding. Decoding is a first step toward comprehension, but it is not comprehension. Comprehension *means* understanding what you have read.

Although some decoding skills are necessary to begin the comprehension process, reading comprehension ability is not necessarily acquired in serial fashion. Once reading has begun, decoding skills enhance comprehension and comprehension, in turn, enhances decoding.

An illustration of the components of comprehension is presented below:

COMPONENTS OF
READING COMPREHENSION ABILITY

STEP 1

Decoding

= word analysis skills, e.g., phonics skills, sight word skills, contextual analysis skills, structural analysis skills

= word recognition skills, i.e., "saying" the word in print

STEP 2

Comprehending

= understanding of:

words	rock
words in context and phrases	on rock music
sentences	Sally gets high on rock music
short texts	Sally gets high on rock music It makes her feel happy and young. It reminds her of her happy youth when she danced the night away
longer texts	Sally gets high on rock music It makes her feel happy and young It reminds her of her youth when she danced the night away But that was long ago. That was before the bad times, before she met Fred, before she met trouble, before she stopped dancing, before...

What might be

A FRAMEWORK FOR DESIGNING
A READING COMPREHENSION CURRICULUM

Purpose: To provide students with a reading program which includes opportunities for *exposure, experimentation, evaluation,* and *expansion.*

General Objective: This program is designed to provide all students with the strategies necessary to become proficient readers.

Procedure: *EXPOSURE*

1. *Students need to practice speaking and listening skills to develop reading-writing abilities because oral language is the base of the reading-writing process as illustrated in the diagram below:*

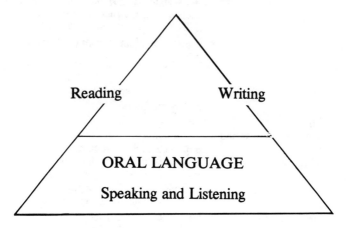

This can be accomplished by developing an oral communications curriculum that emphasizes communication as the primary goal of language (Flood and Salus, 1984, Anderson and Lapp, 1981). The framework for such a program is illustrated below:

2. *Students need to be taught that writers write to be understood by readers*

As teachers we need to explain to children that there is an implicit contract between writers and readers. Writers work at being comprehensive to their audiences. They have an understanding of their audience and they try to convey their message in such a way that it can be understood by their readers. The best way to help students understand their responsibilities as active readers is to encourage them to be writers who write for a specific audience. The two language arts, reading and writing, when taught together, enhance each other and serve to strengthen the child's ability in both areas.

3. *As readers, students need practice in "figuring-out" the writer's purpose, style and organization.* This can be accomplished by exposing and instructing students in ways to comprehend many different types of writing. Students need to learn strategies for reading each of the following types of writing:

A. Narrative
    1. Story
    2. Tall Tale
    3. Fables
    4. Folk Tale

B. Exposition
    1. Temporal (Sequence)
    2. Cause-Effect
    3.
    4. Argument (Position)
    5. List

C. Poetry
    1. Lyric
    2. Narrative Poems
    3. Ballad
    4. Nonsense Poems
    5. Epic Poems

D. Drama
    1. Comedy
    2. Tragedy
    3. Melodrama

E. Representational Writing
    1. Map
    2. Charts
    3. Graphs
    4. Complex Illustrations
    5. Diagrams
    6. Schedules

Mapping is an effective method for teaching children about text organization. Through mapping, i.e., representing the text in a visual pattern, children can improve both reading and writing abilities (Lapp and Flood, 1983).

> 4. *As readers, students need to be aware that there is content/knowledge that the writer is trying to convey.* Because writers cannot predict exactly what readers know, they have to make certain assumptions about the reader's *prior* knowledge. It is important that students have the information/knowledge they need to comprehend written materials. Prior knowledge includes:
>
> A. Vocabulary (concepts) needs to be taught in context, i.e., the way the words are used in the text to be read.

In addition to traditional methods of teaching vocabulary, two activities, semantic mapping and semantic feature analysis, have proven to be effective. Semantic mapping is essentially a structured brainstorming technique that is based on the premise that new words are learned in relation to known words. Giving students a single word synonym does not always work, because students may not know the synonym. A typical map might look like the following:

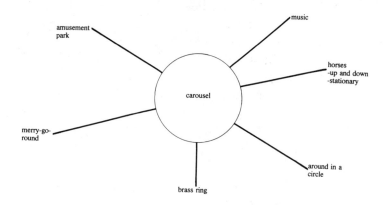

Semantic feature analysis is essentially a system using contrasts to hone the exact meaning of a word. For example, children may not know the ways in which the words "forest" and "jungle" differ in meaning. A feature matrix can be designed to help students "figure-out" how they are alike and how they differ. The matrix might look like the following:

	Vegetation	Animals	Hot/Humid
forest	+	+	−
jungle	+	+	+

B. Background Experience
Students need to be instructed in appropriate background knowledge to ready them for reading texts (Lapp and Flood, 1983). Volumes have been written about ways in which to do this; the most frequently used method is the Directed Reading Activity.

EXPERIMENTATION

6. *Students need to experiment with many different types of writing and reading.* They need to do independent reading by reading whole texts and instructional reading by reading Cloze activities, mad-libs, round-robin stories, and writing personal endings to stories and enhance students' reading/writing abilities.

EVALUATION

7. *Readers need to be made aware that evaluation improves their reading skills.* The goal of reading instruction is the creation of a student who is an independent, self-initiating, life-long learner. Students need to be involved in evaluation through teacher suggestions, test recommendations, and, eventually by becoming self-monitoring text processors.

EXPANSION

8. *Readers need to be encouraged to expand their reading by:* Reading a great deal about the same content; by reading the same content in different types of writing; by reading the same type of writing in different content areas; and by reading about new content areas.

REFERENCES

1 Anderson, P. and Lapp, D. *Language Skills in Elementary Schools.* New York: Macmillan Co., Inc., 1981.

2   Davies, W.J. Frank. *Teaching Reading in Early England.* London: Bowman, 1973.

3   Farr, Roger. *Measurement of Reading Achievement.* ERIC/IRA Reading Research Profiles, 1971.

4   Flood, J., and Salus, P. *Language and the Language Arts.* Englewood Cliffs, N.J.: Prentice Hall, Inc., 1974.

5   Huey, Edmund B. *The Psychology and Pedagogy of Reading with a Review of the History of Reading and Writing of Methods, Texts, and Hygiene in Reading.* Cambridge: M.I.T. Press, 1908, 1973.

6   Lapp, D., and Flood, J. *Teaching Reading to Every Child*, 2nd Edition. New York: Macmillan Co., Inc., 1983.

7   Mathews, Mitford. *Teaching to Read: Historically Considered.* Chicago: University of Chicago Press, 1966.

8   Roser, N. "Teaching and Testing Reading Comprehension: An Historical Perspective" in J. Flood (ed.), *Promoting Reading Comprehension* Newark, Delaware: IRA (in press).

9   Smith, Nila B. *American Reading Instruction.* Newark, Delaware: International Reading Association, 1965.

Notes on Contributors

ARLEEN ARMANTAGE is presently completing her dissertation for the Ph.D. in Education at Claremont Graduate School. JAMES ARMANTAGE consults with industry and academe on design applications of computational environments. Together, the Armantages are founders of DEVTECH: Creative Environments for Human Development, Inc., a non-profit, public benefit corporation. ROBERT COLLIER is presently an Assistant Professor of Education at Western Illinois University, where his special interests are in early childhood development and the role of play in learning generally, but particularly where language is concerned. WILLIAM P.J. COSTELLO is an Associate Professor of Education and the Director of the Division of Learning Services, San Francisco State University, where he is also a happy critic of the public educational system.

MALCOLM P. DOUGLASS is a Professor of Education and Director of the Center for Developmental Studies at Claremont Graduate School. JAMES FLOOD is an Associate Professor of Education at San Diego State University. His publications include *Comprehension Plus* (Prentice Hall, 1983) and *Clues to Better Reading* (Curriculum Associates, 1982).

KENNETH GOODMAN is a Professor of Education at the University of Arizona. He is widely known for his many publications growing out of research he has conducted in miscue analysis. YETTA GOODMAN is a Professor of Education at the University of Arizona and a past president of the National Council of Teachers of English. Her recent research is focused on the preschool years with particular regard to the language acquisition process. GILBERT GREDLER is currently Professor of Psychology at the University of South Carolina, where he is involved in the training of school psychologists. He is on the editorial board of *Psychology in the Schools* and book review editor of that journal. He is also a member of the board of directors of the *Journal of School Psychology.*

DOTY HALE is a Lecturer in Education at Claremont Graduate School and a specialist in literature for children and young adults, with a particular interest in the history of children's literature. DON HAMMILL, an internationally well-known figure in the area of learning disabilities, is the author of five books on that subject. He is past president of the National Council for Learning Disabilities.

RICHARD HODGES is a Professor of Education at the University of Puget Sound. He is widely known for his research in spelling development and has written two recent monographs, one focusing on the elementary school level, the other on the secondary, published by the National Council of Teachers of English, which address classroom applications of recent research findings in the field of spelling. MICHAEL E. JAMES is a Ph.D. candidate at Claremont Graduate School with the Faculty in Education. His special interests are in the field of language and reading. BRUCE R. JOYCE is currently the Director of

239

Booksend Laboratories, Palo Alto, California. A specialist in the education of teachers, he has written extensively on the subject, most recently *Creating Effective Schools* (Longman, in press) and *Staff Development: The Creation of a New System* (Association for Supervision of Curriculum Development, in press).

JANET KIERSTEAD is currently a consultant with the California State Department of Education, specializing in what makes effective schools, while also a doctoral candidate in Education at Claremont Graduate School. HERBERT KOHL is a writer on educational topics, critic, and experimentalist in educational practice. His current interests focus on the role of computers in the schools and upon the generation of creativity in human behavior. DIANE LAPP is an Associate Professor in the School of Education, San Diego State University, where, in addition to her teaching, she continues to be a prolific contributor to the literature in reading.

JOHN McNEIL is a Professor in the Graduate School of Education, University of California, Los Angeles. He is the author of a forthcoming book, *Teaching Reading Comprehension,* to be published by Scott Foresman Co. MARY POPLIN is an Assistant Professor of Education at Claremont Graduate School. She is a specialist in the education of the learning disabled, Editor of the *Learning Disability Quarterly*, and the author of *Methods of Educating the Handicapped* (Allyn & Bacon, 1980).

ARTHUR LEWIS ROSENBAUM is an Associate Professor of East Asian History at Claremont McKenna College. He has a Ph.D. in modern Chinese history from Yale University and has made several extended visits to China and the Far East. He has published the *China Missionaries Oral History Project* (Microfilming Corp. of America, 1973) and has just completed a comparative history of the Chinese, Indian, Japanese, and Indonesian revolutions. ROBERT RUDDELL is a Professor of Education at the University of California, Berkeley, whose research and scholarly writings in the field of reading are widely known. His most recent interests have focused on the effect of master teachers on learning to read.

SAM SEBESTA is a Professor of Education at the University of Washington. Widely known as an effective and entertaining lecturer, he has published for both the professional audience and for children. FEHL L. SHIRLEY is a Professor in the Department of Elementary Education at California State University, Northridge. She has written on the influence of reading on the concepts, attitudes, and behavior of students, and on critical reading. HERBERT SIMONS is a Professor at the University of California, Berkeley, where he has conducted linguistically based research on oral and written language development. HARRY SINGER is a Professor at the University of California, Riverside. A prolific researcher, he has published numerous reports on his studies. He has also been active in the National Reading Conference, and most recently is the author of "Problem Solving Schema with Question Generation for Comprehending Complex Short Stories (*Reading Research Quarterly*, 1981) and *Teaching Comprehension* (International Encyclopedia of Education, in press).

JEANNETTE VEATCH is Professor Emerita at Arizona State University, who has since her formal retirement from teaching continued her career as a consultant, lecturer, and author of books for teachers on individualized approaches to the teaching of reading. Always a popular speaker at professional conferences, she is the author of several books, among them, *Reading in the*

Elementary Schools (Wiley, 1978), *For the Love of Teaching* (International Center for Educational Development, 1973), and *Key Words to Reading: The Language Experience Approach Begins* (Merrill, 1973). McCAY VERNON is a Professor of Psychology at Western Maryland College. One of the nation's leading experts in the education of the deaf, he has managed to publish the results of his extensive research while also serving as the editor of the *Annals of the Deaf.*

INDEX

**Claremont Reading Conference Yearbooks
1936 - 1982**

Alman, John. *Reading Problems of Technical Training in the Naval Air Force,* 1944, *9,* p. 59.

Ames, Jean Goodwin, *Reading Art,* 1941, *6,* p. 1.

Ames, Louise Bates. *Developmental Approach to Reading Problems,* 1966, *30,* p. 78.

Amon, K.L. *Let's Take a Reading on the Flood Menace,* 1955, *20,* p. 85.

Amsden, Constance E. *Oral Language and Printed Word Reading,* 1964, *28,* p. 90.

Anderson, Chloe. *Selecting Objective Reading Tests and Analyzing and Using the Results of Reading Tests,* 1943, *8,* p. 8.

Anderson, Forrest N. *Psychiatric Aspects of Behavior,* 1936, *1,* p. 39.

Anderson, John M. *Improving Reading Skills through Music Experience for the Non-musical Teacher,* 1971, *35,* p. 178.

Anderson, Paul S. *Relationship of Phonetics and Reading,* 1956, *21,* p. 125.

Angell, Joseph W. *Literature and Semantics,* 1942, *7,* p. 1.

Apperson, Sarah, *Effectiveness of Orthoptic Training As a Means of Remedial Instruction in Reading,* 1944, *9,* p. 13.

Armour, Richard. *The Significance of Satire: A Satirist Looks at Books,* 1969, *33,* p. 112.

Armstrong, Hubert C. *What Price Standards?,* 1962, *26,* p. 11.

Atwood, Wallace W. *Audio-Visual Images That Should Widen Our Horizons,* 1947, *12,* p. 26.

Ausubel, David P. *A "Mentalistic" Conception of Word Meaning: Implications for Reading,* 1969, *33,* p. 17.

Ayres, A. Jean. *Perspectives on Neurological Bases of Reading,* 1964, *28,* p. 113.

Baker, August, *Beyond Literacy: Pinfeathers or Wings in Children's Books,* 1966, *30,* p. 60.

Bakjian, Mardie Jay. *Comics and Reading,* 1944, *9,* p. 117.

Balmer, Louise C. *The Reading Act As a Whole,* 1936, *1,* p. 1.

Bamman, Henry A. *Promoting Vocabulary Growth,* 1971, *35,* p. 190.

Barlin, Anne Lief. *Learning through Movement,* 1967 *31,* p. 236.

Blend, Frances. *The Blind Child and His Reading,* 1936, *1,* p. 153; 1946, *11,* p. 87.

Boder, Elena. *Developmental Dyslexia: A Diagnostic Screening Procedure Based on Three Characteristic Patterns of Reading and Spelling,* 1968, *32,* p. 173.

—————— . *Developmental Dyslexia: A Review of Prevailing Diagnostic Criteria,* 1972, *36,* p. 114.

Bong, Nguyen Quy. *Beginning Reading in South Viet Nam,* 1971, *35,* p. 78.

Bonynge, Thomas. *Piaget and Reading,* 1977, *41,* p. 94.

Booth, Graham. *View from the End of a Brush,* 1981, *45,* p. 49.

Bowden, A.O. *Cultures and Conflicts in the Backgrounds of Bilingual Children,* 1943, *8,* p. 29.

Bowen, J. Donald. *Linguistic Competence and Writing Conventions,* 1974, *38,* p. 83.

Boyer, Alta. *Letting Children Raise Their Own Horizons,* 1974, *38,* p. 167.

—————— . *Reading and Creative Writing in a First Grade Classroom,* 1959, *24,* p. 22.

Boyer, Ernest L. *Psychological Stress and the Symbolic Process,* 1965, *29,* p. 102.

Bradshaw, Ralph. *Reading Programs in the Junior College,* 1964, *28,* p. 179.

Brady, Elizabeth H. *The Teacher As Playwatcher,* 1973, *37,* p. 65.

Brayer, Herbert D. *Drug Language—the Binding and the Unbinding,* 1969, *33,* p. 59.

Brengelman, F.H. *Beyond Morphemes and Phonemes: Getting the Meaning from English Spelling,* 1973, *37,* p. 143.

Brenneis, Donald. *"You Can't Say That": Children's Speech Events and Teacher's Rules,* 1976, *40,* p. 147.

Briggs, Raymond P. *The Practical Needs for Survival Literacy,* 1977, *41,* p. 169.

Brill, Richard G. *Implications of a Symbol System As Portrayed by Deaf Children,* 1963, *27,* p. 76.

Bristow, D.A. *Reading Human Behavior,* 1958, *23,* p. 107.

Britton, Jasmine. *Plant To Prosper,* 1939, *4,* p. 1.

Cabrera, Arturo. *Schizophrenia in the Southwest: Mexican-Americans in Anglo-land,* 1967, *31,* p. 101.

Cage, Mabel Vinson. *Practical Classroom Procedures in Secondary Reading,* 1939, *4,* p. 16.

Calfee, Robert C.; Fisk, Leonard W.; Piontkowski, Dorothy. *"On-off" Tests of Cognitive Skills in Reading Acquisition,* 1975, *39,* p. 138.

Calkins, Joan Swietzer. *Language Development in Soviet Programs for Young Children,* 1972, *36,* p. 59.

Campbell, Douglas Gordon. *General Semantics and Behavior,* 1940, *5,* p. 19.

—————— . *Neuro-psychiatric Principles in Education, Counseling and Therapy.* 1939, *4,* p. 20.

Canavan, P. Joseph, *Reading Problem and the Junior College,* 1961, *25,* p. 155.

Caputo, John S. *Becoming a Communicator: A Look at the English Primary School and the Development of Linguistic Strategies in Young School Children,* 1982, *46,* p. 178.

Caputo, John; Cottrell, Eric. *The Anthropology of Reading,* 1976, *40,* p. 142.

Carpenter, Bernice. *Mass Communication: A Reading Process,* 1951, *16,* p. 12.

—————— . *Reading Can Bring Riches,* 1946, *11,* p. 171.

Carpenter, Sandra W. *Literature Is When...,* 1971, *35,* p. 51.

Carrell, Robert E. *Neurophysiological Aspects of Learning,* 1965, *29,* p. 154.

Carroll, John B. *From Comprehension to Inference,* 1969, *33,* p. 39.

Carroll, John S. *Developing Programs of Audio-Visual Education in California,* 1944, *9,* p. 19.

Carse, William T., See Cabral, Dennis L.

Carter, Ethel, *Classroom Teacher and the Aurally Handicapped Child,* 1947, *12,* p. 92.

Case, Keith E. *General Semantics: A Technique in Reading Social Relationships,* 1949, *14,* p. 55.

Caster, J. Edward, *Semantic Aspects of the Reading Process,* 1940, *5,* p. 33.

Clowes, Richard M. *California's New Look in Reading*, 1961, *25*, p. 53.

Coffin, Richard A. *Reading the Normal Adolescent*, 1949, *14*, p. 176.

Coil, Ann. *College Reading Needs: Beyond "Filling the Bin,"* 1978, *42*, p. 219.

Coker, Pamela L. *Problem Solving in Young Children: Conceptual or Linguistic Skills?*, 1976, *40*, p. 153.

Cole, E.C.F. *Reading Personalities through Handwriting Analysis*, 1958, *23*, p. 117.

Collier, Robert. *Play — in the Classroom?*, 1976, *40*, p. 160.

Collins, Gay. See Neff, Priscilla H.

——————. *Recognition of Merit and Announcement of Award*, 1974, *38*, p. 63.

——————. Stalwick, Doreen. *Language, the Basic Ingredient*, 1981, *45*, p. 83.

Conlon, Pamela, *Cognition, Language, and Color*, 1979, *43*, p. 70.

——————. *Is There a Critical Period for Language and Reading Acquisition?* 1978, *42*, p. 60.

Conner, Jay D. *Supplementary Reading Materials in the Social Studies*, 1936, *1*, p. 187.

Conners, C. Keith. *Neurophysiological Studies of Learning Disorders*, 1971, *35*, p. 99.

Conrad, S.J. *Compulsive Reading and Its Psychiatric Significance*, 1947, *12*, p. 114.

Cooke, W. Henry. *The World View*, 1947, *12*, p. 16.

Cooper, Charles W. *Through the Hat and over the Head*, 1942, *7*, p. 37.

Cooper, Elizabeth K. *Writing for Children in a Fragmented Society*, 1972, *36*, p. 85.

Coopersmith, Stanley; Feldman, Ronald. *Promoting Motivation through Inter-related Cognitive and Affective Factors*, 1973, *37*, p. 129.

Coots, James H. *Learning To Read: A Socioinstructional Process*, 1977, *41*, p. 113.

Corbin, Floyd, *Reading without Light*, 1958, *23*, p. 161.

Curran, Clyde E. *Reading As a Moral Process,* 1964, *28,* p. 60.

Curtis, Louis W. *Music of Latin America,* 1942, *7,* p. 55.

Cutsforth, Thomas D. *Problems in the Interdependence of the Senses,* 1937, *2,* p. 12.

Cutts, Warren G. *Reading Today — the National Focus,* 1963, *27,* p. 13.

Cyrog, Frances V. *Self-selection in Reading: Report of a Longitudinal Study,* 1962, *26,* p. 106.

Dale, Edgar, *Clear Only If Known.* 1952, *17,* p. 111.

—————. *Development of International Understanding.* 1958, *23,* p. 27.

—————. *Heart and the Head,* 1952, *17,* p. 31.

—————. *To Invest with Meaning,* 1955, *20,* p. 105.

Dale, Philip S. *Talking and Reading,* 1976, *40,* p. 54.

Dalton, M.M. *Survey of Visual Conditions in a California School System,* 1940, *5,* p. 39.

Dane, Chase. *Presentation of the Eighth Recognition of Merit,* 1972, *36,* p. 94.

Danielson, Cora Lee. *Remedial Reading Procedures in Los Angeles,* 1939, *4,* p.42.

—————. *Teaching of Reading to Gifted Children,* 1942, *7,* p. 59.

Darrow, Helen Fisher. *Reality, Morality and Individualized Reading,* 1968, *32,* p. 278.

Dart, Carroll. *Perceptual Problems with Reading,* 1936, *1,* p. 170.

Davies, Minnie Hawes. *Routine versus Special Instruction,* 1943, *8,* p. 58.

Davis, Harold E. *Education Program for Spanish-speaking Americans,* 1945, *10,* p. 96.

Davis, Homer W. *Reading the Army Training Films,* 1946, *11,* p. 186.

Davis, Irene Poole. *Speech in the Educational Program Today,* 1941, *6,* p. 33.

Davis, Louise Farwell. *Reading the Visual Abilities of Children,* 1948, *13,* p. 46.

Dawidoff, Robert. *Reading and the American Experiment,* 1976, *40,* p. 43.

Douglass, Harl R. *Teaching Reading in the High School,* 1937, *2,* p. 18.

Douglass, Malcolm P. *A Little Revolution Now and Then,* 1976, *40,* p. 29.

_____ . *A Point of View about Reading,* 1963, *27,* p. 5.

_____ .*Does Nongrading Improve Reading Behavior?* 1967, *31,* p. 170.

_____ . *Four Marks of Superior Reading Teaching,* 1959, *24,* p. 2.

_____ . *No Rainbow Pot of Gold — Announcement of the Third Recognition of Merit with an Acceptance Message from Frank Bonham,* 1967, *31,* p. 238.

_____ . *On Becoming a Reader,* 1965, *29,* p. 5.

_____ . *On the Politics of Reading and the Humanizing Experience,* 1980, *44,* p. 33.

_____ . *Reading and Nongrading in the Elementary School,* 1962, *26,* p. 85.

Douglass, Malcolm P. *Reading Around the World,* 1980, *44,* p. 94.

_____ . *Reading As the Earth Writes,* 1958, *23,* p. 49.

_____ . *Reading Between and Beyond the Lines,* 1973, *37,* p. 1.

_____ . *Reading for Life,* 1978, *42,* p. 1.

_____ . *Reading: How the Environment Influences Human Relationships,* 1955, *20,* p. 73.

_____ . *The Many Facets of Reading,* 1971, *35,* p. 1.

_____ . *Writing and Reading in a Balanced Curriculum: Retrospect and Prospect.* 1982, *46,* p. 1.

Douglass, Malcolm P.; Simmons, G.M. *Early Reading and Writing,* 1963, *27,* p. 61.

Douglass, Paul. *"Opposition Is True Friendship": Keeping Spirit and Body Together,* 1982, *46,* p. 65.

Dow, Bertha. *Measuring Blindspots with Remedial Reading Problems,* 1942, *7,* p. 63.

Downey, Lillian A. *Bridging the Gap into the Library,* 1944, *9* p. 93.

_____ . *Reading for Interest Series,* 1943, *8,* p. 67.

Edgar, Clara Lee. *Perceptual Motor Training As an Aid to Development of Reading Abilities,* 1967, *31,* p. 219.

Edmondson, Earl E. *Children's Magazines and Periodicals: A Selective Bibliography,* 1966, *30,* p. 215.

Eisner, Elliot, *Reading and the Creation of Meaning,* 1976, *40,* p. 1.

——————— . *The Kind of Schools We Need.* 1982, *46,* p. 12.

Elkind, David. *Cognitive Development and Reading,* 1974, *38,* p. 10.

Elkins, Herbert. *Third Dimension in Teaching.* 1943, *8,* p. 82.

Eller, William. *Personality Traits As Factors in Reading Comprehension,* 1969, *33,* p. 136.

Elliott, Essie L. *Role of Nutrition in Discriminative Behavior,* 1937, *2,* p. 30.

Ellner, Carolyn. *Stop the Brave New World — I Want To Get Off!,* 1972, *36,* p. 14.

Emery, Leonard. *Visual Processes and Vision Screening,* 1962, *26,* p. 122.

Enright, Gwyn. See Deverian, Margaret Coda, et al.

Erickson, Stephen A. *Signs and One's World,* 1969, *33,* p. 9.

Ernest, Sue. *Oral Avenues to Self-Understanding,* 1952, *17,* p. 43.

Ervin-Tripp, Susan M. *Reading As Second Language Learning,* 1973, *37,* p. 12.

Estupinian, Rafael, *Teaching Reading to the Linguistically Different Student,* 1980, *44,* p. 225.

Evans, Bertrand; Lynch, James J. *High School Textbooks in English: A Summary of a Report,* 1962, *26,* p. 39.

Evans, Vivian. *Reading in the Primary Schools,* 1936, *1,* p. 120.

Eyre, Mary B. *Dynamic Emotion and Reading,* 1936, *1,* p. 199.

Fargo, George. *Framework for Approaching Reading Problems,* 1965, *29,* p. 134.

——————— . *It's a Possibility: Humanism in Reading,* 1973, *37,* p. 53.

Fargo, George; Friedman, R.; Weiss, D. *Grouping for Reading,* 1951, *16,* p. 86.

Flood, James; Menyuk, Paula. *Metalinguistic Development and Reading/Writing Achievement*, 1982, *46*, p. 122.

Forer, Ruth K. *Catch a Falling Star: Early Prediction of Reading Failure*, 1975, *39*, p. 167.

Forney, R.L. *Lest We Forget: The Viable Memory*, 1963, *27*, p. 106.

Forsberg, Roberta. *How To Make Use of Basic English in the Classroom*, 1942, *7*, p. 67.

_____ . *Visual Adaptations Made by Students To Avoid Reading Difficulty: Their Relation to Teaching*, 1938, *3*, p. 19.

Fowles, Barbara R. *The CTW Reading Show: Tailoring Reading Instruction to Television*, 1971, *35*, p. 194.

Fox, Guy. *Some Observations on the Reading Problem*, 1941, *6*, p. 46.

Frasier, Vance. *Visual Motor Phonic Program for the Experience Approach to Language Arts*, 1964, *28*, p. 161.

Friedman, Albert B. *Middle Ages Revisited: Reading in the Electronic Age*, 1965, *29*, p. 11.

Friedman, R. See Fargo, G.

Frostholm, Adrienne; Watt, W.C.; Jacobs, David, *Preliterate Literacy*, 1982, *46*, p. 169.

Frostig, Marianne. *Motions and Emotions: Rhythmics As an Approach to Areas of Reading*, 1948, *13*, p. 111.

_____ . *Respect for Education and Education for Respect*, 1968, *32*, p. 43.

Fry, Brad L. *The Burgeoning Field of Arts Administration: Community Culture Centers*, 1973, *37*, p. 117.

Frye, Northrop. *Sign and Significance*, 1969, *33*, p. 1.

Fryer, Jeanne. *"No, I Can't Read: What Children Think About Reading*, 1976, *40*, p. 135.

Fuller, Leora. *Our Children — Our Challenge*, 1945, *10*, p. 125.

Fuog, H.L. *Developing Seeing for Reading*, 1936, *1*, p. 102.

Gaddis, Marilyn. *Presentation of Special Recognition of Merit*, 1971, *35*, p. 41.

Gardner, Willis Morton. *Vision in Relation to Education*, 1941, *6*, p. 50.

Goble, Norman M. *The Day the Anarchists Were Hanged — Some Thoughts on Literature As an Educative Instrument*, 1968, *32*, p. 140.

Goldmark, Bernice. *Reading As Inquiry*, 1964, *28*, p. 22.

Goetz, Emily. *Hearing Growth and Reading*, 1971, *35*, p. 120.

Gonzalez, Gilbert G. *The Political Economy of Education*, 1977, *41*, p. 104.

Goodlad, John I. *Reading in the Reorganized Elementary School*, 1961, *25*, p. 37.

Goodman, Kenneth S. *Comprehension-centered Reading*, 1970, *34*, p. 125.

_____ . *Manifesto for a Reading Revolution*, 1976, *40*, p. 16.

Goodman, Yetta M. *The Roots of Literacy*, 1980, *44*, p. 1.

Goodsell, J.G. *Eyes in the Act of Reading*, 1937, *2*, p. 59.

Gordon, Elaine. See Craig, Elaine.

Gottesman, Julia. *Humanizing Language Lessons, Grades 4-12*, 1980, *44*, p. 137.

Goudey, Elizabeth, *Radio in Education in Time of Crises*, 1942, *7*, p. 93.

Graham, Lorenz. *Writing for the Teaching Learning Process*, 1975, *39*, p. 96.

Grant, Grace. *Testing vs. Writing: A Critique of Contemporary Composition Curricula*, 1982, *46*, p. 97.

_____ ; Tierney, Dennis. *Perspectives in Multi-cultural Education: Uses of Popular Culture in the Classroom*, 1977, *41*, p. 140.

Grace, C. Delmar. *Incentive for Learning*, 1956, *21*, p. 183.

_____ . *Supplemental Materials for Instruction Illustrated in Science*, 1944, *9*, p. 65.

Gray, Lillian. *Influence of Books on the Child's Personality*, 1945, *10*, p. 115.

_____ . *Reading Oneself and Others through Great Books*, 1949, *14*, p. 44.

_____ . *Value and Use of Basic Readers in a Modern School*, 1943, *8*, p. 86.

Gray, Scott C. *Reading the Vocational Desires of High School Boys*, 1949, *14*, p. 173.

Hancock, Deborah Osen. *Identifying the Reading Needs of the College Student,* 1978, *42,* p. 210.

Hand, Wayland D. *Imprints of American Folklore and Folk Culture,* 1967, *31,* p. 40.

Hansen, Frank A. *Illumination and Efficient Reading,* 1937, *2,* p. 67.

Hansen, Philip A. *Where Have All the Labels Gone?* 1971, *35,* p. 145.

—————. Hansen, Shirley B. *Mainstreaming across Nations,* 1979, *43,* p. 39.

Hardy, Georgiana. *School Board Member Looks at the Reading Program,* 1961, *25,* p. 11.

Hargrave, Willard B. *Adjusting the School to the Child for Aural Reading,* 1946, *11,* p. 52.

—————. *Adjustment of the Physically Handicapped,* 1943, *8,* p. 101.

—————. *Aural Problems in Education: A Re-view,* 1955, *20,* p. 111.

—————. *Aural Reading and Child Maladjustment,* 1947, *12,* p. 85.

—————. *Aural Reading in Educational Development,* 1945, *10,* p. 73.

—————. *Hearing and Reading,* 1942, *7,* p. 100.

—————. *Hearing As a Factor in Behavior,* 1939, *4,* p. 50.

Harnage, Philip L. *Managing the Educational Technology,* 1977, *41,* p. 230.

—————. *Reading: Learned or Taught?* 1978, *42,* p. 84.

Harris, Louise, *Reading to Children,* 1940, *5,* p. 74.

Harris, Margaret N. *A Study of Discriminations Pertaining to Beginning Reading,* 1938, *3,* p. 52.

Harris, Robert L.; Coughlin, Frederick C. *Salvaging Failures through Improved Reading,* 1965, *29,* p. 160.

Harrison, Forest. *Educational Evaluation and Public Policy,* 1976, *40,* p. 203.

Harsh, J. Richard. *Cognitive Style — Facilitator or Deterrent to Academic Learning,* 1972, *36,* p. 102.

_____. *English as a Second Language: The Fringe of Meaning*, 1969, *33*, p. 153.

_____. Sancho, Anthony R. *From Sound to Symbol—a Natural Approach to Reading*, 1973, *37*, p. 49.

Hernandez-Chavez, Eduardo. *The Home Language of Chicanos As a Medium of Instruction*, 1973, *37*, p. 28.

Hess, Robert D. *Maternal Behavior and the Development of Reading Readiness in Urban Negro Children*, 1968, *32*, p. 83.

Higgins, Scott; Cross, Dolores E. *Beyond the Conventional*, 1978, *42*, p. 186.

Hill, George. *Value of Visual Education in the Classroom*, 1936, *1*, p. 46.

Hill, Shirley. *Guiding Young Children in Reading Their Environment*, 1977, *41*, p. 223.

Hinze, Richard. *Who Switches Reading to "Go"?*, 1967, *31*, p. 135.

Hirsch, Joseph. *Tactile Reading*, 1957, *22*, p. 41.

Hockett, John. *Materials and Methods Since the New England Primer*, 1942, *7*, p. 109.

Hodes, Don; Terrell, Jo Evelyn. *Communication Skills Projects: A Community Action Program*, 1967, *31*, p. 156.

Hogue, Harland E. *Coming of Age Spiritually*, 1953, *18*, p. 105.

Hoihjelle, Anne L. *Social Climate and Personality Traits of Able Teachers in Relation to Reading Instruction*, 1962, *26*, p. 114.

Holder, Carol R. *Write, Wrong, and the Wred Pen: Understanding Nonstandard Usage in College Composition*, 1978, *42*, p. 202.

_____. *Writing for Oneself and Others: Contexts For Composition across the Curriculum*, 1982, *46*, p. 76.

Holmes, Jack A. *Brain and the Reading Process*, 1957, *22*, p. 49.

Holt, Raymond M. *Impetus of the Library Region on Reading*, 1957, *22*, p. 151.

Hood, Jane. *Developmental Tasks: A Useful Concept*, 1952, *17*, p. 106.

Horn, Alice M. *Measuring the Outcomes of the Educational Program in Terms of Character Traits*, 1950, *15*, p. 114.

Ihinger, Robert F. *Lateral Dominance and Reading Achievement*, 1963, *27*, p. 126.

Inabinette, Norma. *The Influence of Cognitive Style on Reading*, 1979, *43*, p. 183.

Ingham, Samuel D. *Reading and Functional Sense Reception*, 1936, *1*, p. 158.

Isom, John B. *Some Neuropsychological Findings in Children with Reading Problems*, 1968, *32*, p. 188.

Israel, Marian Louise. *Supplementary Materials for Reading*, 1936, *1*, p. 88.

Iverson, William J. *The Age of the Computer and Reading*, 1967, *31*, p. 159.

_____. *Don't They Teach Children To Read Anymore?* 1953, *18*, p. 94.

Jackson, Philip W. *Reading and School Life*, 1970, *34*, p. 84.

Jacobs, David. See Frostholm, Adrienne.

Jacobson, Virginia. *Movement Experiences and Learning: A Motor Development Program for Young Children*, 1966, *30*, p. 128.

Jacques, Jean. *Old Men of the Desert*, 1943, *8*, p. 111.

Jacques, Louis. *Eye-sight and Learning*, 1937, *2*, p. 82.

Jenkins, Lee. *Reading: Language and Logic*, 1978, *42*, p. 55.

Jenkinson, Marion D. *The Parameters of Knowledge about Meaning in Reading*, 1976, *40*, p. 69.

Jennings, Frank G. *Aspects of Reading*, 1956, *21*, p. 111.

_____. *Of Quietness and Slow Time*, 1975, *39*, p. 1.

_____. *Time Machines, Space Ships and Frog Ponds.* 1966, *30*, p. 7.

Jensen, Arthur R. *Conceptions and Misconceptions about Verbal Mediation*, 1966, *30*, p. 134.

Johnson, Barbah Lee. *Language Experience—Life and Breath of Curriculum*, 1971, *35*, p. 160.

Johnson, James A. *Public Schooling in the Black Ghetto*, 1970, *34*, p. 56.

Johnson, Kenneth R. *Raising the Self Concept of Negro Students*, 1968, *32*, p. 235.

Kellogg, Lydia M. *Relation of the School Lunchroom to the School Program*, 1944, *9*, p. 27.

Kellogg, Ralph E. *An Experience Approach to the Language Arts: Overview*, 1964, *28*, p. 157.

Kelly, B.W. *Training Pupils To See*, 1939, *4*, p. 71.

Kendrick, William. *Comparative Study of Two First Grade Language Arts Programs*, 1964, *28*, p. 173; 1966, *30*, p. 150.

Kennedy, Catherine. *Inability of Disability As Associated with the Reading Problem*, 1942, *7*, p. 121.

Kennedy, Helen. *Aural Reading*, 1946, *11*, p. 26.

——————. *Curing or Causing Reading Difficulties?*, 1978, *42*, p. 78.

——————. *Problems in Aural Reading*, 1963, *27*, p. 86.

——————. *Unusual Auditory Difficulties Related to Reading*, 1981, *45*, p. 133.

Regan, John O.; Ruddell, Robert B. *The Reading Process: A Panel Discussion*, 1971, *35*, p. 96.

Keogh, Barbara K. *An Attentional Analysis of Learning Problems*, 1977, *41*, p. 121.

——————. *Form Copying Tests for Prediction of First Grade Reading*, 1963, *27*, p. 141.

——————. *Perceptual Design As a Measure of Reading Readiness*, 1959, *24*, p. 53.

Kernkamp, Leila M. *School Physician's Approach to the Hearing Program*, 1946, *11*, p. 38.

Kerr, Clare. *Analysis of Reading Disability*, 1938, *3*, p. 57.

——————. *Binocular Coordination and School Success*, 1944, *9*, p. 29.

——————. *Developmental and Remedial Program of Reading in the Elementary School*, 1936, *1*, p. 66.

——————. *Long-Term Planning in the Development of a Reading Program for the Prevention of Reading Disability*, 1938, *3*, p. 25.

——————. *Visual Maturity at the First Grade Level*, 1946, *11*, p. 78.

Kopp, James. *The Individual in a Controlled Society: A Behaviorist's Dilemma,* 1968, *32,* p. 53.

Koppenhaver, Albert H. *The Affective Domain: No Afterthought,* 1976, *40,* p. 103.

──────── . *Reading and the Home Environment,* 1974, *38,* p. 122.

Krakowski, Meyer. *Research in Foreign Language Instruction in Southern California,* 1959, *24,* p. 40.

Krashen, Stephen D. *On the Acquisition of Planned Discourse: Written English As a Second Dialect,* 1978, *42,* p. 173.

Krous, George T. *Visual Analysis Investigation As Part of a Reading Program,* 1947, *12,* p. 66.

Kueneman, Huberteen. *Remedial Work with Reading,* 1940, *5,* p. 85.

Kunz, Jean T. *The Self-Concept of the Young Child As He Learns To Read,* 1968, *32,* p. 114.

LaBrant, Lou. *Genetic Approach to Language,* 1949, *14,* p. 5.

LaCrosse, E. Robert, Jr. *Reading Readiness in the Preschool Years: A Total Preparation by the Environment,* 1971, *35,* p. 27.

Lade, Linda; Lade, John; Weeres, Joseph. *Curriculum Implications of Economic Concentration in the Publishing Industry,* 1976, *40,* p. 198.

Laine, Janice E. *A Community Based Reading Center,* 1975, *39,* p. 152.

Lamson, Robert W. *Allergies and Human Behavior,* 1936, *1,* p. 83.

Lancaster, Julia E. *Function of Orthoptics in Reading Disabilities,* 1947, *12,* p. 75.

Landeck, Beatrice. *Reading Music in the Language of Emotion,* 1957, *22,* p. 87.

Landon, Joseph W. *Music Experiences for Boys and Girls,* 1947, *12,* p. 154.

Lane, Boyd. *Action Research in Reading,* 1961, *25,* p. 67.

Lane, Mary B. *Creating Remedial Readers,* 1972, *36,* p. 150.

Langland, Lois. *The Structure of Feeling: A Base for Developing Strategies in Learning and Reading,* 1975, *39,* p. 36.

Lodge, Helen. *Reading Teachers Can Learn from Listening to the Learners,* 1959, *24,* p. 29.

Lordan, John P. *Visual Ability of Children As a Factor in Modern Education,* 1936, *1,* p. 192.

Low, Anni. *Language Proficiency Testing: Let's Listen to What the Kids Say!,* 1980, *44,* p. 166.

——————. *The Soft Start of the Danish Schools: Learning To Read—Slowly,* 1979, *43,* p. 92.

Lowers, Virginia Bell. *How I Teach Reading,* 1942, *7,* p. 137.

——————. *Selecting Instructional Materials,* 1943, *8,* p. 114.

Lowman, Charles L. *Influence of Body Mechanics on the Learning Process,* 1945, *10,* p. 32.

——————. *Physical Factors Influencing Education,* 1937, *2,* p. 101.

——————. *Reading the Relation of Postural Deviations to Behavior,* 1949, *14,* p. 77.

Lynch, James J. See Evans, Bertrand.

Macaulay, Ronald K. S. *Lingualism: The Real Implications of Lau vs. Nichols,* 1977, *41,* p. 86.

——————. *Linguistic Diversity and the Elementary School,* 1967, *31,* p. 34.

MacCalla, Thomas A. *Some Critical Needs in Teaching English As a Second Language,* 1966, *30,* p. 197.

MacLean, Malcolm S. *Multi-Sensory Approach to Reading,* 1948, *13,* p. 103.

Macomber, F. G. *Developmental Program for Reading,* 1936, *1,* p. 130.

Madden, Richard. *Effect of the Degree of Hearing upon Reading,* 1942, *7,* p. 178.

——————. *Materials for Development of Reading,* 1942, *7,* p. 183.

Mahan, Theodora. *Planning Methods of Improving Vocabulary,* 1943, *8,* p. 122.

Majovski, Lawrence. See Oettinger, Leon.

Maloney, Russell. *Childhood and the Printed Page,* 1947, *12,* p. 144.

McInnes, John. *Teaching Reading with Confidence*, 1980, *44*, p. 57.

McKenzie, Dorothy C. *Our American Heritage through Children's Books*, 1976, *40*, p. 93.

_____ . *Reading and the Fight for Man's Mind*, 1963, *27*, p. 40.

McLean, Donald. *Outline of the Evolution of Communication*, 1941, *6*, p. 74.

McManigal, Craig. *Presentation of the Fourth Recognition of Merit*, 1968, *32*, p. 293.

McNassor, Donald J. *Reading the Students As Individuals: A Story of a High School Class*, 1950, *15*, p. 50.

_____ . *Safe Passage*, 1966, *30*, p. 33.

_____ . *This Frantic Pace in Education*, 1967, *31*, p. 78.

McNaughton, Patricia. *Reading the Language of Teacher and Student in the Classroom*, 1973, *37*, p. 87.

McNay, Allison. *Trends in Audio-Visual Education*, 1947, *12*, p. 103.

McNeil, John D. *Research Strategies in the Teaching of Reading*, 1969, *33*, p. 185.

McQuarrie, Charles W. *Vision Training: An Aid to Better Seeing*, 1947, *12*, p. 80.

Mehan, Theodora. *Planning Methods of Improving Vocabulary*, 1943, *8*, p. 122.

Mehlman, Jewel; Titone, Jon. *Give Us Your Poorest Readers, Your Tired Scholars, Your Muddled Classes Learning without Glee*, 1976, *40*, p. 178.

Mellinger, Suzanne Seabrook. *Tutoring As Educational Therapy*, 1949, *14*, p. 180.

Melnik, Amelia. *Six Characteristics of Effective Reading Instruction in Search of a Perceptive Teacher*, 1975, *39*, p. 43.

Menyuk, Paula. See Flood, James.

Mercer, Jane R. *Imprints of Culture on the Personalities of Children*, 1967, *31*, p. 55.

Merrill, Edith H. *Importance of Basal Text Books in the Teaching of Reading*, 1943, *8*, p. 127.

Moses, Louise. *Reading Interests of Retarded, Reluctant, and Disturbed Children*, 1962, *26*, p. 77.

Moskovitz, Sarah. *How Should the Culturally Different Child Be Taught To Read?*, 1974, *38*, p. 74.

Moss, Andrew. *Writing: A Tool for Learning and Understanding*, 1979, *43*, p. 149.

Nadeau, Adele. *Key Concepts and Instructional Models for Bilingual Education Programs*, 1980, *44*, p. 200.

Nasland, Robert A., et al. *Evaluation and the Reading Program*, 1961, *25*, p. 133.

Nava, Alfonso. R.; Sancho, Anthony R. *Bilingual Education: Una Hierba Buena*, 1975, *39*, p. 113.

——————. *Public Policy and the Limited and Non-English Speaking Student*, 1976, *40*, p. 210.

Neal, Harriet. *Learning from Piaget: Developing Literacy in the Primary Grades*, 1978, *42*, p. 96.

Neely, Charlotte. *Social Reading*, 1946, *11*, p. 113.

Neff, Priscilla H. *A Book and a Teacher*, 1966, *30*, p. 56.

——————. *Children's Literature — An Experiment in Developing Critical Thinking*, 1963, *27*, p. 153.

——————. *Four Boys and Their Boxes*, 1957, *22*, p. 117.

——————. *To Honor a Relationship: Announcing a Recognition of Merit*, 1965, *29*, p. 49.

——————. Collins, Gay. *Children's Literature: An Experiment in Developing Critical Thinking*, 1963, *27*, p. 153.

Nelson, Russell E. *Does Age of Entrance into School Affect Reading Ability?*, 1959, *24*, p. 58.

Nemetz, George F. *Inside California's New English Language Framework*, 1969, *33*, p. 178.

Neufeld, Evelyn M. *Plato, Helen Keller, and the Liberated Reader*, 1977, *41*, p. 80.

Neufeld, Helen H. *Reading, Writing and Algorithms: Computer Literacy in the Schools*, 1982, *46*, p. 133.

Neumann, Henry. *Reading Cultural Patterns*, 1950, *15*, p. 72.

Neville, Ken. *Results of a Remedial Reading Program at the Secondary Level*, 1959, *24*, p. 55.

Papazian, Clement E. *A Pediatrician Looks at Reading Retardation—New Ideas: Conventional and Controversial,* 1967, *31,* p. 212.

_____ . *Common Misconceptions in the Use of Drugs for the Reading/Learning Disabled Child,* 1981, *45,* p. 125.

_____ . *Fact or Fallacy: An Open Line between Doctor and Teacher,* 1973, *37,* p. 167.

Park, George. *Cultural Styles and the Achievement of Literacy,* 1967, *31,* p. 27.

Park, Gordon. *Classroom Approach to Reading Difficulties,* 1940, *5,* p. 117.

Park, Joe. *Vocabulary Burden of Classroom Instructional Sound Motion Pictures,* 1945, *10,* p. 142.

Parkins, George A. *Problems in Visual Re-education,* 1943, *8,* p. 170.

Pattison, Lee. *Fundamentals of Interpretation,* 1941, *6,* p. 89.

Paul, Alice. *Diverse Aspect of Language Development As Related to Reading,* 1974, *38,* p. 97.

Paul, Beulah. *Functional Reading Program for the Elementary School,* 1936, *1,* p. 175.

Perkins, F. Theodore. *Physical Growth Factors,* 1942, *7,* p. 225.

_____ . *Problems Arising from Assertions or Assumptions of Delacato,* 1964, *28,* p. 119.

_____ . *Psychology of the Reading Process,* 1936, *1,* p. 11.

_____ . *Reading and the Psychology of Learning,* 1941, *6,* p. 99.

_____ . *Some Aspects of Perception,* 1938, *3,* p. 32.

Perrelet, Lois. *Reading Activities in the Elementary Grades,* 1942, *7,* p. 232.

Peters, Henry B. *Developing Criteria of Visual Performance for Elementary School Children,* 1956, *21,* p. 75.

_____ . *Visual Efficiency in Relation to Reading Ability,* 1940, *5,* p. 123.

Peters, Joe. *Schools Without Failure: Report of a Success Experience—The Antecedent of Reading,* 1971, *35,* p. 168.

Pfister, Elta S. *Group Harmony,* 1943, *8,* p. 183.

Radnitz, Robert. *Motion Pictures, Children and Books,* 1965, *29,* p. 59.

Ragsdale, Winifred. *Presentation of the Recognition of Merit,* 1970, *34,* p. 115.

_____. *Presentation of the Recognition of Merit,* 1971, *35,* p. 37.

_____. *Recognition of Merit and Announcement of Award,* 1973, *37,* p. 45.

_____. *Presentation of the Recognition of Merit,* 1975, *39,* p. 93.

_____. *Presentation of the Recognition of Merit,* 1977, *41,* p. 76.

_____. *Presentation of the Recognition of Merit,* 1978, *42,* p. 145.

_____. *Presentation of the Recognition of Merit,* 1979, *43,* p. 199.

_____. *Presentation of the Recognition of Merit,* 1980, *44,* p. 127.

Ramirez, Manuel III. *The Bilingual Program Bandwagon and the Psychodynamics of the Chicano Child,* 1970, *34,* p. 68.

Ransom, Genevieve. *From Rags to Riches,* 1977, *41,* p. 217.

Reagan, Bruce V., Jr. *H T P Test: A Reading Aid,* 1949, *14,* p. 154.

Rebish, Della. *Mask of Competence,* 1971, *35,* p. 109.

Reddick, Harry E. *Application of Reading Technique to Soil Conservation,* 1941, *6,* p. 126; 1949, *14,* p. 119.

_____. *Reading the Soil Text in the Book of the Land,* 1942, *7,* p. 253.

Reed, Mary Stevens. *Beyond the Printed Symbol,* 1956, *21,* p. 13.

Reed, Ruth. *Implementing the Curriculum with Audio-Visual Aids,* 1939, *4,* p. 89.

Reeves, Nancy. *Feminine Subculture and Female Mind,* 1973, *37,* p. 19.

Regan, John Owen. *Discovering Thinking by Listening to Language,* 1974, *38,* p. 109.

_____. *Drug Outcomes and Language Programs: A Problem of Communication,* 1969, *33,* p. 168.

Rose, Ivan M. *Initial Teaching Alphabet: Premise and Promise,* 1965, *29,* p. 146.

—————— . *Fostering Logical and Creative Thinking through I.T.A.,* 1968, *32,* p. 286.

Rosenthal, Robert. *Self-fulfilling Prophecies in Behavioral Research and Everyday Life,* 1968, *32,* p. 15.

Ross, Ramon Royal. *Reading and the Nonsense of Play,* 1978, *42,* p. 118.

Rowe, Linda Jo; Rice, Robin. *Oral Language Development in the Preschool Deaf Child: A Two-way Communication Process,* 1968, *32,* p. 247.

Ruddell, Robert B. *Attitudes toward Language—What Value for the Classroom Reading Teacher?,* 1974, *38,* p. 21.

—————— . *Children's Language Development: Research and Implications,* 1965, *29,* p. 115.

—————— . *Language and Early Reading Instruction—Research Based Recommendations for Innovative Schools,* 1971, *35,* p. 135.

—————— . See Kennedy, Helen.

Russell, Sharon M. *Presentation of the Fifth Recognition of Merit,* 1969, *33,* p. 131.

Ryan, John. *Family Patterns of Reading Problems: The Family That Reads Together...,* 1977, *41,* p. 159.

—————— . *The First RX For Basic Skills Students: Imaginative Literature or "The Shaughnessy Approach"?,* 1980, *44,* p. 177.

Saale, Charles W. *Role of Meaning in Reading,* 1950, *15,* p. 19.

Saario, Terry. See Hagerman, Barbara.

Sackett, Gene P. *How Much of Reading Is Really Learned?,* 1963, *27,* p. 110.

Safford, Alton L. *An Evaluation of the Individualized Reading Program in One Elementary School District,* 1959, *24,* p. 60.

Sample, Ina Powers. *Need for Speech Reading.* 1947, *12,* p. 96.

Sancho, Anthony R. *Maintenance and Transitional Approaches to Bilingual Instruction: The Effects on Bilingual Children,* 1980, *44,* p. 218.

Sensor, Phyllis. See Bradshaw, Ralph.

Serrurier, Zenna. *How I Teach Reading*, 1942, *7*, p. 271.

Seven, S. A. *Sex-role Stereotypes in Children's Books*, 1972, *36*, p. 90.

Shallenberger, Alice. *Story of the Blue Horse*, 1953, *18*, p. 11.

Sharp, Alberta. *Project Thrust*, 1979, *43*, p. 68.

Sheets, Millard. *Reading the Art Language*, 1940, *5*, p. 163.

_____ . *Reading the Color Environment*, 1948, *13*, p. 130.

Shelton, E. Kost. *Endocrine Glands As Related to Mental and Physical Development*, 1937, *2*, p. 111.

Shelton, John S. *On Learning through the Earth Sciences*, 1965, *29*, p. 73.

Shepard, Paul. *Nature Study—Indoor Images, Outdoor Reality*, 1977, *41*, p. 206.

Shepherd, Paul. *Reading the Lighting Environment*, 1951, *16*, p. 73.

Shirley, Fehl L. *When Does Reading Make a Difference?*, 1973, *37*, p. 93.

Shockro, Ellen K. *Changing Teacher Behavior in China: The Effects of the Cultural Revolution*, 1980, *44*, p. 119.

Short, Irene T. *Teaching the Deaf and Hard of Hearing*, 1943, *8*, p. 207.

Shrodes, Caroline. *Exploration of the Self through Reading*, 1942, *7*, p. 286.

_____ . *Reading To Extend Experience*, 1941, *6*, p. 151.

Shuck, Lenel. *Applying the Democratic Method to the Selection of Music Materials*, 1942, *7*, p. 295.

Shugarman, Sherrie Lynne. *Moral Dilemmas in Children's Literature*, 1979, *43*, p. 103.

Shutes, Robert E. *Some Individual and Social Contexts of Classroom Learning*, 1968, *32*, p. 131.

Sicher, Lydia. *How To Read Human Minds*, 1942, *7*, p. 299.

Siebel, Cynthia C. *Early Educational Experience: Results and Implications*, 1973, *37*, p. 73.

Spencer, James E. *Reading Behavior in Clinical Testing*, 1949, *14*, p. 159.

_____ . *Selected References from Previous Yearbooks with Regard for the 1954 Conference Theme*, 1954, *19*, p. 135.

Spencer, Peter L. *A Sound Reading Program*, 1945, *10*, p. 69.

_____ . *Broadening the Basis for Reading Instruction*, 1938, *3*, p. 42.

_____ . *Claremont Concept of Reading*, 1953, *18*, p. 143.

_____ . *Developing a Balanced Reading Program*, 1956, *21*, p. 25.

_____ . *Gettsville Becomes Reading Conscious: A Dramatic Panel*, 1940, *5*, p. 165.

_____ . *Human Relations and the Reading Process*, 1954, *19*, p. 11.

_____ . *Mass Communication: A Reading Process*, 1951, *16*, p. 17.

_____ . *Nature of the Reading Process and Building Balanced Reading Programs*, 1961, *25*, p. 1.

_____ . *Reading: A Basic Human Process*, 1950, *15*, p. 34.

_____ . *Reading As Concept Building*, 1952, *17*, p. 13.

_____ . *Reading in a Geophysical Age*, 1958, *23*, p. 15.

_____ . *Reading Is Creative Living*, 1957, *22*, p. 11.

_____ . *Reading Our American Way of Life*, 1949, *14*, p. 99.

_____ . *Reading Process and Types of Reading*, 1946, *11*, p. 17.

_____ . *Reading: The Basis of Curriculum*, 1945, *10*, p. 13.

_____ . *Reading: The Educative Process*, 1942, *7*, p. 314.

_____ . *Reading The Visual Process*, 1963, *27*, p. 68.

_____ . *Reading Things*, 1947, *12*, p. 21.

_____ . *That Man May See*, 1946, *11*, p. 159.

_____ . *The Claremont Reading Conference: Its Message and Educational Implications*, 1973, *37*, p. 205.

_____ . *Vision Education: How Can It Best Be Accomplished?*, 1946, *11*, p. 65.

_____ . *Visual Training: A Remedial Reading Technique*, 1943, *8*, p. 215.

Strang, Ruth. *Personality Development and Reading Problems,* 1945, *10,* p. 43.

——————— . *Reading in This Age of Television, Radio, and Motion Pictures,* 1951, *16,* p. 22.

——————— . *Reading Observed Behavior,* 1954, *19,* p. 21.

Stout, Robert T. See Guthrie, James, et al.

Strickland, Ruth G. *Language Learning: Modes, Models, and Mystique,* 1965, *29,* p. 81.

Stringfield, Lamar. *Orchestral Techniques for Schools,* 1942, *7,* p. 321.

Stuart, Sylvia. *Reading the Anecdotal Behavior Record,* 1949, *14,* p. 169.

Sturman, Douwe. *Reading and the Creative Life,* 1957, *22,* p. 143.

Sullivan, Elizabeth T. *Some Aspects of the Reading Program,* 1941, *6,* p. 161.

Swift, Hildegarde Hoyt. *Emerging Cultural Values in Children's Books,* 1964, *28,* p. 67.

Taba, Hilda. *Human Relations in Educational Programs,* 1951, *16,* p. 53.

Tabachnick, B. Robert. *Reading English in Nigerian Primary Schools: Gateway to Opportunity; Barrier to Understanding,* 1968, *32,* p. 267.

Tager, B. N. *Personality Changes in Endocrine Disturbances,* 1940, *5,* p. 191.

Tarjan, George. *The Child, the Parent, and the Teacher: Implications for Mental Health,* 1962, 26, p. 26.

Tallman, Norman O. *Administration of Aural and Visual Reading,* 1953, *18,* p. 82.

Tax, Sol. *Self and Society,* 1968, *32,* p. 1.

Taylor, Halsey P. *Beyond "Literal" Meaning: Step One,* 1977, *41,* p. 172.

Taylor, Harris A. *Organizational Schemes and the Improvement of Reading Instruction,* 1961, *25,* p. 45.

Taylor, Linda. See Adelman, Howard.

Taylor, Mark. *Realms of Reality,* 1966, *30,* p. 67.

Taylor, Mary Stuart. *Readers Theatre: A Creative Experience,* 1978, *42,* p. 130.

Tierney, Dennis S. *Reading the Social Studies*, 1982, *46*, p. 139.

——————— . See Grant, Grace.

Tipton, Elis M. *Language One Means of Improving Mexican-American Relations*, *1944, 9*, p. 160.

——————— . *Problem Children or Problem Communities: Minority Groups*, 1943, *8*, p. 224.

Titone, Jon. See Mehlman, Jewel.

Titus, Eve. *Author of Anatole Tells All*, 1972, *36*, p. 77.

Trainor, M. E. *Unity in Hearing Conservation*, 1943, *8*, p. 248.

Treadway, Gerald H., Jr. *Effects of Redundancy on Reading Comprehension of Second and Fifth Grade Children*, 1971, *35*, p. 127.

Trillingham, C. C. *Reading Problems in the Secondary Schools*, 1936, *1*, p. 28.

Trueba, Henry. *Microethnographic Research in Bilingual Classrooms: An Inside Analysis of the Teaching/Learning Process*, 1981, *45*, p. 152.

Truher, Helen B. *Relationship Between Reading Achievement and Patterns of Reading Instruction in the Primary Grades*, 1959, *24*, p. 50.

Turner, Ralph H. *International Understanding: An Exercise in Reading National Perspectives*, 1955, *20*, p. 13.

Tyler, Louise. *Reading and Persons: The Creation and Discovery of Meaning*, 1982, *46*, p. 29.

Upton, Albert W. *Reading and Intelligence*, 1964, *28*, p. 137.

Vanderpoel, Edith. *Remedial Reading*, 1966, *21*, p. 171.

Van Gundy, Justine. *Exploration of the Social World through Reading*, 1942, *7*, p. 323.

Van Metre, Patricia D. *Syntactic Characteristics of Selected Bilingual Children*, 1974, *38*, p. 102.

Veatch, Jeannette. *Education and Brainwashing*, 1975, *39*, p. 19.

——————— . *Sign and Significance: The Jabberwock Rides Again*, 1969, *33*, p. 100.

——————— . *Key Words and Other Ways To Teach Beginning Reading*, 1982, *46*, p. 53.

Vernon, McCay. *Relationship of Thought, Language and Nonverbal Communication to Reading*, 1972, *36*, p. 137.

Waterman, David J. *Reading Intelligence Quotients*, 1949, *14*, p. 133.

Watt, W. C. *On the Notion That Sense Is in the Eye of the Beholder, with Special Reference to the Horror Movie*, 1974, *38*, p. 67.

—————— . See Frostholm, Adrienne.

——————; Jacobs, David. *The Child's Conception of the Alphabet*, 1975, *39*, p. 131.

Wedberg, Alma. *Relation of Speech to Reading Readiness*, 1947, *12*, p. 98.

Weida, Ethelyn Yount. *How I Teach Reading*, 1942, *7*, p. 340.

—————— . *Providing Maximum Opportunity for All Students To Learn To Read the Printed Word Commensurate with Individual Capabilities*, 1951, *16*, p. 105.

—————— . *Reading Program of the Compton Union Junior High School*, 1937, *2*, p. 113.

Weiss, D. See Fargo, G.

Welch, Dorothy J. *Assisting Problem Readers through Individualized Reading*, 1959, *24*, p. 62.

Wells, Vera R. *Open a Book, Open the World*, 1956, *21*, p. 103.

Wepman, Joseph M. *Learning and Learning Disabilities*, 1977, *41*, p. 50.

West, Edna A. *Effective Reading in Business*, 1953, *18*, p. 132.

Weymouth, Frank W. *Some Aspects of Visual Perception As Related to Education*, 1955, *20*, p. 117.

Whitcomb, Irene. *Self-selection in Reading (Panel)*, 1956, *21*, p. 33.

White, E. B. *Acceptance Message*, 1970, *34*, p. 117.

Wibberly, Leonard. *History for Those Who Couldn't Care Less*, 1963, *27*, p. 24.

Wiese, Mildred J. *Teaching Reading to Adult Illiterates with Films*, 1945, *10*, p. 93.

Wilcox, J. C. *Community Reading Clinic Program*, 1939, *4*, p. 106.

Wilcox, John C. *Physiological Impediments to Learning*, 1940, *5*, p. 216.

Wilde, John E. See Wagner, Steven R.

Worden, Jack D. *Visual Considerations in Learning Performance,* 1966, *30,* p. 175.

Work, Henry W. *Reading Personality Development in Children,* 1956, *21,* p. 165.

Wright, Clifford A. *Influence of the Ductless Glands on Education of Children,* 1943, *8,* p. 251.

Yager, A.H. *Reading in a Correctional Institute,* 1947, *12,* p. 132.

Yang, You Chan. *Russia: A Problem To Be Solved,* 1958, *23,* p. 35.

Young Ethel. *First Things First—Nurturing the Root Experiences in Reading,* 1975, *39,* p. 53.

Zetterberg, Stephen I. *Peripheral Reading, a Factor for Survival,* 1954, *19,* p. 115.

Ziajka, Alan. *The Child As Symbol User: The Early Origins of Reading in Infancy and Early Childhood,* 1981, *45,* p. 106.